Advance Praise For
He's Just No Good for

"Finally, here is a guide for freeing women who are ensnared unnecessarily in relationships that are emotionally abusive. A must read."
—John Gottman, author of *The Seven Principles for Making Marriage Work*

"Women of all ages need to read this book! Beth brings a fresh approach to the topic and a compassionate voice, focusing on women's empowerment and learning to trust ourselves, especially in relationships."—Lisa Fredriksen Bohannon, author of *If You Loved Me, You'd Stop Drinking!*

"Beth Wilson's words fire with arrowlike precision to help women penetrate the layers of programming keeping them trapped in unhealthy relationships. This book is a true friend to women because it tells the truth."—Elizabeth Diane & Andrew Marshall, authors of *Listening with Heart 360: Wisdom Women Have Forgotten*

"*He's Just No Good for You* is a comprehensive, well-written book for women who will recognize themselves, their relationships, and their partners' destructive patterns. The author knows her material, and offers hope and spiritual sustenance without judgment while nudging us to make better choices."—Karen Fiester, Ph.D., Stanford University, Clinical Psychologist

"Written with compassion and humor, *He's Just No Good for You* is a must-read for every woman who gets involved with the wrong kind of men. It's also a fun, and insightful, read for everyone else."
—Riane Eisler, author of *The Chalice and The Blade* and *The Real Wealth of Nations*

"Beth brings to light the subtleties of how many of us have found ourselves to be in damaging relationships, not by knocking us over the head with bricks of 'how could you *not* know' or laying blame that we brought this on ourselves, but gently lifting the fog that we've been living in by shedding light on all the little glimpses of a dark reality that we too easily have rejected as our imagination. The pain of acknowledging this reality is softened by Beth's understanding and wisdom. She holds the belief and hope that we can learn from our experiences, trust ourselves to make better choices, and journey towards a better life . . . and she gives us the tools to do so!" —Audrey L. White, M.P.H., Stanford University Research Coordinator, Health Educator, Nia Technique Instructor

"He's Just No Good for You is a unique approach to destructive relationships, providing much needed wisdom and insight for women who just aren't certain what, exactly, is wrong when it comes to their intimate relationship. Beth extends a trusted hand to help these women find their way back to themselves; to find their way home." —Judith London, Ph.D., author of *Connecting the Dots: Hope for Advanced Alzheimer's Patients*, clinical psychologist specializing in addictions recovery and Alzheimer's Disease

"A groundbreaking book, *He's Just No Good for You* reassesses the basis for female relationships. By unpacking the characteristics of problematic individuals, Beth Wilson creates a roadmap that allows women to free themselves of destructive influences." —Sylvia Ann Hewlett, Economist, author of *Off-Ramps and On Ramps: Keeping Talented Women on the Road to Success*, President of the Center for Work-Life Policy

"Beth Wilson uses her keen mind and alchemical skills to create concise formulas that help women distance themselves from toxic relationships that devalue and suppress them."—Dr. Ramona P. Rubio, author of *The Alchemical Woman: A Handbook for Everyday Soulwork*

"Beth Wilson has done a great service to womankind by bringing awareness to the damage done by controlling relationships and identifying the "red flags" which erode self image. Women don't have to feel like they're crazy or less than competent any longer. This book is a roadmap out of a toxic situation and onto a life of well-being, autonomy, and joy!"—Barbara Scala, J.D.,Transformation & Divorce Coach and co-author of *Sanity Savers: Tips for Women to Live a Balanced Life*

"Beth Wilson has spent a lifetime empowering women, and her newest book, *He's Just No Good for You*, is a provocative triumph; daring to go where few authors do in exploring dysfunctions in relationships. Almost every woman reading this book can directly relate to her incisive profiles, or knows someone who does. Beth carefully weaves through a painful subject of abusive behaviors in men with raw honesty, sprinkled with humor, and clearly filled with a passion to help women find the inner strength to rise above their circumstances."—Kari Henley, Founder, GatherCentral

"As a psychotherapist, I was often shocked and saddened with the many forms of battering women accepted in their daily lives. We women seem satisfied and even grateful with what I came to call 'the absence of awful' in our relationships. In *He's Just No Good for You*, Beth Wilson has done us all a service in describing patterns, symptoms, and syndromes and pointing ways to reclaim, restore, and recreate ourselves. A must read."—Anne Wilson Schaef, Ph.D., *New York Times* bestselling author of *When Society Becomes An Addict, Meditations for Women Who Do Too Much, Women's Reality*, and *Escape From Intimacy*

Other Books by Beth Wilson

Meditations During Pregnancy

Meditations for New Mothers

Meditations for Mothers of Toddlers

Restoring Balance to a Mother's Busy Life

Creating Balance in Your Child's Life

He's Just
NO
GOOD
for You

A Guide to Getting Out of
a Destructive Relationship

BETH WILSON
with Mo Therese Hannah, Ph.D.
Foreword by Rita DeMaria, Ph.D.

life

Guilford, Connecticut
An imprint of The Globe Pequot Press

GPP Life gives women answers they can trust.

Copyright © 2009 by Beth Wilson

GPP Life is an imprint of The Globe Pequot Press

Design by Libby Kingsbury

Library of Congress Cataloging-in-Publication Data

Wilson, Beth, 1960-
  He's just no good for you : a guide to getting out of a destructive relationship / Beth Wilson with Mo Therese Hannah.
    p. cm.
  Includes bibliographical references and index.
  ISBN 978-0-7627-4934-8
  1. Man-woman relationships. 2. Mate selection. I. Hannah, Maureen Therese. II. Title.
  HQ801.W7245 2009
  646.7'7—dc22

                                                      2008041012

Printed in the United States of America

10 9 8 7 6 5 4 3 2 1

Contents

Contents

FOREWORD

As a practicing marriage and family therapist for more than 25 years, I have learned that men and women can have truly extraordinary, loving, and caring relationships no matter how bad their marriage was when we began to work together. Because I am considered "marriage friendly," I receive calls every day from individuals who want to get married or wonder about getting married, and from couples who want to fix their marriage. When I expanded my practice and included relationship-skills training to deal with conflict and other issues, more and more couples came to see me with seriously troubled relationships—in particular, married couples at the brink of divorce who wanted to attempt reconciliation. Providing both therapy and education had a positive impact for the majority of these couples and they were able to reconcile and move on with their lives. As my practice grew, my husband gave me the name "the marriage doctor." I have great satisfaction in knowing that the majority of couples that I see are able to reconnect with each other in healthier and more loving ways.

But I also work with couples where emotional abuse is severe and chronic, as well as with individuals—usually women—who come to see me because they are in marriages or relationships that are very troubled. These women are often unsure about whether they want to, or should, consider leaving. It's a very difficult and heartwrenching decision, even though they know that abusive relationships are unhealthy. In *He's Just No Good for You*, Beth Wilson describes with depth and sensitivity how to gain freedom from destructive love relationships that manifest as abuse and turmoil in a woman's life and the lives of her children.

Women need a way to become more understanding about themselves and their relationships and find a way to change these cycles. Just because we fall in love doesn't mean it will all work out. The chemistry of love is a wonderful experience, but sometimes the person we are attracted to has issues and problems that they are unwilling to address. With this book Beth Wilson digs deeper, unafraid to call out the experiences of many women and expose destructive relationships for what they are: unhealthy and, at times, abusive. She goes into detail about the myriad ways that women become captured in toxic relationships with men who are not interested in pursuing genuinely healthy and loving relationships, and offers concrete steps for disengagement. *He's Just No Good for You* provides a comprehensive look at the psychological, social, and historical reasons that women get stuck in destructive relationships and outlines the anatomy of destructive relationships by identifying the types of men to watch out for, while encouraging women to take a look at any patterns that might get them ensnared in seriously troubled partnerships. Unhealthy and abusive relationships are not one-type-fits-all, so a big picture approach is important for women searching for answers. The journey to recreating a life requires knowledge and hope so that motivation and courage can be maintained through the tough spots.

Family life today isn't what it was in my mother's or grandmother's eras. In those times marriage was a given. Today there are choices. But choices don't necessarily get us into the best relationships. Unfortunately abuse and violence are still prevalent problems for families, despite more attention and better services offered throughout many communities. In these situations many women stay in destructive and abusive marriages for years. They stay because of the impact on children. They stay because of financial or family or even religious considerations and impacts. They stay out of fear of the unknown. Compound these factors with low-self esteem, limited social support, and a relationship history filled with trauma and, leaving an abusive relationship can be a formidable challenge.

Together, Beth Wilson and Dr. Mo Hannah have gone beyond academic discussions of intimate discord and theories of abuse straight to empowering women. They succeed in this by providing essential information while validating women's gut feeling that "something isn't right." They clearly outline a process that women can use to navigate beyond the destructive forces of their intimate relationships so that they can move toward personal health and wholeness.

What I have learned as a "marriage doctor" and as a wife, mother, daughter, sister, and friend is that there are no easy answers in life. But, there *are* answers. We do know what a healthy relationship is and isn't. We do know something about love. We do know something about change and growth. We do know something about resolving trauma. So when a woman decides that she is worthy and deserves to love and be loved, it is essential that she have caring, knowledgeable, and compassionate guides and mentors for the journey. Luckily, Beth Wilson is here to help women take charge of their lives again.

Rita DeMaria, Ph.D.
Senior Staff and Director, Relationship Education
Council for Relationships, Philadelphia, PA
Coauthor of *The 7 Stages of Marriage*

September 12, 2008

Introduction

Power without love is reckless and abusive, and love without power is sentimental and anemic. Power at its best is love implementing the demands of justice, and justice at its best is power correcting everything that stands against love.

—MARTIN LUTHER KING JR.

Destructive relationships make women small. They eclipse the vitality and expansiveness of our spirit, reducing the parameters of our world. They make us feel unworthy and "less-than," eventually leading to a hunger in our soul as we inhabit a relationship that doesn't nourish us. Instead of being as luminous and full as the feminine moon, we become too constricted to bring forth our light—and may no longer feel the right to shine.

In more than twenty years of working in private practice, both Dr. Hannah and I have seen the damage done to women in destructive relationships. In fact, we've experienced the toxic results of these unions firsthand and know that no matter how strong, how smart, how creative, and how worldly a woman is, these and other admirable qualities cannot save her when she is involved with a controlling, verbally abusive, and psychologically domineering man. At first he may seem to be all you had hoped for in a mate; a perfect fit. Yet as time passes, a different reality emerges—one that is often confusing, maddening, and above all painful. Before you realize it, you don't feel quite like yourself, but you're not sure what's wrong. You communicate your concerns to him, and although he may feign understanding, things go back to the way they were. If you try to convey your thoughts and feelings with the hope of improving matters, he has a way of making you feel wrong. Or he simply doesn't want to talk about it, and you are left with a problem that he's not working to resolve. And why should he? While you're attempting to forge a loving bond, an intimate connection, and a compatible partnership, he's sabotaging your every move. The arrangement works for him, but it doesn't work for you. Nevertheless, you try harder, determined to fix a situation that, to him, is not even broken. In *The Verbally Abusive Relationship: How to Recognize It and How to Respond,* author Patricia Evans writes: "There are two kinds of power. One kills the spirit. The other nourishes the spirit. The first is Power Over. The other is Personal Power." When you're in a destructive relationship, you and the man you're with are working at cross purposes. For this reason it's difficult, if not impossible, to change the dynamics. He wants power. You want a relationship.

If you think you might be involved with a controlling man, you're not alone. Most women's lives have been touched by a destructive individual—some for months, others for years. If you are one of these women, the good news is that you can make things change. In *He's Just No Good for You: A Guide to Getting Out of a Destructive Relationship,* we show you how.

In the first chapter we start with you. Take a look. If you experience the thoughts and feelings so common in unhealthy relationships, you will see yourself in the first few pages. Dr. Hannah and I then provide profiles of different types of toxic men and describe how they operate, to help you understand their maneuvers. Though these men often wear different guises, their tactics are strikingly similar, and it's essential to know more about the particular brand you're contending with so you're not so easily deceived. At the end of chapter 2, we offer a "Where Do I Stand?" Quiz so you can better determine whether you're with a bad-news individual or not. If you are . . . read on, for the rest of the book is devoted to you.

Indeed, we always bring the focus back to you, not only to help you identify how you get hooked by these individuals but also to encourage you to build a stronger bridge to your inner wisdom and self-authority. We invite you to use this opportunity to make conscious contact with your authentic self, so that you can become stronger, wiser, more empowered, and a better version of the woman you were. Rather than allowing a problem person to decimate your spirit, you will become richer in knowledge and understanding, both of these men and of yourself.

Relish the aha moments—there will be many in this book! Trust yourself. And rest assured that although you may feel crazy at times—dealing with destructive men will do that to you—you're not. Rather, you are learning to navigate a complex and abusive way of living that can be tricky to sort out, especially if you're unaccustomed to these behaviors. Or because of your family of origin, you may have grown *too accustomed* to them and only recently begun to realize that there are better, more life-affirming ways to relate and communicate. At times you may feel stuck, but remember, you're not. We can tell you with the utmost confidence that many women have moved beyond these unhealthy partnerships and have found good relationships and fulfilling lives.

> **Rest assured that although you may feel crazy at times . . . you're not.**

This will be a step-by-step process, one that we will take you through. Be patient with yourself and remember, *there is no one right way to move on*. Only *you* can decide what actions to take and how quickly to take them. We will make sure you possess all the necessary pieces of the process so you can put them together in a way that works for you.

He's Just No Good for You provides information and support to help you come to terms with "the nature of the beast." Once you are well on the way, you can begin the process of sanity and self-care, which includes the decision to go or to stay, eventually growing beyond your current predicament.

Involvement with these men shapes us, but it does not define us. You can move forward, beyond their grasp. You can start anew. The time is ripe for all women to elevate the quality of their relationship bonds and to no longer settle for less. Our goal is not only to nourish women and create a healthy environment for children, but also to activate the highest good in us all. If women become more whole, so will the world.

In the end, all human beings are woven together by relationships. Wouldn't it be far better for all of us if these relationships were based on mutual empowerment, instead of domination?

| 1 |

It's Not Just You

Let's face it, as women we're relational. It's natural for us to think twice, once for ourselves and once for others. Our relationships are important to us. We cultivate them, nurture them, and count on them. But what if a relationship becomes toxic to our spirit and dangerous to our well-being?

What if it's our most intimate adult relationship that's wearing us down, whittling away at our sense of self, leaving us feeling worthless and depleted? What if it's destructive?

What if it's our most intimate adult relationship that's wearing us down, whittling away at our sense of self, leaving us feeling worthless and depleted? What if it's destructive?

This Is You . . . This Is You in a Destructive Relationship

Picture what you love most about yourself; what you like to share with others. Think about what you're good at. Think about the contributions you make to your children, your career, your friends, and your place of worship. Think about the ways in which you enact your personal vision, whether in politics, in business, in the arts, in nature, or in the home. Picture the light in your eye, your inimitable features, your distinctive laugh, the length of your fingers, and the color you like most when painting your toenails. Then picture yourself in your favorite outfit or in your most flattering clothes; swimming in the ocean; painting a canvas; tending to your children or working at the office. Think about your generosity, intelligence, perceptiveness, or simply that signature walk that belongs exclusively to you. Do you like to dance? Wear cowboy boots? Buy hats with feathers? Read historical novels? Play bingo? Do crossword puzzles? Golf? Invest? Cook? Travel? Really remind yourself of the unique compilation of qualities that you and you alone possess and enjoy every one of them because, when brought together, they are you; they are who you are.

Now picture yourself reacting to a comment from your partner that left you off-center and shut down. Think about conversations where you ended up feeling invalidated or nuts. *Is it just me?* you've wondered. *Does everyone walk away from conversations with him somehow feeling like they missed the point? Like they were just dismissed and subtly treated as less-than though they're just not sure how or why?* You've wanted to ask the person next to you, "Did that sound as ludicrous to you as it did to me?" But instead you're making excuses for him. *He's having a bad day*, you tell yourself. *I'm overreacting . . . he didn't mean to make me feel bad.* Or did he? *No one else seems bothered by his witty comments or deprecating humor.* Or are they?

Is it just me? you've wondered.

Think about the times when his response to your questions didn't quite make sense. Remember when he purposefully undermined your efforts to teach your kids to clean their rooms by poking fun at you in front of them? And when you asked him to stop, he replied, "I'm only joking, lighten up"? What about when you called him on the phone, eager to share news of a new job offer, and his response was: "That's great . . . congratulations . . . uh . . . how are you going to be able to have dinner ready for me and the kids? This could really have a negative effect on the kids . . . have you thought about that?" As your "intellectual superior," has he ever informed you that your dreams had no basis in reality and thus should not be pursued, leaving you feeling ridiculous for even thinking you could achieve your goals?

Of course he rarely flat-out criticizes you; he simply assaults your emotional stability with the smallest of cuts until, suddenly, you realize you're bleeding. "No," a good friend might say, "he really loves you and believes in you. I think you're just being overly sensitive." But that proud smile he gave your friend over dinner, boasting about your achievements, disappeared once you headed home and were out of the public eye, to be replaced by steady, small, but cruel criticisms. And so you think, *I must be crazy. Everyone loves him. He's smart. He's funny. He seems so perfect. How come I feel like shit?*

It's because your many wonderful traits are withering, diminishing one by one. Some changes are obvious. Others are gradual—you've stopped singing in the shower, stopped listening to *your* music while fixing dinner—little shifts until you no longer feel quite like yourself; you no longer feel like the woman you used to know. You're on edge, anxious, uncertain, confused, frustrated, angry, depressed, and powerless to fix the situation—although you're not certain what, exactly, the situation is that you'd like to fix. You wonder silently and sometimes out loud: "Is it my fault?" "What have I done wrong?" "Why is he acting this way?" "Why does he now fault me for a quality he used to say was one of his favorite things about me?" "Why do I feel so defensive? Shut down? Under attack?" "Why am I unhappy when, on the surface, everything looks so good? What's going on? Is it me or is it him?"

> You no longer feel quite like yourself; you no longer feel like the woman you used to know.

Like it or not, this could be you, this could be any of us, in a destructive relationship. If you're in such a relationship, over time you reach a point where you don't completely recognize yourself. Then you begin to focus much of your energy and time on simply staving off the effects of an unhealthy union that, quite literally, erodes your spirit and reduces your ability to fully engage in life. It's not a pretty picture. And it's more common than most of us think. You are certainly not alone.

Although the details may vary, one thing is certain: When we're entangled in a destructive relationship, we must contend with an array of corrosive tactics designed to undermine our self-worth, confidence, and dignity. This book is designed to help you fight back.

Educator and author Lawrence J. Peter once wrote: "If we lacked imagination enough to foresee something better, life would indeed be a tragedy." I'm quite confident that every one of us has a formidable imagination and an inner strength that can be put into action to create a new future. Understanding what, exactly, we are contending with and then learning to make better choices are essential to constructing a life that belongs to us and lovingly reflects the best of who we are. We can, indeed, save our own lives and build our own beginning for today, tomorrow, and the days to come. Remember, you have choices. You can get your life back.

> Remember, you have choices. You can get your life back.

The Many Forms of Control

As we move through this book, we will look in detail at the many ways a problem person keeps you down. After all, most of us weren't taught how to identify this type of relationship; as a result we may not be familiar with the all-too-common tactics used. So let's look quickly at the hallmark tools of the destructive individual:

Control ■ Possessiveness ■ Lying ■ Mind Games ■ Isolation
Emotional Terrorism ■ Manipulation ■ Corrosive Criticism
Denial ■ Deception ■ Minimizing ■ Projection

Any of these sound familiar? Destructive people view relationships in terms of power politics instead of cooperative unions based on mutual love. Control is their primary concern. Part of your uneasiness with them is because they rarely engage in an authentic way. Why? Because genuine relating requires sustained intimacy, emotional honesty, connection, and vulnerability, all qualities that undermine efforts to control the relationship and the other person.

It's not that the destructive individual is incapable of having feelings for the woman in his life; it's just that he's often confused about what it means to love a woman as opposed to possessing her. Certainly all of us can be thoughtless. We can speak in anger and lash out with hurtful words. We can be condescending and flip, insensitive and irritable, manipulative and stubborn. We can even shut others

Destructive people view relationships in terms of power politics instead of cooperative unions based on mutual love.

down in a moment of frustration. Yet while we are all guilty of acting in these ways from time to time, for the destructive individual these behaviors are his modus operandi—his bag of tricks—the subtle tools he uses to quietly control others . . . and that can mean *you*.

Physical and Verbal Abuse

In this book we're not focusing on the very overt and visible forms of control: physical abuse and verbal threats of violence. These are well known, much discussed, and in another category of abuse all together. Women enduring domestic violence have to struggle to keep themselves and their family members safe, often feeling like they have no options. In high school I remember watching a lab rat being shocked over and over in a metal cage. It was agonizing to see this helpless creature endure random zaps of electricity in order to prove what women in destructive relationships have long known. In such an environment the victim develops a conditioned response. She either gives up, lying down and simply taking the painful treatment, or she develops neurotic behaviors that, if they persist, can lead to a nervous breakdown. Either way she breaks under the pressure, and unless she can escape the cage, the situation only gets more damaging.

This book is about the more subtle behaviors that, unchecked, systematically disintegrate a woman's vitality and self-confidence. Verbal abuse coupled with cruel behaviors are the main culprits we're focusing on.

Verbal abuse is tricky. Unless it's blatant—threatening physical assault or direct character assassination—it can be more likened to a razor blade than a machete. In the hands of an extremely skilled man, it can be a scalpel of control, with each incision creating a small but significant wound that must be perpetually mended in order for a woman to remain intact. And because these people want to avoid being labeled "abusive"—and many of them have convinced themselves that they are not—their first line of offense is to undermine, manipulate, confuse, invalidate, and dismantle a woman's sense of self, and her self-confidence. This they do very well. The more easily you can spot words and actions that undermine and invalidate you, the better off you'll be. This book will help you understand his maneuvers and sleight-of-hand tactics so you can make better sense of a crazy-making situation—and see things for how they really are. It will help you learn how to differentiate between thoughtless words and actions and those devised to undo you.

At first, it's difficult to put your finger on what is happening; you feel crazy. Then, once you know what you're dealing with, it's difficult *not* to see it.

In my work I have seen brilliant women, creative women, enlightened women, loving women, perceptive women, even tough-minded women succumb to these tactics in the same way sound health can erode with disease. And often because of the words of a brilliant, creative, seemingly loving man. You may be reluctant to admit that your relationship is destructive, or you may simply be confused by the cyclical nature of the demeaning behaviors and aren't certain how to describe your experience. Here Dr. Hannah and I will lay out the various forms of control, whether in words, actions, or a combination of the two. Familiarizing yourself with the anatomy of a destructive relationship is the best way to come to terms with the nature of the beast. As one woman told me, "At first, it's difficult to put your finger on what is happening; you feel crazy. Then, once you know what you're dealing with, it's difficult *not* to see it."

Why Do I Feel Like the Crazy One?

In a partnership the goal is to nurture closeness and cooperation, not to create distance and dissonance, right? Of course this is a fair assumption for a woman to make. However, it's usually not an assumption that is shared by the destructive individual. When you're investing in a relationship and your currency is primarily love, respect, and emotional integrity, yet the man in your life places a higher value on control, power, and psychological domination, then it's nearly impossible to be on the same page. After all, you're working toward different goals. His words may deny this but his actions will indicate otherwise—and this can be crazy making.

Lies and Deception

Being lied to and deceived feels horrible. It belittles us and in a short period of time erodes our trust—in ourselves, in the other person, and in the relationship. If we do not know what's true and what's false, it's nearly impossible to avoid feeling bewildered, off-balance, and tense. As one client told me, "Lies and deception are women's kryptonite." They zap our vitality, hurt our hearts, and can turn us into lunatics as we frantically try to ferret out the truth day after day. If your partner is a destructive individual, lies and deception keep you in the dark and allow him to stay in control. You may sense that something isn't quite right. You might even confront him, hoping he'll 'fess up. But more likely than not, he'll avoid being held accountable—especially if he's hiding addictions, illegal activities, infidelity, financial problems, or simply other lies. Of course no one wants to believe that the man she's in love with would intentionally deceive her and withhold the truth. *Why would he lie to me about the amount of gas in the car as if he didn't want me to know where he's been?* you wonder. *Why would he want to conceal his financial affairs or the sites he visits on the computer?* The reason is plain: He doesn't want you to know. There may not be much behind the secrecy, or there may be a whole other life. Either way, knowledge is power—and if he's in the know and you're not, *he's* in power.

Lies and deception are women's kryptonite.

Manipulation and Mind Games

Like lies and deception, manipulation is a form of dishonesty. But rather than an outright lie, it's designed to conceal the truth in an effort to control the power in a relationship. And like lies and deception, manipulation is demeaning primarily because the underlying assumption is that your feelings, values, and preferences have little worth. They will only be placed in the equation when they do not directly threaten the agenda of the destructive individual. Moreover, he will unilaterally renegotiate the terms you've agreed to on a whim, completely disregarding a previous negotiation. One mother of four put it this way: "Manipulation is a self-centered ruse that treats others as though they are simply puppets in someone else's play. It can really kill your self-esteem, especially when it happens in an intimate relationship."

While mind games are also tools of manipulation, their main purpose is to fragment us with psychological warfare. Broken women, anxious and uncertain women, and women who lack confidence, no matter how high their IQ, no matter how many college degrees, no matter how prestigious their athletic awards, are much easier to control. With such unrelenting invalidation you can become plagued with self-doubt and susceptible to the chipping away of your dignity and positive self-regard. You end up feeling as though something is wrong with *you* when, in reality, it's the man you're involved with— he's simply no good for you.

Emotional Terrorism

Emotional terrorism is a certain type of mind game that is worth mentioning here, since it is a very effective tool of control that can turn a sane woman into an emotional wreck in record time. It goes like this: Your husband picks up the children from school since you have to stay late at the office. He calls to tell you that the school counselor pulled him aside to "discuss what happened to our son, Nathan." His tone is serious, and so you're worried. "Was Nathan hurt? Molested? Is he in trouble?" He says he cannot discuss it on the phone but he is very concerned and urgently needs to talk about it with you. Hardly able to focus, you rush home . . . only to learn that it wasn't the school counselor but the teacher who spoke to him, and she only wanted to discuss Nathan's difficulty with math. When you confront your husband, and say that you hurried home to deal with the problem, he insists that you misunderstood him and clearly "made something out of nothing." Cruel, yes, but he got you to leave the office, didn't he? The emotional terrorist will use your love of your children, your love of your family, your love of your pets, even your love of treasured belongings to unseat you—and that is the only element of this game you can be sure of. His ability to manipulate you emotionally and cause distress makes him feel powerful and in charge—and it can destroy your self-confidence to the point where you feel as though you're walking on eggshells anticipating the next episode.

Twisting the Facts

Destructive individuals have the most curious memories. As Mark Twain once quipped: "I remember things whether they happened or not." Well, that's what it's like living with someone who chronically twists the facts. Although this maddening behavior often sounds ludicrous, it's not so easy to laugh off. It's a tactic that can be applied to small matters such as "You told me you didn't care if my friends came over" when he actually never asked the question and is now unhappy with your response, or big ones: "I think you heard me wrong. I told you I could *not* pick up the children from school today" when you're certain he said he could. Either way, we are often accused of saying or doing things we didn't or that our version of events and conversations is, unequivocally, "inaccurate."

But I Was Only Joking: Denial, Minimizing, and Projection

Ever feel like everything you say is put back on you? When you attempt to engage your mate in problem solving or ask him to do something differently because it's hurtful, rude, or simply inconsiderate, does he act as though the problem is with you, not him? Or perhaps he denies any wrongdoing on his part, turning events around so you end up being blamed for something when you're clearly not at fault? Problem people have a knack for evading responsibility for their words and deeds.

> Hostile teasing, insults couched in "jokes," refusal to accept responsibility for destructive actions, and false accusations are hallmark traits of toxic relationships.

If your partner refuses to be held accountable, one of his favorite ways to do this is to lie to himself—otherwise known as denial. Sadly, he may genuinely believe what he's telling you. He really may think that you're the one who's acting erratically and that he is "just kidding." Another way he might respond to your questioning is to turn it back on you: projection. Thus you are the one at fault. Finally, minimizing is also very commonplace. It often goes like this: He insults you, or makes fun of you in an underhanded way, yet as soon as you say "Hey, that hurts," he tells you, "Relax. I was only joking." In other words, if there wasn't something wrong with you, his disparaging comments and refusals to act in a more loving way wouldn't bother you. Hostile teasing, insults couched in "jokes," refusal to accept responsibility for destructive actions, and false accusations are hallmark traits of toxic relationships. It couldn't be him . . . so it's all about you . . . it's all about what's wrong with you.

Behind Closed Doors

A sure sign that you're involved with a destructive individual is when he acts very different in public than he does at home. Out with others he's careful to project a certain persona—family and friends only see what he wants them to see, and most of the time he comes off as the greatest guy. However, once you get into the car or arrive at the house, the tune changes and he becomes surly and demanding, impatient and intolerant. Perhaps he treats you with contempt. Sometimes the personality shift is abrupt while at other times it's more like a slow frame-by-frame transformation.

> Having a public persona and a private one that only you are privy to is one of *the* defining features of a destructive individual.

Whichever way he goes, you can be sure that the fun you were having just minutes ago stops. And if you were nervously anticipating the change in persona, you probably weren't enjoying yourself that much anyway, knowing it was just a matter of time before he slipped back to toxic behaviors. Having a public persona and a private one that only you are privy to is one of *the* defining features of a destructive individual. He doesn't want "outsiders" to discover what he's hiding from everyone *but* you. Unlucky you.

Jealousy, Possessiveness, and Isolation

Jealousy, possessiveness, and isolating behaviors are common tools of control. These are powerful tactics precisely because they pressure us to adhere to the terms he sets forth by requiring that we relinquish those people, places, and things that having meaning to us to prove that he matters more. Talk about sacrifices to a false god! When we're ensconced in such an arrangement, our "loving partner" monopolizes our time because he is jealous of time spent with anyone but him. In these scenarios he usually exerts his power over us by acting in possessive ways, the message being: *She belongs to me.* If these behaviors persist, we can become isolated from friends and family, even giving up appearing at favorite haunts as he tightens his grip. It's not unusual for destructive individuals to be jealous of anyone from our closest family members to a friendly store clerk, and use tactics to alienate us from those people. I even heard of one man who tried to get rid of his girlfriend's dog!

Not surprisingly, these men often find ways to justify their jealous and possessive behavior in an attempt to be the main influence or, better yet, the *only* influence in our lives. Why? It's because they want to call the shots and they don't want others interfering with their agenda of being number one. However, they may not be obvious and overt. Asking that you be "the perfect wife" and co-opting your unspoken agreement to

Slowly your individual identity slips away until you appear to be an extension of him.

do as he wishes with disapproving glances and hostile scowls when you pay attention to someone or focus your attention elsewhere can achieve the same results. After all, nonverbal communication can be just as powerful as the spoken word and, you tell yourself, you *do* love him. You want him to know that he comes first. But if you're not careful, his opinions can become your opinions; his political affiliations can become your political affiliations; his favorite restaurants can become your favorite restaurants. Slowly your individual identity slips away until you appear to be an extension of him. Such a blurred sense of self can make you feel alone and lost—your personal power obfuscated. Destructive individuals know this, and they know that a woman alone is much easier to manage than one who is kept buoyant by others—friends, relatives, and professionals—who support her independence, value her opinions, and care about her individual happiness. Don't let this happen to you.

Taking Aim at Your Heart: Purposefully Disrupting the Relationship Bond to Fuel Insecurity

As women, we want to be the recipients of genuinely caring acts that enrich our relationship, and bad-news individuals are well aware of this fact. They have remarkable talent when it comes to dismantling the security of a relationship in order to disrupt our bond and sever feelings of trust. Since most of these men are connection-averse, they act in ways that undermine closeness and genuinely loving emotional contact. They are abusive to the relationship instead of being supportive of it. For example, if you begin to settle into the relationship and feel comfortable, he will purposefully take action to cast doubt on his affection by commenting about attractive women on the TV, "reminiscing" about past girlfriends, and "joking" about the advantages of being a bachelor. He may distance himself after periods of relative tranquility; or he may choose times when you are gaining in strength, happiness, or in some way getting ahead to undermine you and keep you down. You end up knowing that if you have personal success, there's a price to be paid.

> The goal is to get you worrying about the relationship.

The goal is to get you worrying about the relationship because, as women, any threat to something so important to us makes us feel upset. Your energy is focused away from his assaults and instead you attempt to rescue the relationship, alter your behavior, and frantically try to please.

One of the most disconcerting things about these men is that they themselves can buy into their own games. They have been operating in destructive ways for so long that they may not know how to relate in a healthy way. If it's true that thoughts create our reality, then the reality these men live with inside their heads is not one we would want to be privy to, much less entangled in. As one family law attorney put it: "They have a tendency to believe their own bullshit, and that's dangerous." While you're wanting a relationship that engenders trust, security, and love, the destructive individual is busy sabotaging. He may have once admired you for your confidence, but now he does what he can to make you insecure about the relationship—and, ultimately, about yourself. As Harvard psychologist

Dr. Daniel Goleman points out in *Social Intelligence: The New Science of Human Relationships:*

> *The more strongly connected we are with someone emotionally, the greater the mutual force. Our most potent exchanges occur with those people with whom we spend the greatest amount of time day in and day out, year after year—particularly those we care about the most . . . To a surprising extent, then, our relationships mold not just our experience but our biology . . . That link is a double-edged sword: nourishing relationships have a beneficial impact on our health, while toxic ones can act like slow poison in our bodies.*

It's not surprising to end up feeling diminished, lost, and shut down when partnered with the wrong man.

I Used to Be so Confident

We all have moments when we catch a glimpse of ourselves in a store window that snaps us to attention and we realize that, somehow, we've changed. We used to be so confident. What happened? How did it vanish? Did someone take it or did I lose it? One minute you're self-assured and now this. *What's wrong with me? Where did my happiness go? How come I feel paralyzed?* No matter what you do, you can't make things better.

If you feel you're often walking on eggshells and have noticed that decisions you used to make easily now make you uneasy, as though you no longer have the authority or the capability you used to, you can't help but ask, *When did that happen?* Think about it. All the crazy-making behaviors, like a virus, have compromised your well-being, subtly, insidiously; they've changed you. Even if you weren't the picture of confidence previously, what daring you did possess seems to be lost. One woman put it like this: "I may not have been an adventurer and traveled to all corners of the earth, but at least I could book an airline ticket to travel home for the holidays. After a couple of years with my husband, I felt unsure about whether I was capable of getting us the best deal and handling the details. It was so strange. Those things never intimidated me before!" You find yourself apologizing for things you aren't responsible for—and trying, unsuccessfully, to improve the situation. As one professional woman expressed it: "Sometimes I felt so badly about myself, as though I was apologizing for my very existence." Destructive relationships will do that to you, to any of us, until we begin to turn things around and opt for sanity.

Put It All Together and What Do You Get?

It's hard to argue against a manipulative partner. Destructive men can argue quite convincingly that you are the problem, not them. They often invalidate your feelings, refuse to believe your side of the story, and tell you that your perceptions are wrong. When you point out that their words and behaviors are hurtful, they'll blame you for your response instead of acknowledging any cruelty on their part. They are also notorious for telling you what you want to hear. They have an uncanny ability to get you to believe them—face it, you *want* to believe them. As a counselor for family court once said: "The less-than-noble goals and motives that are the daily preoccupation of destructive people don't even enter the minds of decent folks. As a result, the healthy person can't even conceive of such motives and will tend to misread the problem person's character in a more positive direction, much to her own detriment."

The Five C's of a Destructive Relationship

If, after reading this, you still have doubts whether your relationship is destructive, remember the *Five C's*. Despite differences in personalities and predominant profiles, *all* destructive men share these five characteristics.

Control: They want to control you. Period. The methods may vary, but the goal is the same.

Containment: Once they find what works to control you, they use these tactics to maintain control.

Calculating: Destructive men spend an inordinate amount of time figuring out ways to keep you off-balance so they can hide outside activities, addictions, lies, and avoid being found out for who they really are.

Condescending: Criticism, put-downs, sly, demeaning jokes . . . they are all part of the attitude he holds toward you—yes, regardless of the fact that he tells you he loves you. The word is *contempt*.

Connection-Averse: Destructive individuals aren't really looking to relate to you. Though they may have loving moments, communicate honestly for brief stints, and occasionally show affection that is not part of a larger manipulation, their main objective is control—and this makes an authentic relationship impossible.

■ ■ ■ ■ ■

In the next chapter we'll take a closer look at these men so we can more readily identify the various wolves in sheep's clothing. They're a colorful bunch, and I suspect you already know a number of them. In addition, Dr. Hannah and I have assembled a list of questions so you can score your relationship and then be better able to connect the dots.

| 2 |

Know Any of These Guys?

Like the woman in the previous chapter who was initially bewildered by the destructive behaviors she was facing, most of us have no context to properly identify and understand what, exactly, is happening. Yet once the proverbial gumball dropped, ". . . it was difficult *not* to see." Keep in mind that these bad-news guys come in many guises, and learning how to identify them—as well as developing your bullshit detector—is essential. Behaviors that might, at first glance or to the untrained eye, appear quite innocuous, benign, or even benevolent can hide quite another story underneath.

The truth is, rarely do any of these men fit neatly into one category. There can be overlap and interrelations among the types outlined below. So it's helpful to use these profiles as pieces to a puzzle that you can put together yourself. I'll leave it up to you to determine which tactics, traits, and characteristics best describe your particular scenario. A teenage client who eventually left a high school boyfriend who turned out to be more than she bargained for once confided, "I kept listening to his words until I finally realized that they had nothing to do with what he was saying." At a rather young age she, like Dorothy in *The Wizard of Oz*, decided it was best to pull back the curtain of deception to reveal what, and who, was behind it. This allowed her to short-circuit the power the charade had over her. If this is your situation, you'd be surprised how easily you can blow the whistle, too.

I'll begin with some of the most obvious offenders, then move on to the less conspicuous ones who have perfected their disguise and may even have come to believe that the image they project is who they truly are. As we often say in my line of work, "They've been conned by their own con," making the deception all the more difficult to penetrate. But it can be done. I can guarantee that the problem people such as the ones described below rarely want to

> "I kept listening to his words until I finally realized that they had nothing to do with what he was saying."

be identified, because for you, too, knowledge is power. Knowing his true nature will allow you to reclaim control over your own life and decide whether or not you want him in it.

Again, bear in mind that there are many overlapping characteristics and parallels to the personalities. Nevertheless, the packaging is quite distinct, and once you identify a type of man you catch on to his tricks more easily. So let's take a look at these "wolves in sheep's clothing," "snakes in suits," or "hyenas in pajamas." I think you'll find some of them familiar.

The Control Freak

Control freaks spend an inordinate amount of time and energy paying attention to your every move. At first this type of man may seem like he's attentive and simply wants to be with you—very flattering! But soon the dichotomy starts. Perhaps he calls your cell phone or e-mails you repeatedly, as if to prove his love and offer signs of affection. But the questions are always the same: "Where are you? Who's with you?" If you tell him he sounds suspicious, he denies it and either becomes irritated by your "rebuffs" or continues to insist that he misses you and lays on the sweet talk. In actuality he's grooming you to respond to his beck and call whether it's through cyberspace, phone signals, or face-to-face conversations. If you don't comply, he may resort to anger, guilt, or shame to bring you to heel . . . all under the auspices of wanting to be your one and only man.

When you are apart, he often gets a little rattled. It may not be obvious in the beginning, but if he's feeling threatened—by your independence, your friends, your family, an old boyfriend you haven't contacted in years—he'll call to purposefully pick a fight or to plant a negative thought in your brain that will deflate your fun and make you feel anxious and obligated to leave your family or friends and return home to find out what's wrong. Of course, he presents his controlling behaviors as concerned overtures or love. And even though you and your friends may catch glimpses of subplot, it's easy not to actively connect the dots. As a result it can take a while before the bigger picture becomes clear. This is not your fault. But remember, once you know what you're dealing with, you can take steps to stop the cycle. More on this later.

While it doesn't take long before you feel trapped by a control freak's attention, smothered by his love, and exhausted by his repetitive tactics as he exerts them over and over in an attempt to keep you in line, you may find it easier to just go along. You might feel something is out of whack, yet you also feel wanted. You're receiving attention, he's good in bed—there are any number of reasons to gloss over his tactics and simply tell others, "It's an intense relationship," when they can already see that you can hardly breathe. Turns out, with his one-pointed focus, he's adept at keeping the target always in view. We wake up every morning wanting to include him in our day while unbeknownst to us, he's been *planning* ours!

The Corrector

This is another version of the control freak. The corrector is always amending your opinions to fit his own; he always insists you like the same things when he knows that isn't really the case; and he readily hints about his preferences until you catch on and comply—whether it's in the way you dress, how you vote, or what books you read.

While you may think of him as particular or fussy, the truth is, he cannot tolerate views that differ from his. Your independent choices often lead him to pout, withdraw his love and attention, or seek out ways to make you look wrong in order to gain the emotional and psychological upper hand. "Why don't you wear the red dress?" he may ask. This seems innocent enough . . . until you realize that he rarely compliments your choices but is quick to make suggestions for his preferences. "Why do you read such drivel when you're supposed to be so smart?" The onslaught of questions such as these can be never ending. The corrector isn't really looking for answers so much as trying to herd you into submission with criticism and verbal intimidation.

The Abuser

These guys are hard to miss. They're Marlon Brando in a wife-beater T-shirt—if not literally, then figuratively. Their world view can usually be summed up into a few basic principles, not the least of which is that men are superior to women. Yes, even when we see these fellows depicted in movies and wince at their obvious larger-than-life behaviors on screen, we might still finish our popcorn and head to our own "old lug" (as we affectionately call him) at home. "So he loves sports, drinks beer, leaves dirty dishes in the sink—that only proves that he's *all man*," you might say, knowing full well that plenty of men who possess these traits don't have a habit of berating, threatening, or chastising their wives or girlfriends. These men have gained a reputation precisely because they built it.

They often have dangerous tempers and can easily form a fist if a woman will not bend to their will. While the control freak uses words to break a woman down, the low-life abuser backs up his words with physical threats that he carries out when needed—even if they're disguised as playfully rough instead of overtly battering. In fact, these men are notorious for grabbing too hard, accosting with "love taps" to remind us who is stronger, pulling hair, throwing objects close to us, and so on. As an attorney once described it: "These guys usually lack interpersonal skills, though they might be quite intelligent. As a result, they only have a hammer in their proverbial tool belt . . . and for that reason, they treat every situation as a nail—sometimes they only tap with the hammer and at other times they swing it. Either way, their only tool is one of control."

But if he did possess better tools for communication, it is doubtful the abuser would be asking you what you want because your opinion counts so little. He thinks men should receive

The rules are plain: Do what he wants, when he wants, and nobody gets punished.

preferential treatment as part of the natural order of things—or at least how things should be. These guys insist on taking power where they can get it—usually subjugating the women and children in their lives—and feel justified doing whatever needs to be done to keep order. "I wouldn't have to yell so loudly if you would just do what I tell you" is an often-used phrase. After all, the rules are plain: Do what he wants, when he wants, and nobody gets punished. Too bad the rules can change so abruptly, especially when he's been drinking.

It is important to note that abusers—regardless of social status or economic class—have a high rate of alcohol consumption. As Dr. Donald G. Dutton writes in his book *The Batterer: A Psychological Profile:* "We found that assaultive men . . . have very high alcohol use scores. Indeed, the more a man matched our gauge for having an abusive personality, the greater his alcohol consumption." Keep in mind that alcohol doesn't cause the destructive behavior; it simply relaxes a man's inhibitions, dismantling any restraint that may have prevented a verbal or physical attack.

For the abuser, verbal, psychological, and physical violence are simply a way of life. He's the quintessential brute, the common batterer, and other people's feelings mean little to him. Whether he resides in a mansion, a condo, or a houseboat, he sees himself as king and expects full cooperation from his loyal subjects. Or else.

The Charmer

A dictionary might describe a charmer as someone who has the power of pleasing others through his personality; someone able to act upon others with a magical force. The charmer is funny, engaging, clever, responsive, and, at least at first, polite and considerate. You may feel lucky to be his choice of companion. But in a destructive relationship, you need to know that this type is in the business of image management and will dismiss or attempt to alienate you from those who do not buy into his game. Sadly, most of your friends and family will refrain from telling you they think he's a phony because (1) it's "not any of their business"; (2) they don't want to burst your bubble; or (3) they're afraid you'll be upset since, clearly, he appears to be so wonderful in your eyes.

While he's adept at figuring out what you like, once the charmer attaches himself, flattery and humor can be and often are used to manipulate. The charmer works quite hard at creating his pleasing persona, but it's often behind closed doors that you will discover the truth. His outgoing or attractive personality can lure in intelligent women, educated women, professional and nonprofessional women alike. Regardless whether he's a Don Juan, New Age progressive, established professional, or any other version, beware. He will charm his way into your home, your bank accounts, your children's lives, your co-workers' hearts, and more as he carries out his well-thought-out agenda. When you discover his abuse—siphoning money out of your savings, lying to your children, misinforming employers, and so on in an attempt to disrupt your life and hold you hostage to "bigger plans"—you may well be in disbelief. How could you have mistaken charm for love?

> How could you have mistaken charm for love?

Sadly, when you try to tell others what you're experiencing, they often don't believe "such a great guy" can be doing such bad things. "Are you sure?" they ask. "Maybe he borrowed it and intends to pay you back?" If he's charmed them, too, they'll think you're exaggerating and jumping to conclusions. After all, he makes everyone feel good . . . his compliments, helpful suggestions, and considerate overtures win almost everyone over. So if the problem isn't with him, the implication is that it's you. This, of course, fuels your own self-doubt; something he's counting on. Once you have caught on to his charming facade, it can be maddening to see him charm the pants off others. You want to shake them and say, *Don't you see?* But they seldom do—and then again, neither did you, at least at first.

The Passive-Aggressive

Karen, a bright and engaging woman in her midforties, recently came to see me for a session. "I'm confused," she told me before I had a chance to offer her a seat. "The man I've been dating for the past four months is about ten years my senior, he's been fairly successful in corporate America, is attractive, and at least at first appeared to be mature and together. But as time's gone on I've found that he negotiates and renegotiates everything—often like we're business partners instead of a loving couple—and says one thing but often means another. He can contradict himself in the same sentence!" Instantly I knew what we had on our hands: a passive-aggressive who never said exactly what he meant and, in a few short months, was driving her crazy! As clinical psychologist Dr. Scott Wetzler writes in his book *Living with the Passive-Aggressive Man: Coping with Hidden Aggression from the Bedroom to the Boardroom:* "Problems arise with the passive-aggressive man because of his fatal flaw: an indirect and inappropriate way of expressing hostility hidden under the guises of innocence, generosity, or, more likely passivity."

Decoding the Mixed Messages

Passive-aggressive men habitually send mixed messages. They like to keep you guessing so they can string you along. As Karen explained: "When we first went out to dinner, he spent a lot of time telling me how he enjoys paying for meals, opening the door, and basically 'being the gentleman,' which was fine by me, except that by the third date he kept repeating himself as though he was trying to sell me, to persuade us both. I thought he was describing who he is, you know, telling me his preferences for conducting his life. Boy, was I wrong! One night after dinner he starts making hostile comments about paying for the meals . . . yet even when I brought it up to him, in midsentence no less, he actually renounced it as it was happening or quickly claimed that was not what he meant!"

Dr. Wetzler puts it this way:

Passive-aggressive tactics aren't that easily read at first; it takes a while to figure out what this guy is getting at: the blur of meaning lies in his genius for creating discrepancies between how he pretends to be and how he acts . . . You're always receiving mixed messages because he wants you to guess what he wants almost as much as he wants to fool you or string you along.

Like many women, though, Karen was hooked into the relationship in two ways. First, "He seems like such a nice guy," she insisted, despite all the hostile words and actions that contradicted this statement. Second, she liked it when he consulted with her, asking for help in picking out clothes for weekend trips or joining him for grocery runs, because it appealed to her giving nature. Yet the deeper into the relationship she got, the more passive *and* aggressive his words and actions became. Over time she discovered that he really wanted to be taken care of—a bit too much—and emotionally acted more like a child than an adult. Although Karen eventually understood the personality type she was dealing with, she wasn't quite ready to leave the relationship until a few weeks later. "When he offered to open a joint bank account to pay for meals out—telling me we'd simply have to negotiate how the money was spent—as a solution for our 'communication problems' over who pays for dinner, it was like a window opened up in my mind and I got it. The new arrangement wouldn't solve any real problem, it would just be a bigger, messier version of what I was contending with—which, in reality, wasn't about food . . . it was about him!"

Karen hadn't invested much and could quickly extricate herself. She was lucky. Women who are enmeshed with passive-aggressives risk being pushed over the edge. These men "accidentally" throw out important

> These men need an adversary, someone whose demands and expectations they can resist in order to work out their aggression and feel powerful in some small way.

documents you need for work; they "forget" to show up for your children's piano recital; they purposefully make you late for appointments and then deny any wrongdoing. In short, their hostile antics wear you out, belittle you, and make you feel stressed, frustrated, and angry. Like a perpetual teenager, these men need an adversary, someone whose demands and expectations they can resist in order to work out their aggression and feel powerful in some small way. As Dr. Wetzler says, "Passive-aggression is often expressed through relationships and so appears to be a 'relationship' problem. But more often than not, it is one person's problem: *his*." It sure can feel like it's yours, though!

The Pillar of the Community

The news is full of these types: pillars of the community. When their wives file for divorce, or they're caught with their hands in the company cookie jar, or they're picked up on multiple DUI charges, we hear neighbors say in dismay, "He was a leading member of our church, he coached the baseball team, he volunteered at the homeless shelter . . . how could this happen? We never heard him raise his voice at anyone. He was such a good person." Over and over journalists interview citizens who attest to the destructive individual's "good character," all different versions of the same story. Graduated from college with honors; loved by his management team; pitched in to help orchestrate the local holiday parade . . . the profile is perfect. However, it's woefully incomplete.

These seemingly credible men possess many of the same traits as the abuser, the passive-aggressive, the charmer, and the control freak—except they have money, or prestige, or power, or all three. This makes them look very good on the outside. To the women in their lives, however, they are emotionally dangerous. These men often use subtle forms of verbal abuse, mind games, and emotional terrorism as tools of control that go completely unnoticed by others who are too busy admiring the new car, addition to the house, extravagant gifts, art collections, and rare bottles of wine picked up in France. Besides, as Dr. Susan Weitzman points out in her book *"Not to People Like Us": Hidden Abuse in Upscale Marriages*:

"How could this happen? He was such a good person."

> *The man of means has more resources to protect his rights, his privacy, and his "castle." Expansive living quarters are not merely luxurious; they also make for an insulated existence, affording more privacy for engaging in physical and emotional tyranny. And on the rare occasion when the wife involves the police or other outside authorities, the upscale husband can retain skilled legal representation to defend his actions with little retribution or fanfare.*

After all, men who have prestige don't behave like that, right? Actually they do. They're just dressed differently. For women involved with this type of man, especially those raised in privilege, such abuse goes against the perception of being upper class, thus increasing the chances for isolation, shame, and quietly soothing the pain with prescription medication or alcohol. If there is little to no physical abuse, you may feel that you lack hard evidence and may question whether you're actually in a bad situation. *If he struck me, I'd be gone,* you reassure yourself, not realizing that the systematic tactics he's using are eroding your sanity—indeed are dangerous—and that abuse is not just for the underprivileged. Even if you're not embedded in an upper-class code of

You will very quickly learn that because of his wealth, connections, and power, it isn't difficult for him to get and hold on to the upper hand.

silence, you will very quickly learn that because of his wealth, connections, and power, it isn't difficult for him to get and hold on to the upper hand. In addition to placing you at a severe disadvantage, this can add to a feeling of helplessness, a sense that you've lost the battle before it's begun. Besides, he looks so handsome in his designer suits, Italian leather shoes, leaning against his Mercedes before he takes off for the hospital as head surgeon; the courthouse as a magistrate; the airport to take his seat in a congressional office. It's intoxicating and easy to remind yourself that as the woman by his side you're envied by many. But they don't know the image isn't real, and that there's an abuser under that Armani.

The Self-Righteous Progressive

A variation on the pillar-of-the-community type, self-righteous progressives tend to travel in academic, social justice, and political circles. These men are usually quite bright, educated intellectuals who have decided what, in their mind, the new world order should be. They are the men who rally for peace, equal rights, and reverence for life, yet fail to practice what they preach, particularly when it comes to women. They're much better at talking about high principles than actually incorporating them into their lives, yet this hypocrisy seems to be of little concern. In fact, these progressive types have an uncanny ability to gloss over their own behavior as they focus on the wrongdoing of others who display the same psychological and emotional warfare on the international stage. Remember Jenny's militant boyfriend in the movie *Forrest Gump*? He was a self-proclaimed hero when it came to saving those less fortunate on the other side of the world, all the while shaming and verbally attacking Jenny. He treated her with contempt as he railed against "The Man"; "The Man" that unjustly kept *him* down. As a friend of mine who's a physician at a prestigious college medical center once remarked: "Ladies, be careful of these men who are gonna save the world while they're destroying yours. Maybe it's time to wake up and smell the diplomas!" Author and Harvard psychologist Dr. Daniel Goleman has defined *emotional intelligence* as self-awareness, impulse control, persistence, zeal, self-motivation, empathy, and social deftness. And it's easy to assume that it's the same as intellectual prowess. It's not, and the misconception is common among women who enjoy theorists, philosophers, academics, geniuses, and smart guys who seem to care.

> Ladies, be careful of these men who are gonna save the world while they're destroying yours. What's at work here isn't selflessness, but an eroding of your self.

Understandably, this type of man is alluring because it appears that he wants to make the world a better place. He rides his bike instead of using a car; he filters his water; he refuses to dry-clean his clothes; he gives money to National Public Radio and international charities. Yet he doesn't want to afford you the same rights he fights for so vehemently. Instead, he may use these righteous stances as a weapon, forcefully turning off the television during your favorite show because he's decided it's "mind numbing." Or he may ask why you don't ride your bike more often to cut down on auto emissions. When you answer, "Because I have to take three children to and from school, ballet lessons, science camp, and friends' houses . . . ," he replies that if you were truly dedicated to the cause, you would solve this problem; a problem he perceives as yours and yours alone. While you may realize that the guilt is unwarranted, you still can get hooked in. After all, you want to save the world, too. Yet what's at work here isn't selflessness, but an eroding of your self. One mother put it this way: "When it finally occurred to me that I'd rather go to hell in an Armani gown than tolerate any more of his sanctimonious, guilt-inducing diatribes, I felt better. I could see them for what they were . . . a tactic designed to make me feel bad about myself. But honestly, it took a while, and you want to know why? Because I, too, was in love with the image of being good, living my values . . . I had to get real."

The New Age Man

A close cousin of the self-righteous progressive is the New Age man. This problem person cannot be pegged solely by his Birkenstocks and ashram beads. Like the progressive, he has ordered his life around a particular philosophy, in this case a spiritual or metaphysical one. He has probably been in therapy to "work on himself," and he's attracted to a wide range of feel-good pseudo-religions. But rarely does he actually do the hard work. Like any destructive individual, he simply wraps up old behaviors in newer, prettier packaging. He's an adept salesman, but the image he's peddling doesn't match his actions. If he has problems with substance abuse, obsessive-compulsive behaviors, infidelity, anger management, controlling and manipulative behaviors, he manages to avoid dealing with them and instead prays harder, meditates more frequently, and indulges in yet another self-help book. Sadly, these are usually temporary fixes that do little to improve the treatment of those around him. Rather than taking a look at themselves, these men "correct" our views, invalidate our feelings, and belittle us in condescending tones with their superior intellect and "spiritual knowledge."

When it comes to the treatment of women, New Age men are anything but enlightened. Although they view women as inferior and subservient, they are quick to give examples of the workshops they've attended specifically to develop their "feminine side." Women who've been with this type of man know that no matter how many visits to the guru, no matter how many trips to India, no matter how many workshops or spiritual practices he incorporated into his life, there was little authentic change when it came to his actions within the relationship. As a client in her thirties put it: "He was more in love with the idea of being a spiritual man than actually being one. And who could blame him? Cultivating compassion, patience, presence to others, love, respect, gratitude, and so on is hard work—and putting it into action is even harder! Yeah, when I encouraged him to go out and get in touch with his feelings, that's exactly what he did. He went out and got in touch with *his* feelings—no one else's!"

The Narcissist

One of my favorite Bette Midler lines goes like this: "Well, enough about me, let's talk about you . . . what do you think of me?" That's what it's like living with the chronically self-absorbed. The focus is always on them and their needs, and even when the attention shifts to others, it doesn't stay there long. Inevitably the narcissist finds a way to bring the focus back around to him. Undoubtedly there are plenty of self-centered women on the planet—most of us have met them, and some of us were even raised by them. But the *Diagnostic and Statistical Manual of Mental Disorders*—the bible of the mental health professions—has estimated that 75 percent of narcissists are men. Of course there are a lot of theories about why this is the case, and Dr. Hannah and I certainly have our own, but suffice it to say, if you think you're dealing with a narcissist, you probably are.

> Trying to connect with narcissists is abusive to your essential self precisely because they're not that interested in you, except for what you provide for them.

As an astute Hollywood physician I know once confided: "Narcissists are naturally psychologically and emotionally abusive because they have almost no room to accommodate others. Any needs you have, even for basic things like love and affection, are experienced as impositions and can bring on hostility and what is called narcissistic rage. In other words, they throw tantrums that are quite nasty. In my practice I see the mental and health problems that are a product of these kinds of marriages." In other words, as I like to tell my clients, repeatedly trying to connect with narcissists is abusive to your essential self precisely because they're not that interested in you, except for what you provide for them. While they may not engage in criminal activities like the narcissistic expressions of "the predator," they have their own vices: ignoring schedules and court-ordered visitations; being chronically late (because whatever they're engaged in takes precedence); forgetting birthdays and other causes for celebration; and blatantly judging others in their household for annoying behaviors that they themselves may have exhibited just a few minutes earlier. In addition, when narcissists feel you are not providing them with your full attention, they respond with guilt-inducing tirades, put-downs, and reasons to dramatically leave the house so they don't have to put up with your foul treatment of them. From a certain perspective, narcissists' behavior so closely resembles that of a two-year-old that it can be downright funny. Yet when you're feeling alone and trapped in an emotionally vacant union, your laughter may turn to tears.

The "Nice Guy"

Dr. Hannah and I are both pleased to say that we're close to a number of genuinely nice guys. A lot of women are. They are kind, considerate, loyal, loving, playful, humorous, sweet individuals who genuinely like women. And as with anybody else, they can have bad days, grouchy moods, and occasional tempers. They can be impatient, bossy, judgmental, and self-absorbed. Sometimes. The difference between real nice guys and destructive men who successfully play the nice guy is that for the latter, the negative characteristics are the norm. Perhaps more importantly, there is an underlying agenda designed to keep a woman down.

"He Seemed Like Such a Nice Guy"

I once had a client call in for a phone session. At the time she was living in Paris and would be relocating back to New York City in a few months. The trouble was, she had recently met this really nice guy—an American who worked for *The New York Times* and was in Paris for a six-month sabbatical. I listened to her describe the relationship, and while everything on the surface sounded fine . . . I wasn't so sure. I pointed out a few things to keep an eye on, and she agreed that she would.

A couple of weeks later, she called to ask me if it was normal for a guy to always extend a hand to other women, some he hardly knew. Could it be that he was just "too nice"? Two months later she phoned to tell me that she discovered he'd been cultivating sexual relationships with other women—which he had lied about. He had a girlfriend at home—which he had also lied about. "Helping women" was his method for making inroads into their lives and, eventually, their pants. Luckily, on a hunch, she'd refrained from being intimate with him, but that hadn't prevented her from being seduced, and emotionally she was on a trajectory of building a meaningful relationship that might be continued in New York. "No wonder he accepted the fact that I prefer to wait to have sex after I get to know a guy. I thought he was being respectful because—" We both said it in unison. "—he was such a nice guy!" He had been carrying on with other women behind her back, and his girlfriend's. Painfully, she accepted the truth, but it took her months to stop saying, "He seemed like such a nice guy . . ."

The Predator

Predators can range from callow and calculating con men to full-blown sociopaths. No matter where a man falls on the spectrum—and even though he may not blatantly exhibit the extreme behaviors commonly thought to be the providence of the sociopath—the core characteristics are the same: ruthless, coldhearted, deceptive, narcissistic, and devoid of genuine empathy and compassion. Though the word *sociopath* conjures up images of ruthless criminal assailants, it's important to remember that an estimated one in twenty-five people is a sociopath with no capacity to love or empathize. Whether he's a plastic surgeon who secretly stalks women he eventually intends to seduce so no one will suspect, a presidential aide who ruins his wife financially, or a businessman who ends up in jail for battery, he leaves a destructive wake behind. The defining characteristics of a predator—of any kind—can lead to serious problems for women involved with these men. In her book *The Sociopath Next Door: The Ruthless Versus the Rest of Us*, Dr. Martha Stout—a clinical psychologist and member of the Department of Psychiatry Harvard Medical School faculty—sums up a predator succinctly:

> *Imagine—if you can—not having a conscience, none at all, no feelings of guilt or remorse no matter what you do, no limiting sense of concern for the well-being of strangers, friends or even family members. Imagine no struggles with shame, not a single one in your whole life, no matter what kind of selfish, lazy, harmful, or immoral action you had taken. And pretend that the concept of responsibility is unknown to you, except as a burden others seem to accept without question, like gullible fools. Now add to this strange fantasy the ability to conceal from other people that your psychological makeup is radically different from theirs. Since everyone simply assumes that conscience is universal among human beings, hiding the fact that you are conscious-free is nearly effortless. You are not held back from any of your desires by guilt or shame, and you are never confronted by others for your cold-bloodedness. The ice water in your veins is so bizarre, so completely outside of their personal experience, that they seldom even guess at your condition.*

In another informative book, *Snakes in Suits: When Psychopaths Go to Work,* authors Dr. Paul Babiak and Dr. Robert D. Hare describe the deplorable tactics of men who lack a moral conscience, and the

Predators are skillfully adept at emulating a real emotional, psychological, and even spiritual connection. far-reaching implications their actions have in the corporate world. Certainly most of us have seen white-collar criminals in the news. Their callous, selfish, and manipulative grandiosity has impacted millions of people in gut-wrenching ways: the loss of pension funds, the waste of taxpayer dollars, the destruction of entire companies.

The Predator at Home

And what happens when these men come home, to us? Well, first and foremost, they lack empathy and are incapable of intimate bonding. Yet these faults can seem incomprehensible while you are under the spell of their charms. You may even feel as though you've found your soul mate, and that your unhappiness must be of your own making, since predators are skillfully adept at emulating a real emotional, psychological, and even spiritual connection.

Natural narcissists, these individuals view those around them solely in relation to their own needs and, as a result, prey on others for their own personal gain. They can be ruthless. They lie without compunction and are highly unpredictable in their behaviors. Notorious for huge mood swings, first raging and then being abruptly sweet, they may leave us feeling cautious and tentative around them. It's not uncommon for a woman in relationship with a predator to be both miserable and enamored, terrified that if she lets go, "No one else will ever me know the way he does."

That may be true. After all, these men work hard to study us, to analyze our likes and dislikes, our attachments and values . . . but not because they love us and want to be close. Rather, they do it so they can use us as a means to *their* ends. Inevitably, once we've outgrown our usefulness, they will abandon us because, as forensic psychologist J. Reid Maloy puts it: "They don't have the internal psychological structure to feel and relate to other people. Sometimes they can imitate it, so they can fool other people, but there will come a point when they can't maintain it."

While you may be reading this thinking, *My guy isn't that bad,* keep your eyes open. Types like this spend an inordinate amount of time and energy deceiving not only their intended mark but also the friends, associates, and communities affiliated with the woman they have targeted. In the instance of a sexual predator, they not only cultivate a relationship with the child they intend to sexually violate but also make great efforts to secure their image among those in their church, their place of work, their neighborhood, and even at the local grocery store, so everyone, including the victim, finds it hard to believe that "someone like this" would be capable of such horrible actions.

We, too, may get caught up in protecting and defending this type of man until we have the courage to open our eyes to the uncomfortable truth, and painfully realize that we were only serving him. That's when hindsight makes it easy to ask *Why didn't I see it?* In all fairness, predators are very effective when it comes to deceiving others, especially when they're physically attractive and socially charming. As one client put it: "I know it sounds silly, but at first, while getting to know him, I felt like one of those women depicted in commercials dancing in a field of flowers. Then the inconsistencies in his story, the strange, aloof, and often callous behaviors started to emerge. He was very seductive, yet there was hollowness to his words and actions . . . like he was reading a script. I was deeply in love with him until I discovered he didn't really exist—at least not as I knew him. It was a horrible realization."

The Addict

Al-Anon's preamble says in part: "Living with an alcoholic is too much for most of us, and soon our thinking becomes distorted, our lives become unmanageable . . ." Addictions are generous diseases. They not only change the addict but also "infect" those close to him.

Addictions are generous diseases. They not only change the addict but also "infect" those close to him

His behaviors become extreme and uncharacteristic—and how he feels about himself usually turns from bad to worse. His unpredictability, his withdrawal from those close to him, his verbal battering and mercurial moods all create a tense environment with which those who remain nearby must contend. In no time at all, though you may barely notice, you start to behave in ways that make you say to yourself *That's not me*. The main focus of your life has now become the addiction.

You attempt to manage it so neighbors won't see him drunk on the lawn. You try to control the drug habit by hiding available cash. You try to become a better wife and mother to reduce the stress, thinking that, perhaps, you might be the cause of it. Your intentions are good, but you're still on the road to hell. You feel desperate, out of control, and often abandoned as you try to fix the problem alone. And you usually are alone—sometimes physically, at other times emotionally. After all, the man you've been living with, dating, or married to has his primary relationship with whatever the addiction is, not with you.

While we traditionally think of addicts in terms of substance addictions, namely alcohol and drugs, it's clear that highly compulsive and addictive behaviors can move into other arenas: food, sex, exercise, work, gambling, video games, and so on. No matter what the "drug" of choice is, the impact on the addict is strikingly similar—as is the impact on those close to him. An Al-Anon member put it quite succinctly: "The details of the narrative may be different, but the story's the same." No matter what the addiction, the addict's preoccupation with his drug of choice interferes with all of his intimate relationships.

When the person you love becomes someone you hardly recognize, it can be extremely painful and disorienting. As a recovering alcoholic said, "These ugly moods would come over me and, after a while, I couldn't tell whether they belonged to me or the booze." Addicts are notorious for avoiding being held accountable and invalidating others' responses to their abuse, preferring to make us wrong instead of taking responsibility for their actions. They often withhold love and affection and use it as a punishment if we don't play along in their games of denial. "I didn't drink that much last week, so get off my case!" they may say, and although the intoxication was reduced, the

> No matter what the addiction, the addict's preoccupation with his drug of choice interferes with all of his intimate relationships.

alcoholic behaviors were as prevalent as ever. An array of tactics are used to blame others for their inability to stop the cravings; for driving them to drink, use, snort, or act out sexually; for making their life miserable.

Addiction is an insidious disease that, little by little, creeps in and disrupts both of your lives, taking with it your dignity, self-esteem, and serenity. Sadly, most of the approaches we might take to remedy the situation are ineffective. It's important to remember when dealing with an addict that you didn't cause it, you can't control it, and you won't cure it.

> It's important to remember when dealing with an addict that you didn't cause it, you can't control it, and you won't cure it.

The Sex Addict

I think it's important to mention this particular type of destructive individual, since sex addiction and other sexually compulsive behaviors can be harmful to women on so many levels. As one client put it, "As far as I'm concerned, it's beyond destructive. It screwed up my mind, my heart, my sexuality, and I ended up with a host of STDs" (sexually transmitted diseases). Along with many psychologists, sexual abuse therapists, and counselors, I see this addiction as the next social epidemic. Dr. Elaine Brady, a

He's Just No Good for You

doctor of clinical psychology as well as a certified sex addiction therapist well versed in this disease, notes: "The proliferation of porn on the Internet has created an epidemic of addiction, and it shows no end in sight."

While to most of us the term *sex addict* conjures up visions of a depraved sexual predator or a pathetic dirty old man in a trench coat, he can also be the successful attorney whose wife serves tea to the prostitutes he regularly hires to come into their home. Or perhaps it's the really nice guy who appears to be a gentleman when he's out on a date, but then goes home and indulges in porn while he masturbates since, in actuality he prefers chronic fantasies to real relationships. And what about the pharmaceutical researcher who is notorious for his chronic infidelity? The college president who cannot curb his hunger for phone sex?

The sad truth is that men who have a problem with sex addiction, like any other addicts, make attempts to hide it out of shame and feared retribution. But the signs are clear once you know what you're looking for . . . Does he sneak time on the computer at all hours of the night? Does he insist on controlling finances so you can't look up certain charges on your credit card? Does he alternate between wanting you and then acting aloof in bed? And does he subtly make disparaging comments about your body, your weight, your appearance to keep you shut down? Does he flirt at parties when he doesn't think you're looking, or treat you as though you're invisible when introduced to a woman he finds attractive?

> The blame, the put-downs, the claimed inadequacies are all designed to keep the focus off his behavior and squarely on you.

As with all addictions, the blame, the put-downs, the claimed inadequacies—yours, not his—are all designed to keep the focus off his behavior and squarely on you. He will deny it when confronted; lie as necessary; tell you you're exaggerating, that "All men need to look at porn," "All men feel restrained by commitment," "All men have extramarital affairs if they're not being satisfied at home, so what's the big deal?" or simply claim, "I love you. I would never do anything like that, really. I have no idea where those charges came from/why porn sites are on my computer history/why you'd think I'd ever cheat on you when you're all I want" (and then the next day he "jokes" that your pants are looking a little tight).

Sex addicts can also be quite possessive, since it is inconceivable to them that other men aren't lusting over you the same way he's lusting over other women. Innocent flirtations or platonic friendships between the sexes are, for him, impossible to imagine. Judy, despite being a therapist herself, had no idea what she was dealing with in her own personal life until she found books on sex addiction; then it all started to become clear. She says: "Dealing with a sex addict made me feel horrible about myself. In a short period of time, I felt unattractive, unloved, unworthy, and was so confused, always confused, until I eventually became depressed and knew I either had to find help or live miserably forever."

The Ultimate Question: Is Your Relationship Destructive?

Admittedly, we have just scratched the surface here. Volumes of books, psychological profiles, and case histories have been written about each of these characters. These profiles are meant to give you some vocabulary to identify the toxic man in your life. As a mother of two little girls put it: "It was vital for me to know what, exactly, I was contending with in terms of my husband's behaviors. Once I could put names to the behaviors, then the tactics of verbal abuse became easier to figure out so I didn't always take them personally and could develop more effective ways to deal with them. When I realized that I could take the first steps toward my own recovery; my own self-care; and then decide what I wanted to do in terms of what was best for me and my children, my life began to change."

Take the following quiz and see where your relationship comes out. It will give you an idea of the level of difficulty you're contending with so you can get a better sense of where you stand—and make a more informed decision about whether this is what you signed up for or not. Remember, if it looks like a duck and it quacks like a duck, it's probably a duck. And you don't deserve a duck as your primary relationship.

> "Once I could put names to the behaviors, I could develop more effective ways to deal with them."

Where Do I Stand?—A Quiz

- ☐ Do you walk away from interactions feeling confused or crazy?
- ☐ Have you stopped doing some of your favorite activities because you're concerned about his reaction to them?
- ☐ Do you find yourself thinking about the same conversations and behaviors over and over in an attempt to figure them out?
- ☐ Would you say you feel depleted, rather than energized, after interactions with the man in your life?
- ☐ Does he act differently when you're in public than when you're alone?
- ☐ Does he often accuse you of flirting, not being where you said you would be, or engaging in suspicious activities?
- ☐ Does he behave in ways that make you feel like he's a rebellious teenager and you're his mother?
- ☐ Do you catch him in lies that he won't admit to even when you have proof?
- ☐ Is he likely to blame things on you whether you have a hand in them or not?
- ☐ Is he prone to flying off the handle over something minor or inconsequential?
- ☐ Does he often turn discussions about issues important to you into discussions that are all about him?

☐ Has he frequently put you down or criticized you and insisted he was "only kidding"?

☐ When he hurts your feelings with unkind words or deeds, does he tell you that you're too sensitive or are overreacting?

☐ Did his behavior change once you moved in together or got married and he now feels at liberty to have you change to his liking?

☐ Do you feel he owns you, rather than relates to you?

☐ Do you find yourself biting your tongue to keep the peace or yelling and arguing in ways that are uncharacteristic?

☐ Does he come up with expectations that you are required to meet even though they may have never been negotiated between the two of you?

☐ Have you caught him lying? Does he cheat on you and hide his activities?

☐ Is it common for him to charm the people around you so thoroughly that, when you tell them about some of the painful things he has done or said to you, they don't believe you?

☐ Does he compare you with his mother or with former girlfriends or wives in ways that insinuate you're not making the grade?

☐ Has he ever touched you in ways that are rough and aggressive while he insists he is only being funny or playful?

☐ Have you ever found mysterious credit card, cell phone, or Internet charges that might be related to sex calls, affairs, or porn sites although he denies knowledge of these "mistaken" charges?

☐ Will he agree to various terms in your relationship and then completely disregard them without a reasonable explanation?

☐ Have you noticed any problems with alcohol or drugs? Does he seem dependent on them as a social lubrication when you're out with others? Does he insist on using before you're intimate or sexual?

☐ Does he instigate arguments and then, when you get angry, act as though he's the victim and didn't have a hand in the conflict?

☐ Do you often find yourself making excuses for him or his behavior?

☐ Do you try to talk yourself into giving him the benefit of the doubt even though you may have concerns about his behavior?

☐ Are you often saying, "But he loves me . . . ," in order to excuse hurtful and demeaning behaviors?

☐ Even though he's considered to be "a great guy," do you often experience him as being unkind? Playing mind games? Hiding information or lying to you?

If you find yourself saying yes to many of these questions, read on . . .

| 3 |

Which Me Am I Supposed to Be?

Most of us come into relationships with expectations. Some we may be aware of; some we may not. In a mature and respectful union, expectations are discussed and negotiated. They are not simply orders passed down to the rank and file. Unfortunately, most destructive individuals seem ill informed on this point or, more likely, they believe it doesn't apply to them—and this can lead to serious problems as we contend with a plethora of unspoken rules, attitudes, and standards we often only learn about once the relationship is well under way.

To say that a destructive individual is more interested in shaping you to his liking than liking the unique shape you come in would be an understatement. While he may favor a particular trait or even admire qualities you have, he will certainly come to find fault with them, upset that you are not meeting his expectations. Though unreasonable, most toxic men feel justified in criticizing you when you fail to achieve their standards or to act in a way they deem appropriate and correct. Sometimes they are subtle about their discontent,

> While he may favor a particular trait or even admire qualities you have, he will certainly come to find fault with them, upset that you are not meeting his expectations.

and at other times they are blatant in their shaming of you. The result? You feel rejected for who you are, certain he wants you to be someone else.

Expectations That Destroy a Woman's Sense of Self

It's common for a destructive individual to view the woman in his life as merely an extension of him. Rather than being a person in your own right, you are expected to say and do what is required of you, attempting to live up to standards you probably knew nothing about. These internal narratives live in the minds of these men. They are ambiguous, often based on immature and inaccurate notions—even fantasies—of how a woman should be. Initially he tells you how great you are, how he enjoys your quirks and funny little habits. He convinces you that it is *you* he wants, glossing over any personal differences. Yet as time goes on, another reality emerges.

Watch for the signs. Does he spend more time stamping ownership on you than making an effort to get to know you more deeply? Does he only go so far when supporting your endeavors, often trying to steer you in a different direction because it's more lucrative or "would better suit you"? Or perhaps he insists that you take a baking class even though he knows you're a frozen-foods connoisseur. Holding you hostage to unfair and in some cases unconscious expectations is demeaning. In some cases it's clear that he wants you to be sexier and act more like a pinup girl. Then he may chastise you and insist that you act like "a real mother" instead of a provocative flirt. Perhaps he corrects your manners or gives you disapproving looks when out with business associates as if to say, *You're embarrassing me with your low-class antics.* The problem is that he can change on a whim, wanting you to be one way and then another.

> He can change on a whim, wanting you to be one way and then another.

The Perfect Wife

Many destructive men, whether they admit it or not, hold fast to ideas of male superiority and traditional roles of power, expecting "their woman" to acquiesce even if, initially, qualities such as being independent and having a wild streak were considered part of your allure. But soon he would prefer you act like his ideal wife and lets you know in subtle and not-so-subtle ways, expecting you to relinquish aspects of who you are to fit an image he holds in his head. His demands are usually contradictory, unclear, and inconsistent, yet he will act as if you are the one who doesn't understand and are therefore being unreasonable.

An executive's wife who came to see me said her husband enforced domestic role structures in their home by unilaterally announcing the rules to her once the honeymoon phase had passed. All along he had expected her to use her intelligence not to pursue her own goals, but to help him rise in the ranks of his company— a marital requirement he carefully kept hidden—and though they could easily have afforded to hire domestic help, he insisted that she cook, clean, entertain, and do the laundry in order to fit his image of the perfect wife. He actually told her that "I'll do the thinking and all I need you to do is keep yourself well kept and attractive." At one point he suggested she color her hair to please his boss: "He prefers redheads." When he decided she wasn't meeting his expectations, he started writing out lists she referred to as "The Executive Orders." They read: "Do not walk the dog without my permission; have the bed made by 8:00 a.m.; never refuse my sexual advances . . ." Perhaps the movie *The Stepford Wives* comes to mind? The ideal wife, though a machine without the capacity for love, was preferred to a real woman.

Nowadays this scenario is heavily played out in the arena of professional success and presents an impossible bind

Your partner may tell you he wants you to achieve your dreams. He may also resent it.

for women. Your partner may tell you he wants you to achieve your dreams. He may also resent it. While he likes the extra income your work brings in, in all likelihood he still assumes that dinner will be on the table by six o'clock. He pressures you to be the quintessential mother while also expecting you to excel in the workplace—without it disrupting his idea of the tranquil home. Again, you are caught in a no-win situation, and if you're not careful you can drive yourself nuts, make yourself sick, and lose what's best in you by trying to meet these unrealistic expectations. "Don't let him invalidate your actions or before you know it, he'll invalidate *you*," was a grandmother's advice to her granddaughter on her wedding day—the grandmother had endured a damaging marriage for thirty-seven years to a Fortune 500 CEO.

Marrying His Mother

Has your boyfriend ever compared you with his mother? Has he congratulated you for acting like her? Or let you know that she used to have the same bad habits and ways of saying or doing things that he grew to disdain? Whether they were actually close to their mothers in real life or not, it's not uncommon for destructive individuals to want you to be the mother they never had or mimic the one they thought they had. On the surface his requests may seem innocuous: to use his mother's recipes; to go with an artificial Christmas tree at Christmas "just like Mom's"; to take up the hobby of scrapbooking. But slowly you realize that each is just one in a series of modifications designed to turn you into someone else.

Bit by bit he's determined to mold you into a woman you are not—and chances are, it's a poorly constructed, overly idealized rendition of his mother; a mother who, in all likelihood, never revealed all her true feelings and may have hidden away aspects of herself and private details of her life he simply wasn't privy to. In fact, she may have concealed affairs, problems in her marriage, family feuds, and money problems just to sustain family harmony. No matter how the image of her was manufactured and no matter what limited perspective formed it, the underlying message is the same: *You're not being who I want you to be!* You are left with a vague sense of unhappiness because his words and behaviors indicate that you're inadequate next to the image he holds.

These men are badly conflicted when it comes to women. If their own psychological and emotional needs weren't adequately met, they may not have had healthy bonding experiences with the female figures in their life.

> The underlying message is the same: You're not being who I want you to be!

Jim's Story

A man whom I will call Jim felt incredibly loyal to his mother and protective of her because his father had numerous affairs, yet once he married, he began to act out the same behaviors. When I asked him why he thought it was all right to inflict the same kind of pain on his wife that his father had inflicted on his mother, he replied, "I didn't really think of it like that at first. I felt sorry for my mother, yes, but I also felt that she shouldn't have put me in the middle of a situation she could have left. I realized I viewed women as victims and also manipulators who deserved what they got. Slowly, I'm beginning to straighten this out for myself . . ."

Jim's mother, who eventually came to realize that she had played a part in his confusion, described her mistakes like this: "I told him to be a good son and stand up for me all the while encouraging him to be 'a real man' just like his father. It's no wonder he felt confused and troubled inside." No surprise that he was ambivalent about bonding: Closeness, to him, was wrought with an overwhelming sense of responsibility for someone whom he thought should be capable of saving herself. His actions were juvenile attempts to sever the emotional connection with his wife since he didn't want to be consumed by another woman's problems, though he longed to be close. He had to learn how to see his mother for who she really was, and to separate his internal conflict with her from his relationship with his wife. Unfortunately, Jim found emotional connection to be too threatening and continued to act out his aggression toward his mother both inside and outside the relationship until his wife finally left him.

The Imago

Freud claimed that women marry their fathers. More recent studies conducted by Harville Hendrix's Imago Relationship Therapy suggest that we are romantically attracted to partners whom we perceive as having traits similar to both of our parents or early caretakers. According to Hendrix, as a heterosexual woman, I will be attracted to men who unconsciously remind me of my parents—not just my father, but my mother as well. Hendrix believes that our early life experiences with our caretakers form an unconscious model or definition in our minds of what love looks like, or at least what it's supposed to look like. Hendrix calls this unconscious model "the Imago," which is the Latin word for "image."

What's especially intriguing about this notion of being attracted to partners who match our Imago is that those partners will share not only the positive characteristics of our parents, but the negative ones as well. If I grew up with a father who was outgoing, charming, and generous toward people outside the family but emotionally distant and critical toward me, his daughter, my Imago will draw me toward men with both sets of features—the upside and the down. Of course, while falling in love with this kind of man, I will be convinced that he possesses only the *positive* characteristics of my father and none of the negatives. (Who falls in love with someone's bad side?) Since just about everyone is a mixture of positives and negatives, it's just about certain that I'm wrong. This offers a compelling answer to the question of why so many of us end up with men who seem at first to be perfect for us but whose destructive traits, hidden beneath the irresistible surface, emerge slowly but surely.

Likewise, if a man's Imago contains the image of a perfect mother (which, of course, doesn't exist in reality), he may see those same perfect features in the woman he's dating, at least at first. But eventually he will either try to force the woman into conforming to the image or reject the woman outright for not being as perfect as his mother.

> **Many destructive men aren't clear, from one minute to the next, about how they want you to look or behave.**

The problem is, many destructive men aren't clear, from one minute to the next, about how they want you to look or behave. The experience can be bewildering and damaging to your self-esteem until you decide not to respond so readily to his demands and insist on being yourself. But then you face another problem: narcissistic rage.

Narcissistic Rage

When science discovers the center of the universe, a lot of people will be disappointed to find they are not it.
—BERNARD BAILY

What happens when reality interferes with the expectations of a toxic man? Look out! In psychological circles it's known as narcissistic rage, and it closely resembles a temper tantrum served up by an enraged two-year-old. The problem is, this "child" can humiliate, intimidate, and lash out, sometimes violently. Inside, he is feeling threatened and vulnerable

> **What happens when reality interferes with the expectations of a toxic man? Look out!**

since you're no longer perceived as being with him, and therefore must be against him. While venting his anger offers a temporary solution for his internal instability, it only serves to make you feel attacked. In the end, if he can't resolve these issues with you due to a growing sense of entitlement—a continued sense of having the right to tell you how to be and who to be—there is little you can do to reconfigure the destructive dynamics. His narcissistic rage is clearly indicating, *I deserve to have what I want despite the unreasonableness of my demands.* The two-year-old translation would be: "Mine!"

| 4 |

Now, How About You?

Truly recognizing and valuing your life force energy and the various currency expenditures it entails could in fact be the first step toward moving out of denial, opening your eyes, and calling yourself home—whether you remain in the relationship or not. In the end, the real question you must ask yourself is: *Is this relationship worth the cost of my life and essential well-being?* Author Helen Rowland once quipped: "In olden times sacrifices were made at the altar, a custom which still continues."

While relationships require compromise and sacrifice, it's important to take an honest look at what kind of sacrifices you're making. Read the small print. Does the relationship require that you give up something essential? Have you been able to hold on to your most beloved self? Be honest. Is your life force diminishing, and no matter what you do, you can't seem to fully revive it? And, though painful, ask yourself the hard questions: *Am I more in love with the* idea *of our relationship, the imagined possibility of what it could be, if only . . . rather than the actual reality of it? Does it enhance my life or detract from it? Is it a convenient way for me to avoid growing up and becoming my own person?*

> Ask yourself if one of the sacrifices you're making for the relationship is you.

Who Am I Now?

Chances are, if you're in a destructive relationship, a lot has changed. Try to remember. What was different? Try to feel yourself as you were before . . . less constricted, perhaps? Not as tense and chronically worried? Did you laugh more? Feel as though you could breathe more easily? If you find yourself on edge as though something is amiss, it's helpful to reflect on the before and after as though looking at photos to compare how you were *before* him, and how you feel now. It may be a painful assessment, yet it's essential if you are going to get an accurate perspective on the price you're probably paying. Has his behavior toward you become more negative—even if it's intermittently—so that you feel more defensive and reactive in response to his words and actions? Are you often on an emotional roller coaster that doesn't seem to be of your own making? Do you ruminate over conversations you've had, comments he's made, and veiled accusations endlessly trying to figure them out? You may feel drained and depressed or alternate between feeling hopeful, and that life is good, only to have another invalidating response throw you into despair. But you're not sure why.

All couples have disagreements, you might tell yourself. *After all, no one is perfect. All families are dysfunctional, and that means everyone comes with baggage, right? Men and women have issues that have to be ironed out. It'll get better.* But what if it doesn't? What if little changes—or if things do change, they inevitably swing back to the same old behaviors that are causing you stress? What were you like before the relationship? Was your self-talk less anxious, less filled with self-doubt? Did you spend more time figuring out how to make money, plan a vacation, find time to have lunch with friends rather than focusing on how avoid conflict and keep things on an even keel? Think about it. Try to remember. Something essential in you may be slipping away . . .

Life Force Energy and How it Works

As women, we're notorious for giving our energy away. We forget that it's a valuable commodity—our life force. So we often act as if it's infinite and can forever be drawn upon without any repercussions. As a matter of course, we offer it up, overextend it, with little or no reciprocity, often failing to make a conscious decision about who we want to receive it and how much we can dole out before we have none left for ourselves. Far too often we run our lives on the assumption, *If you're okay, then I'm okay.* One of my favorite jokes goes like this: "What happened when the co-dependent woman fell off the edge of a cliff?" Answer: "Someone else's life flashed before her eyes!" Humorous, yes, yet it makes the point.

If we're not careful, we can distribute our time as well as other important currencies—emotional, psychological, spiritual, and economic—too freely, depleting our life force energy in an effort to be in connection with others. It's a common dilemma for women. I dedicated one of my Internet radio shows to the value of women's currency because, often, we forget how worthwhile our contributions are— most of what we do isn't counted, at least not in traditional economic terms such as the gross national product. And this has had a tremendous impact on the ways in which we view our interpersonal outlays, especially when it comes to meeting the needs of and responding to others. In many cases we may be driven to tend to others, even if it's at huge cost to ourselves. As financial guru Suze Orman writes in her best-selling book, *Women & Money: Owning the Power to Control Your Destiny:* "So many women—from professionals to stay-at-home moms—treat themselves, their services, and their abilities as if they were always on sale. I have always said that if you undervalue what you do, the world undervalues who you are. And when you undervalue who you are, the world undervalues what you do. My experience is that women are, unfortunately, masters at both."

Many of us were socialized to devote ourselves to the care and empowerment of others while remaining selfless, and we forget to put ourselves in the equation. Unfortunately, for many of us "putting ourselves in the equation" creates an uncomfortable internal conflict because we fear that if we develop our own personal power, it will be at the expense of others. In the book *Women's Ways of Knowing: The Development of Self, Voice and Mind*, the authors write: "Women worry that if they were to develop their own powers it would be at the expense of others . . . they also worry that if they excel, those they love will automatically be penalized. Conventional sex-role standards establish a routine for settling self–other conflicts when they occur. Men choose the self and women choose others."

Many women in destructive relationships become more combative to be heard or resort to self-silencing to avoid conflict.

Our life force energy goes into tangible acts such as scrubbing pots and pans and building a business, as well as less tangible ones such as rocking children to sleep, creating union with our lover, and making a house feel like a home. We need not be rocket scientists to know that, in general, women are in a bind. Juggling work and family life has become overwhelming, not because anything is wrong with our organizational or time management skills, but because we are undersupported and overwhelmed. Chronic stress—and the guilt that often accompanies it—takes a toll. Even if we have a loving partnership, we're still likely to feel depleted from time to time due to the complex nature of our lives. However, when we are in a toxic union, we are more likely to suffer from chronic mental and physical health problems. Many women in destructive relationships become more combative to be heard or resort to self-silencing to avoid conflict.

When Silence Isn't Golden

Arguing is, of course, an inevitable part of married life. But now researchers are putting the marital spat under the microscope to see if the *way* you fight with your spouse can affect your health. One study of nearly four thousand men and women from Framingham, Massachusetts, asked participants whether they typically vented their feelings or kept quiet in arguments with their spouse. It was discovered that the women who suppressed their feelings, or self-silenced, were four times as likely to die during the ten-year study period than were those who always told their husbands how they felt. Further research by Dana Crowley Jack—a professor of interdisciplinary studies at Western Washington University—found an association between women's self-silencing and a variety of physical and mental health problems, including depression, eating disorders, and heart disease.

When we are repeatedly undermined, maligned with a smile, and lied to, it's not surprising that we experience exhaustion and burnout, thyroid problems, chronic fatigue, anxiety, and insomnia. Being in a relationship that's not good for you means that your energy gets siphoned off more readily and more rapidly due to the emotional, psychological, spiritual, and intellectual turbulence you're experiencing. In fact, problem people have a tendency to suck the life right out of others. They exhaust you with mind games, emotional terrorism, and constant demands; some are subtle, while others are quite blatant. "Honey, can you come with me to look at the car I want to buy?" when you just took a test drive with him yesterday and he knows you have a report due at work—and you notice that he always manages to find clever ways to "include you" in a special activity whenever you are focused on deadlines. "I need you to clean up the kitchen. I just don't have time before the guests arrive." The truth is, neither of you has time, but his schedule is clearly more important, always.

Problem people instinctively know about life force energy. They feed off it with little concern for the toll this takes on others. Ever notice how your energy seems to go down after interactions with certain people? Even if they're not overtly negative and they never complain, they somehow manage to zap you. That's why one of their favorite tactics is to simply wear you down, siphoning off your energy with controlling tactics, confusing accusations, manufactured conflict, passive-aggressive acts, and invalidating jokes.

You must ask yourself, *Is this relationship worth the cost of my life and essential well-being?*

Remember the idea of "women's kryptonite" from chapter 1? Men who want to control women become experts at wielding weapons that they know are emotional, psychological, physical, and spiritual kryptonite. They know, consciously or unconsciously, that disentangling mixed messages is draining; running inconsistent stories over and over in your head, digging for the truth, distracts you so that you lose focus; and unkind putdowns couched as humor leave you deflated. "Oh, I can handle it," you hear yourself saying in an attempt to ward off uncomfortable feelings of inadequacy—and you certainly don't want to blame your partner unfairly. And so you refuse to place the situation in its proper perspective, forgetting that even Superman was adversely affected by such a negative force!

Sadly, these men care little whether they use you up or not. As Dr. Elaine Brady can attest: "The rate of illness is higher and the life expectancy is lower for a woman involved with an addict or abuser because she's actively dealing with the problems he's creating, but avoiding through his alcohol or drug abuse." The result? You become resentful—and resentments can use up a lot of mental and emotional energy. In the end you must ask yourself, *Is this relationship worth the cost of my life and essential well-being?*

Making Contact with Your Authentic Self and Trusting Your Instincts

No matter what experiences you've had in childhood or later years, whether joyous or painful, a deep resilience pulses within that cannot be snuffed out—though in some instances it may be hidden from view. I truly believe that most of us have an innate sense of who we are—an essential self, an authentic self, an essence that resides within regardless of any fragmentation or emotional wounding that has occurred at the hands of others. Though a destructive individual will systematically chip away at your self-esteem and can make you feel incredibly distant from your authentic self as he finds more repressive ways to exercise control, you need not allow him to damage what is best in you . . . at least not permanently. In some instances you may develop a false persona—no longer sharing your real self or being automatically vulnerable—with the man in your life to protect what is real within you; your essence, though concealed, remains intact. You may be careful to spend time with positive people as a way to keep yourself buoyant and inspired so that your internal well continues to be refilled.

Slowly, as you begin to trust your instincts and inner knowing that something is indeed wrong, you can make shifts within yourself and the relationship as though pulling a plane out of a nose dive so it can soar once again. In *Women's Ways of Knowing*, the authors echo the same thoughts:

> . . . *As a woman becomes more aware of the existence of inner resources for knowing and valuing, as she begins to listen to the "still, small voice" within her, she finds an inner source of strength. A major development transition occurs that has repercussions in her relationships, self-concept and self-esteem, morality and behavior. Women's growing reliance on their intuitive processes is, we believe, an important adaptive move in the service of self-protection, self-assertion, and self-definition. Women become their own authorities.*

Listening to the "small still voice" inside—the voice of God, the voice of intuition—is a powerful move toward self-assertion, self-protection, and self-definition.

> ## Listening to the "small still voice" inside is a powerful move toward self-assertion, self-protection, and self-definition.

However, don't expect any newfound strength to be celebrated by the destructive individual. On the contrary, he has expended a lot of energy making certain that your personal power and confidence are greatly diminished, and changes such as these are threatening. Undoubtedly, he'll sabotage your efforts and make attempts to distance you from people and activities that encourage this inner connection to your authentic self and its wise voice. In his world someone always has to be one-up and someone else has to be one-down . . . and he has no intention of being the less powerful player in this game.

When you can move away from self-talk that revolves around the destructive individual and instead begin a more constructive dialogue with your authentic self, then you can grow more stable, more trusting of your own authority. Sure, he will still attempt to confuse you and convince you that you're wrong, but you can maintain your sanity, and perhaps some serenity, as you anchor yourself from within rather than depend on the destructive individual or the relationship to validate you. You'll grow more stable and trusting of your own authority. Admittedly, maintaining a strong inner identity can be a challenge. Luckily, it's not an impossible task.

■ ■ ■ ■ ■

Everything in our lives can wake us up or put us to sleep, and basically it's up to us to let it wake us up.

—PEMA CHODRON

And even if there are few others with whom we can express our authentic self, there are many ways to strengthen the connection by cultivating a spiritual practice, developing self-love, being in nature, and participating in nurturing activities such as a women's gathering group. Take time to meditate and actively listen to the messages that emanate from deep within in order to fortify your personal power and innate wisdom.

Finding meaningful ways to hold our center and remain connected to our authentic self has been an ongoing challenge for women and is especially tough to achieve when we're under daily assault. Instead of being a sanctuary, our relationship often leaves us feeling alone—a common occurrence in a toxic union—and this can be crushing to our sense of self. Trust your instincts, your intuition, your internal wisdom . . . you probably know more than you think you do. Step by step you can more easily come to identify what you're dealing with, over time developing a broader range of skills to contend with denigrating and invalidating behaviors. Remember, it may not feel like it now, but in truth you're capable of saving your own life. You have only to remember who you truly are. "Technology is not going to save us. Our computers, our tools, our machines are not enough. We have to rely on our intuition, our true being." Never were Joseph Campbell's words more applicable.

■ ■ ■ ■ ■

A rock pile ceases to be a rock pile the moment a man contemplates it, bearing within him the image of a cathedral.
—Antoine de Saint-Exupéry

Ladies, if you're even remotely contemplating a cathedral, and you're reading this book, you've already taken an important step toward building something different, something better. Keep in mind that as new structures emerge, often old ones must be altered, torn down, dismantled, and rebuilt, including those foundations that no longer serve. In the following two chapters, we will look at beliefs, attitudes, and convenient myths that have become enemies of the state—that is, your state of well-being. Freeing yourself from a relationship that is simply no good for you requires personal change. Why not welcome it?

| 5 |

Know Any of These Women?

To move forward within ourselves, whether any physical relocation ultimately takes place or not, it's essential to bring our own patterns in attitude, emotional orientation, and nonserving behaviors into view. Otherwise they can abscond and distort our authentic selves, trapping us in scenarios that are simply not good for us. Ask yourself if your family encouraged you to tolerate, accommodate, and normalize destructive behaviors. Were you given messages by family members, friends, clergyman, educators, or the media that encouraged you, as a woman, to put up with harmful and demeaning behaviors from men because "that's what guys do"? If you have adopted these culturally approved belief systems about what it means to be a woman, now would be a good time to make them conscious, dismantling their hold over you so you can define who you really are from the inside, out.

As you read through the various profiles in this chapter, decide for yourself, discriminate for yourself, which aspects of these women you possess and the ways in which you might want to transform them into someone who truly stands for you—or perhaps a more empowered you. "I never thought I had the right to question the status quo. It simply never occurred to me." These words were spoken by Mary, a lovely older woman, when I asked her if she thought "always being nice" was worth the price: a load of resentments she carried around with her constantly. Her preconceived notions that it was a woman's job to behave certain ways and to forgive men's transgressions made her susceptible to the maneuvers of destructive men. No matter what she did, no matter how hard she tried to please, she could never win their approval. Her conditioning had set her up, making her a prime target for men who use and abuse women. Mary said it best when she told me: "My early training primed me to be with a man who played on and preyed on my desperate need to be a nice person—meaning, being nice to everyone but myself."

It is worth noting that according to research, girls who are raised to accept male privilege—who are told that "boys will be boys" and, when boys behave badly, girls should just "put up and shut up"— grow to become women who will stay in a relationship with a man no matter how badly he treats her. Then people look at her and wonder, "Why does she stay?"

I wish I could honestly say that the cultural conditioning I saw in Mary is uncommon among women in younger generations, but I can't.

It's time to reclaim our core identity and reunite with our true essence.

Despite the women's movement, entry into high-level positions, the accumulation of college degrees, and new models of femininity represented in mass culture, women are still struggling with many of the same issues faced by their grandmothers. In fact, the conflicts and pressures bearing down on the average woman today may be more intense and pervasive than in previous generations.

Mary Pipher, Ph.D., author of the groundbreaking book *Reviving Ophelia: Saving the Selves of Adolescent Girls*, contends that most women begin to lose contact with their authentic selves early in adolescence, when the pressure to conform closes in on them from all sides. The media's portrayal of women, parents' pressures to be a "good girl," our culture's double standards—these and many other forces may not merely affect how we develop our identities but derail the process altogether, moving us farther from our real natures. This wreaks havoc on the psyche, making it harder for women to express the kind of personal power that comes from a strong inner core. Dr.

Pipher writes: ". . . the loss of wholeness, self-confidence, and self-direction can last well into adulthood."

In addition, our family of origin can also influence our susceptibility and attraction to destructive relationships. Certainly, if we grew up in a family where there was alcoholism, substance abuse, emotional anorexia, neglect, verbal abuse, or invalidating behaviors—or if we simply weren't seen or heard by members of our family—we may be more likely to find ourselves in destructive relationships later on. Although I have met a number of women who grew up in functional families but nevertheless ended up in a dysfunctional intimate relationship, I more often see a strong relationship between a woman's early family life and her current romantic partnership.

The extent to which any of us may have lost connection with our authentic selves during our childhood or adolescence, however, is less important than how we've dealt with the loss and how much we have been able to heal from it during our adulthood. I can assure you that prior conditioning aside, the corrosive nature of a destructive relationship can erode whatever personal strengths and resources we managed to gain earlier on, pulling us farther and farther from our real selves. The fact that now we feel diminished and confused and may be apologizing for our very existence means something is very wrong and changes are in order. If we've become or are fast becoming anything like the women described below, it's time to open our eyes and learn to reject whatever inauthentic aspects or false personas we've adopted so we can reclaim our core identity and reunite with our true essence.

Co-dependency Re-examined

Dr. Hannah and I include co-dependence in this book to highlight a syndrome that can be likened to a deep sleep that a woman must wake up from if she is to develop a healthy and autonomous self-identity. Though it may sound simple, it isn't. Keeping the focus on our own needs while being in service to and intimately relating to others—especially those who take as much as we can give and may even "take us over" with psychological domination—is challenging and can become a personal journey in and of itself.

The concept of co-dependence has found its way into the popular vernacular in recent years, and while it is helpful in understanding certain behaviors, attitudes, and proclivities, it is often misunderstood. In some cases I find that the concept of co-dependence is used to pathologize women's nurturing natures, making the milk of kindness into a deplorable act—yet another way to malign women and keep them in a double-bind. In other instances, I find those who abhor the term since they mistakenly believe that it somehow means a woman is responsible for the behaviors of a destructive individual and she brings them on herself—a "blaming the victim" stance that is completely inaccurate. While a co-dependent can enable and help to perpetuate certain addictive and toxic patterns in another, she is not the cause of them! Too often, being nice is mistakenly perceived as co-dependent behavior, since one of the main characteristics of co-dependence is to strive to do just that, to be nice. However, there is an important distinction to be made. The "nice" behavior often exhibited by a co-dependent belies the need to control others consciously or unconsciously. With their overwhelming need to be perceived as unselfish and devoted to the well-being of others, co-dependents frequently minimize, alter, or deny their true feelings, making it easier to put others' needs before their own—and easier to conceal any resentments they may have for feeling taken for granted, used rather than loved, and always giving out. In fact, co-dependents are capable of denying their needs and desires so deeply that they can lose conscious contact with them and, instead, spend a lot of time and energy trying to become better mothers, better wives, and better employees—ostensibly not in service to themselves, but in service to others. Whether coined "co-dependence" or not, whenever a woman identifies more readily with those external to her, side-lining herself, she suffers. Co-dependence, then, can be thought of as internalized oppression. Dr. Mary Pipher puts it this way:

Even sadder are the women who are not struggling, who have for-gotten they have selves worth defending. They have repressed . . . the betrayals of self in order to be pleasing. These women come to therapy with the goal of becoming even more pleasing to others. They come to lose weight, to save their marriages, or to rescue their children. When I ask them about their own needs, they are confused by the question.

Unfortunately, by dismissing their own needs and protecting those around them from the consequences of their own actions, co-dependents can and often do enable others to remain immature, irresponsible, and unaccountable. Instead of empowering themselves, they spend their time and energy being doormats, believing that they are helping those close to them. As one minister's wife remarked, "We do unto others what others should probably be doing for them-selves." The result is that their identities become too closely aligned with the successes and failures of others. This makes it easier to put others' needs before their own and to conceal any resentments that accumulate.

Those of us in a destructive rela-tionship may discover that, perhaps, we never really knew our true needs and desires, or only partially knew them. Or they may have become obscured as we struggled with worry, pain, conflict, and a persistent feel-ing that something wasn't quite right.

Somewhere along the line we distanced ourselves from our needs, usually in an attempt to appear agreeable.

Somewhere along the line we distanced ourselves from our needs, usually in an attempt to appear agreeable; to maintain harmony or the illusion of harmony; to stay out of the line of fire; or as a middle-aged schoolteacher put it: "to become invisible in the hopes of protecting ourselves and staving off the uncomfortable truth."

Sadly, one of the most pervasive images of "a good woman"—selfless, or always there for others—is also one of the core traits asso-ciated with co-dependence. As a result, many of us are trained into these behaviors in subtle and not-so-subtle ways. It's not surprising, then, that we end up with problem people who want to keep us down. After all, if we're co-dependents, we need others' approval; we often accept others' opinions of us more readily than our own and tend to be overly loyal, remaining in unhealthy situations much longer than is sensible or wise. Although we can become controlling, and our harsh judgments of ourselves can eventually turn outward toward others, we continue to try to be the "ideal woman," responding to images of the 1950s housewife or perhaps the so-called liberated career woman who kills herself making things work at home after killing herself all day at the office. We feel we have to take care of every sphere, to be the perfect wife, loving mother, and helpful friend who never says no.

Many women who are considered co-dependent have many years' experience being defined by others. So, whether you want to think of it in terms of a larger syndrome called "co-dependence," or internalized oppression resulting from others defining who you are, or, perhaps, looking outside instead of within for an identity, all paths lead to an empty sense of self; a feeling that you're not sure who you really are. In her book *Controlling People: How to Recognize, Understand and Deal with People Who Try to Control You*, Patricia Evans notes what occurs:

> *People . . . who have been told what they want, what they feel, and so forth, who haven't had their experience clearly reflected back to them, are usually unsure of their experience or what it means . . . How then do they develop their identity? . . . Which "self" would one bring to a relationship or to the world if he or she was in fact disconnected from his or her true self?*

A Prescription for Misery

If you think co-dependence is a prescription for misery, you're right. Yet many of us push ourselves to make the impossible happen—not because we think we're worth it, but because we believe everyone else is. As a co-dependent, our identity can be so wrapped up in the caretaking of others that we may forget how to identify or solve our own problems. If we're not careful, the person we knew, the authentic self inside, may wither as we attempt to live up to an image of Superwoman that simply doesn't exist in the real world. As one of my clients said, "I thought if I was nicer, he would be nicer. If I was more loving, he would be more loving. If I complimented

> "Regardless of what I did, how much I compensated for all that was lacking in our home, in our marriage, I was powerless to fix it; I was powerless to change him."

him, he would compliment me. But it never worked. Regardless of what I did, how much I compensated for all that was lacking in our home, in our marriage, I was powerless to fix it; I was powerless to change him. Coming to terms with this went against everything I had been taught. It didn't make sense at first, but there it was plain as day. To adjust to my new revelation, I had to reexamine my entire identity and come to terms with the real me—warts and all—and make her stronger . . . building from the bottom up."

A friend of mine once joked: "Co-dependents aren't born, they're made." Nature-versus-nurture arguments aside, when we're involved in a destructive relationship, any co-dependent tendencies we may have harbored within can grow exponentially, and new ones may develop. In an attempt to fend off put-downs, try harder to make things work, and preserve our increasingly fragile identity, we may work to placate, to control interactions and to counter the actions of the problem person. Yet more often than not, our thinking becomes distorted and we may find ourselves reacting and overreacting to, well, just about everything. After all, one of the hallmark traits of co-dependent behavior is to become a reactionary. Instead of coming from a position of power, choosing the course of our actions, we instead create crisis and chaos by reacting to others' actions, feelings, and problems. We worry and obsess, ricocheting between anxiety and self-hatred, caretaking and controlling. We are not in charge of our own destiny since we have so few internal moorings and have difficulty staying centered on self.

Co-dependence doesn't cause a destructive individual to act the way he does, but it can perpetuate negative patterns that keep us focused on pleasing everyone but ourselves.

You might want to ask yourself: *Do I obsess over the problem person in my life? Do I alternate between denying his actions and reacting to them? Do I worry too much about the relationship and worry too little about myself? Do I feel jittery inside, unstable, on edge? Am I always trying to figure out what's wrong? Determined to fix things?* If so, you're in good company.

Keep in mind that when she's in a relationship with a destructive man, a woman feels so anxious, so doubtful (with good reason) about his commitment, and so uncertain about his love that she takes responsibility for both sides of the relationship—both his and hers. It's as though she's in a relationship with herself rather than him. Co-dependence doesn't cause a destructive individual to act the way he does, but it can perpetuate negative patterns that keep us focused on pleasing everyone but ourselves.

The Respondaholic: "Yes Woman"

Respondaholics can be co-dependents, and co-dependents can be respondaholics. In fact, being a respondaholic can be one aspect of co-dependency. The difference between the two is that respondaholics may have healthy boundaries in some areas of their lives but not others. They have a reflexive habit of always saying yes and then having to find a way to retract the yes and change it to a no—often getting themselves into trouble in the process. They feel guilty for having responded so hastily and, if they're not careful, others can play on these feelings, manipulating them to go along with something they really don't want to do. For example, when asked if she wants to get married, a respondaholic will automatically say yes. Then she'll go and think about it. Usually, after having some time to reflect, the respondaholic will decide whether she's ready to get married or simply in love with the idea of marriage.

Unlike more full-blown co-dependents, a respondaholic doesn't usually have such an overwhelming sense of obligation that she'll compulsively override her own sensibilities—even if it's embarrassing or uncomfortable to renegotiate. However, when dealing with a destructive individual, it may be more difficult for her to wiggle out of an initial commitment or simply change her mind. He may have tipped the scales in his favor by using either charming manipulations that hide his true personality, or head games that cause her self-doubt and confusion, so that a clear decision is not easy to make.

> Destructive individuals capitalize on insecurities.

Like the co-dependent, respondaholics want approval; they want to be liked. Destructive individuals capitalize on these insecurities. Despite the development of some personal boundaries, if we're caught in a cycle of saying yes, we become more susceptible to the tactics of an abuser who will try to wear us down until we say yes and mean it, or make us feel too afraid to say no. Being centered on self is a position of strength; it is not a selfish stance of being self-centered.

The Savior: Rescuing Others, Wanting to Be Rescued

Men aren't the only ones who like to be thought of as heroes. As women, we have our own version of playing the hero, and although it usually involves fewer horses, evil wizards, and swords, it's playing the hero just the same. We cleverly find ways to save a man from himself or to change him for the better, whether or not he has asked to be saved or changed. We're determined to control him, to make him the man we want him to be—all for his own good, of course! If we're not careful, he can turn the tables on us, ensnaring us in "the rescue" even though he has no intention of changing a thing.

Once we're hooked into the heroine role, his empty promises to change, to do better, to stop himself before he says something hurtful, and to live up to our new and improved image of him can keep us locked into a vicious cycle that is detrimental to us and plays right into his hands. As a loving mother figure, we win points for taking care of him as though he were an infant. (Okay, okay, he may act like one. But all you have to do is check his driver's license to remember his real age!) Besides, our acts are usually not selfless, and they certainly aren't respectful. Instead, our efforts to control often come across as condescending, and when he reacts negatively, or pushes us away, we feel genuinely hurt. After all, we were only trying to help.

More often than not, efforts at rescuing behaviors turn into enabling behaviors, which prevent him from taking responsibility for his own actions, from experiencing the consequences of his behavior, and from growing up. In my practice I've seen warm, nurturing women, outdoorsy women, socially conscious women, and hard-core, coolheaded professionals exert great effort to convince me that their husband, boyfriend, or partner couldn't survive a day without them. While they may have some justification for feeling this way, it's apparent that their identity is wrapped up in saving him.

Playing the role of savior can distract us from claiming our own life.

For the savior, this brand of caretaking has a superhero or saintly aspect to it. Saving others makes her feel good inside, makes her feel like somebody, especially if she doesn't believe she is worthwhile on her own. It also distracts her from taking charge of her own life, living out her own passions, realizing her own success, and meeting her own potential. She can avoid dealing with herself since the focus is on someone else—especially her man. The truth is, deep down, most saviors secretly want to be rescued. Gloria Steinem once said: "Many of us are becoming the men we wanted to marry." Well, saviors attempt to become the Prince Charming they always wished would come and whisk *them* away.

The Optimist: Falling in Love with Someone's Potential

While it would be convenient if all destructive individuals were complete monsters, the truth is, they're not. Many of them are wounded; many of them come from abusive homes, were raised by domineering tyrants, or developed into troubled people for any number of reasons that weren't their fault. Like the rest of us, they have some good qualities, their own special brand of intelligence, and often a great sense of humor. The optimist falls in love with every one of the good qualities, whether imagined or real, that such men possess. Often her view of the man she loves discounts his dark side, his tendency to disrespect her, his all-too-frequent slights.

It can be confusing. We may feel deeply connected to the problem person. Yet over time the less-than-desirable aspects of his personality start to show through, and we're not sure how to reconcile this emerging and troubling dichotomy. Consequently, we may deny the negative while focusing on his unmet potential. It's a dangerous place to be in a relationship, and it becomes only more dangerous when we discover he isn't the man we imagined him to be. He fooled us with a persona that he conjured up to entrap us. But the eternal optimists among us often refuse to give up even when it has become clear that the only real potential our beloved has is to hurt us, degrade our self-esteem, and cripple our dreams. Once the illusion is shattered, it can be difficult to disengage from him because we've invested so much in the hope of what he *could* be, of how good we would feel, how great our lives would be, if he were the man we once envisioned.

The Invisible Woman: Without Him, What Am I?

It doesn't seem to matter how successful, independent, liberated, creative, or financially secure we are; all of us tend to see ourselves in relation to others. In and of itself, this is a wonderful trait to have! However, when we don't express our need for connection in socially intelligent ways, we can run into problems. To hold on to a relationship simply because without it, we would feel incomplete is one of the worst reasons for being in a relationship. After all, desperation is hardly a solid foundation to build on. If we feel fragmented and believe that someone else will make us feel happy and whole, we're not only placing unfair expectations on him but also putting ourselves in a very vulnerable position, especially if we've become involved with a controlling man. In no time at all, he'll figure out that all he has to do is threaten to leave and we'll acquiesce and give him anything he wants. Our fear—or in some cases our genuine terror—of being alone, being abandoned, or being without a man makes us easy to manipulate and dominate.

> Fear of being alone, being abandoned, or being without a man makes us easy to manipulate.

Why we feel so unworthy if we're not attached to a mate is a question worth asking. Certainly tying ourselves to a man, any man, means we will always have company when we go to the movies or out to a restaurant. But solving this one problem creates many others, including a lowering of our self-esteem and our failing to learn how to love the one we're with—that is, ourselves.

You Complete Me: Emotionally, Financially

It's not uncommon to seek out a partner who's everything we're not. If we lack patience, we may try to find someone who's patient. If we aren't physically active, we do our best to attract someone who is. If we're good at math, then we look for someone who has strong writing skills. The theory here is that together, our two halves will create a whole. The combination of our opposite qualities will result in a match made in heaven. Right?

While it might sound good in theory, it usually doesn't pan out in real life—especially when our "other half" is a destructive person. After all, many of these guys are adept at figuring out what we're looking for in a mate, and once they know what we're after, here come the promises. He shapes himself into the likeness of someone we think we want, someone whom we believe will make us complete. That's how he hooks us in emotionally.

When it comes to money, he may make elaborate, if false, claims of financial wealth in order to ensnare us. Whether financially comfortable or dirt poor, for most women—especially those who want to raise children—financial security is a looming concern and the fear of being without is an emotional hot button that can easily be exploited. Surprisingly, even those with substantial trust funds can have a deep-seated fear of poverty as well as an ingrained belief that a woman cannot adequately provide for herself despite bank statements to the contrary and thus get involved with a wealthy man to ensure their continued financial stability. In any event, we can rest assured that the delivery of goods will come with a hefty price tag. Even if we're wealthy and find someone who matches our status, so that together we share a lifestyle of privilege, the illusion of security, of being "the perfect couple," may blind us to the reality of our situation. Completing each other isn't a sound basis for any relationship. It's a complete disaster when it comes to a destructive one.

> Completing each other isn't a sound basis for any relationship. It's a complete disaster when it comes to a destructive one.

■ ■ ■ ■ ■

Hopefully, recognizing ourselves in any of these women can help us to better understand the reasons why we became attracted to and involved with a destructive person. Remember, there are many reasons for becoming enmeshed in a relationship that's just no good for us. In the next chapter we'll examine more messages, myths, and mental tricks that may have gotten us here and are keeping us stuck. Awareness is the first step toward change. Let the revelations begin!

| 6 |

How Did I Get Here?

David Byrne, lead singer of the rock group Talking Heads, caught the world's attention when he dressed in a theatrically oversize suit in the film *Stop Making Sense* and sang what are now some of his best-known lyrics. Performing the song "Once in a Lifetime," Byrne jerks his body as though attempting to wake from a dream and shake himself out of his own disbelief that the life now surrounding him is not an apparition—it's real. He vaguely seems to understand that he's had something to do with it, but he's not quite sure what.

Many of us also wonder how we got here. "I felt like I was living someone else's life, as though I was in a dissociated state looking in on everything instead of feeling a part of it," is the way a young mother described it to me as she was waking up to the truth of her circumstances—a reality she'd managed to keep at a distance for more than ten years.

Certainly we can use a variety of methods to deal with our situation. The problem is, many of them don't work, and they won't ameliorate the erosion of our self-esteem. In truth they can dig us farther into a hole until we begin to notice that we're standing in a potential grave—and could get buried. But as soon as we wake up and stop letting the days go by, we can better see through the myths, through the false, negative beliefs we have about ourselves as well as the disempowering ways of thinking and acting that can perpetuate a destructive situation. They're usually more common than we think, and once we become aware of them operating in our lives and place them in their proper perspective, we can begin to replace what doesn't work with what does.

What is especially astonishing is how many of us go through our love life unaware, doing the same thing over and over while hoping for a different outcome. Relationship after relationship, we repeat self-defeating patterns over and over again—different man, same relationship. Only when we become aware of what we're doing and are ready to instigate a new plan does it become possible for us to change.

> So many of us live our love life unaware, doing the same thing over and over while hoping for a different outcome.

A well-known observation bears repeating here. Rats can be quickly trained to find the corridor within a maze that has a piece of cheese at the end. Once the rats find that corridor, they no longer go down the paths without the cheese. We cannot say the same for so many of us, who keep getting stuck in unhealthy relationships, doing the same things with the same types of men with the same disastrous results.

Denial of What's Real

Denial is everywhere. Politicians use it; corporate executives use it; common thieves use it—everyone uses it. It's a common strategy for avoiding the truth. And for those of us in destructive relationships, it's an effective way to discredit our feelings, instincts, and intuition. What we often know in our gut is simply too painful to admit, so we make up excuses for the man in our life. We tell little lies on his behalf, and we even minimize the severity of his actions, often telling ourselves stories that are renditions of the truth so that we can continue to endure what's going on. Denial prevents us, and the problem person, from taking responsibility for any actions or consequences we are too uncomfortable to acknowledge. If it doesn't exist, nothing needs to be done to change it—right? Ultimately, the message we're

giving ourselves is: *It's not real.* We
want to believe the relationship is
okay, and that we're okay in it, and
so we bolster our false sense of security with internal mind games in an
attempt to convince ourselves that
everything is copacetic.

Rose, a stage actress who often
jokes about life with her former
husband, relayed a story to me: "I
kept wondering why he seemed

Denial prevents us, and the problem person, from taking responsibility for any actions or consequences we are too uncomfortable to acknowledge.

so dissatisfied with me as a woman. My shape was incredible; my
legs rivaled a model's. I dressed in flattering ways and was not, like
many in my profession, a scattered mess. I had a successful career
and still managed to handle life at home with the help of a nanny. I
was very loving and attentive, yet he would find ways to comment
on my weight, or a tiny scar—mean-spirited comments directed
at my appearance. He often rejected me in bed. Then one day I
found a pair of woman's gloves tucked under his side of the bed, an
enormous bra stuffed with padding, and a dress that could have fit
two of me inside. I couldn't decide which was worse—his having an
affair with a very large woman or the fact that he might be wearing
women's clothes—so I told myself he was saving them as a gift for
his mother! Well, when the truth finally came out that he was a gay
cross-dresser, the denial I thought would save my sanity came back
to bite me in the ass, and hard!"

Denial affords us the opportunity to normalize the abnormal. We
see a white elephant standing in the center of the living room, yet we
walk right on past. In certain moments we might stop long enough
to dust off its nose, but that's probably the extent of our acknowledg-
ment, since the elephant, like the problems in our relationship, can
appear to be too enormous and overwhelming to handle. In essence,
denial enables us to fake it until we decide to do something different.
The problem is that the very act of faking it can further perpetuate

our inability to act. Why? Because day after day we're losing more life force energy, the very force that is needed to feed our authentic self so that we are able to act from a place of personal power rather than fear. Jungian analyst Clarissa Pinkola Estes, author of *Women Who Run with the Wolves: Myths and Stories of the Wild Woman Archetype*, writes: "In 'being good,' a woman closes her eyes to everything obdurate, distorted, or damaging around her, and just tries to 'live with it.' Her attempts to accept this abnormal state further injure her wild instincts to react, point out, change, make an impact on what is not right, what is not just."

In essence, denial enables us to fake it until we decide to do something different.

It's important not to condemn ourselves for using denial, since it can be a necessary coping strategy for enduring difficult situations. However, we often remain in denial too long, long after it has outlived its usefulness, and as a result we run the risk of losing track of what is real and what is fiction.

A corporate attorney who had recently made partner came to see me because she wanted to discuss her suspicions about her husband's extracurricular activities: an affair, a cocaine problem, and illegally siphoning off donations paid to his company. When I confirmed her suspicions, she broke down in tears and cried for a few minutes before she finally spoke again: "You know, my son and I used to play a game called Not Me, Couldn't Be. It was an innocent way to pretend. Whenever he'd leave his toys out and I'd have to remind him to pick them up, I'd ask him, 'Did you leave those toys on the floor?' and he'd respond, 'Not me, couldn't be . . . ,' and then go put them away. It took me fifteen years to figure out that my husband was playing the same game with higher stakes."

So this woman, too, despite being at the top of her Ivy League class, effortlessly passing the bar exam, and achieving the status of partner, had been in deep denial as far as her relationship was concerned. She had lost touch with her inner wisdom and the deeper voice inside. Turns out that she had confronted her husband on several occasions, and when he denied any wrongdoing she quickly accepted his response—because "I didn't want to believe he might be capable of such things. My ability to lie to myself overpowered my ability to be in touch with the truth. Luckily, too much evidence piled up, so that even an attorney who was ignoring the facts of her own case eventually had to open her eyes!"

Here's an interesting paradox: One of the things that makes it so hard for us to see the destructive things that are going on in our relationship is, ironically, our survival-oriented drive to maintain homeostasis. In general, like the human body, the psyche craves balance, safety, predictability. It strives to maintain the status quo and feels threatened by the prospect of change. Homeostasis, therefore, motivates us to believe that our partner is operating from the best intentions, is playing on the same playing field, and has the same goodwill toward us that we have toward him. Often we are just fooling ourselves. This explains why so many of us are reluctant to conclude that our partner is cheating on us, lying to us, or otherwise abusing us until we get hit over the head with some kind of indisputable evidence.

> **Like the human body, the psyche craves balance, safety, predictability.**

Is It Really Abuse?

Another form of denial can come into play when we're experiencing genuine confusion about what's actually taking place. Until recently, abuse was thought of as strictly physical . . . which is simply incorrect. Psychotherapist and author Dr. Jill Murray—herself the survivor of a destructive relationship—points out in her book *But He Never Hit Me: The Devastating Cost of Non-Physical Abuse to Girls and Women*:

> *Popular wisdom suggests that all abuse is physical, so if a woman doesn't have a black eye or a broken arm, she doesn't consider herself*

*abused, and neither does the outside world. In fact, physical abuse—
hitting, shoving, choking, grabbing, and assaulting by any means—
constitutes the vast minority of abuse. The vast majority consists of
verbal, emotional, psychological, financial, and spiritual abuse.*

We may not really know what's going on, we're not sure what's
wrong, and we may talk incessantly to our friends about his bad habits and rage on about his transgressions to get relief, yet we never
take action. "Do you believe he suggested that I get liposuction when
I just completed breast augmentation surgery?" we ask, rhetorically.
"Why do you think he compares me with his old girlfriends and his
ex-wife, always making me feels like they're better than me? But when
I ask him about it, he immediately reassures me that I'm his favorite person." Our friends may confront us, ask us why we stay, and
let us know they would never put up with such demeaning behavior
. . . and in the moment we may acknowledge how miserable we are
and that they're right, but then we go right back into the cycle and
minimize our suffering, denying that things are as bad as they really
are. Though deeply unhappy, we may not be ready to face the truth
because, honestly, we're not mentally or emotionally able to believe
it. *Maybe he's right, I'm just insecure,* we tell ourselves, because in some
strange way that rationalization makes more sense—at least in the
moment.

The situation may be crystal clear to those around us while we,
on the other hand, wobble back and forth, sincerely perplexed, feeling that the real truth is elusive. "I couldn't settle on the real answer,
I was too confused. I'd lost all confidence in my ability to distinguish
fact from fiction and open my eyes to unfamiliar possibilities. After
all, I'd never been involved with a man like this before . . . it was all
too foreign to me. It took me two years to break through . . . I felt so
stupid when I finally got it."

When the dynamics of a destructive relationship are so far from
our awareness, we may not be sure how to think about them. Regardless of socioeconomic or social standing, regardless of intelligence or

training (yes, therapists find themselves in destructive scenarios and aren't always certain what steps to take to get out), if we don't have an accurate way to think about what's happening, we may, for a time, get stuck; sometimes in ignorance, other times in misinterpretations. Barbara, a wealthy banker's daughter, explained it this way: "I thought toxic men wore T-shirts, drank beer, cursed, and sported tattoos. That was my idea of an abusive man. As far as I was concerned, the verbal attacks and sly defamations of my character from my live-in lover were simply a *communication* problem. I couldn't comprehend that a woman with my intelligence, social standing, and elite background could ever be dense enough to end up in a situation like mine. What a humbling experience!"

Five Main Beliefs that Perpetuate Denial and Disbelief

"He must be right" We take his word over our own no matter how ludicrous, nonsensical, and deceptive his claims, excuses, or rebuttals.

"It's not hitting" Only physical abuse is considered a real violation and harmful act. Other forms of destructive behavior "don't really count."

"Someone who says he loves me can't be abusing me . . . besides, he's not hitting . . ." We refuse to wrap our mind around the apparent dichotomy.

"Other people get themselves in messy and troublesome relationships, but I'm too smart, alert, savvy, seasoned, sophisticated . . ." We contend that it's only *other* people who could fall for the tricks of a toxic troublemaker—it could *never happen to me!*

"It can't be abuse . . ." It has to be a communication problem; a relationship problem; an introvert–extrovert problem; differences in temperament; "he's a morning person and I'm a night owl; he's an Aquarius and I'm a Capricorn . . ." You get the idea.

Another reason why many women don't recognize their partner's words and actions as destructive, abusive, or otherwise unacceptable is the well-known male privilege that permeates many cultures, including our own. In my experience, male privilege, which logically is accompanied by a lowered status for women, can be especially predominant within many church denominations, especially those that relay on literal interpretations of biblical phrases such as "Women, be obedient to your husbands." As Dr. Grace Ketterman points out in her book *Verbal Abuse: Healing the Hidden Wound*, often the pastors and other clergy whom women seek out for counseling are blinded by their own possibly unconscious gender biases. This may be why there are relatively high levels of intimate partner abuse in certain religious sects.

Denial is a way of safeguarding the illusion that we're not contending with what we're actually contending with . . . or what we hope we're not contending with. It serves many purposes and is a powerful coping mechanism. It staves off our fear of change. It postpones coming to terms with reality so we are protected from confronting the uncomfortable facts of our lives. It's important to keep in mind that denial doesn't stave off the harmful effects of a destructive relationship. It only allows us to pretend that they're not really happening. "I had headaches, stomach problems, my skin was breaking out and my hands developed small tremors, and I kept acting as though I had no idea why my health was deteriorating until my physician asked me how things were at home. Thankfully, she was astute enough to see that my body was screaming for help even though I was afraid to. The truth about my husband's behavior was too painful. I felt ashamed that I couldn't handle it."

> **Denial doesn't stave off the harmful effects of a destructive relationship. It only allows us to pretend that they're not really happening.**

Minimizing Red Flags and Giving Others the Benefit of the Doubt

"I often saw red flags," confided Connie, a college senior whose mother had referred her to me, "and instead of running the other direction, I charged forward. I just had to find out what *kind* of red flag it was!" How many of us can relate to her story? When it comes to red flags, here is what all my closest male friends advise: "If the guy says he's had problems with lying, anger, infidelity, or women in general, he's letting you know right off the bat. Don't stick around to find out exactly what he means!"

> If the guy says he's had problems with lying, anger, infidelity, or women in general, he's letting you know right off the bat. Don't stick around.

In all likelihood, however, the destructive individual in our life did not lay things out for us right up front. Instead, he probably worked hard to show us his good side until we became enamored, charmed, touched, or attracted—or simply enjoyed his company. Unsurprisingly, the more heavily involved we become, the more difficult it is to pull away—and the more likely it is that whenever we *do* see a red flag, we give him the benefit of the doubt.

"Don't you trust me?" "What have I ever done to make you suspicious?" "How could you ask me that question? I'm insulted you could even think that about me." Any of these sound familiar? They should. They're some of the most common tactics used by a troublemaking man. Most times they get us to withdraw so we're distracted from the truth, and then feel guilty for doubting him—even if it's clear that we caught him in a deception. By taking the focus off the action, the false words, and the obvious inconsistencies—and instead putting it on our love and trust of him—we're emotionally manipulated so he isn't held accountable. "I hated the thought of insulting the man I

loved and so I always took it back—the 'accusations,' the confronta-
tions, the moments I caught him in the act. It was crazy-making . . ."
In essence, we put his word above our own. We minimize what we
know, and the sanity-threatening twists of the truth persist.

Romantic Mythologies That Get Us Into Trouble

Romantic mythologies permeate our culture. Corporate empires
are built on them and generate them . . . we can't get enough.
While fairy tales and romantic comedies are wonderful, some of
us take them a little too much to heart. Somewhere along the line,
we turned a romantic notion into an entitlement of dependency,
thinking that someone *out there* will ensure our happiness instead
of understanding that we must create it for ourselves. It's not that
we're lazy or ill equipped; it's just that we buy into the idea of being
rescued in such a way that anyone posing as a prince could profess his love and we'd be all too ready to abandon ourselves for the
promise of a dream.

Allison married a man who owned a Mercedes dealership, and
though at some point in their rela-
tionship she knew she no longer
loved him and could barely tolerate his treatment of her, she had
to admit: "Losing the privilege of
driving the latest model every year
was really difficult for me. The car represented a dream—a dream I
was terrified to give up even if it meant further lowering of my self-
esteem. It's sad, but true." To Allison, the coveted automobiles gave
her status, respect in the community, and a sense of worth; things she
had not fully cultivated within herself. "And why would I have?" she
once asked. "My mom was already looking for a prince to match me
up with right there in the hospital on the day I was born. I was taught
that I mattered little without a man."

> "I was taught that I mattered little without a man."

Another aspect to this romantic myth has to do with financial security. No matter where we sit on the socioeconomic spectrum, the majority of us still believe, deep down, that we need a man to support us. Even when we earn more money, psychologically we may still feel we couldn't do it without him. Our financial security, or perceived financial security, is tied to him in one way or another . . . and the fear of going it alone can be paralyzing, especially if we have children. Granted, the reality is that postdivorce women's economic status declines while men's increases, making money a serious issue to consider. Yet the trappings of the psychological myth must be overcome first in order to clearly determine the role finances actually play in the decision to stay. Breaking through the deep-seated notion that we need a man—and we want a prince—isn't always easy even when we have evidence to the contrary.

Being rescued; finding a Prince Charming; being swept away by a handsome man on a horse or driven through the streets of Europe in a Bentley . . . these myths can deeply influence our unconscious, driving us toward forming certain relationships without questioning our real motives. The illusions we then build around us could end up being a prison instead of a castle. After all, some princes are handsome, polite, and kind while others act as though they're self-crowned tyrants. It's our job to dismantle the myth that, because of its nebulous and often elusive nature, can be influencing us in ways we could never have imagined when it comes to forming relationships with men. Once we've done that, we can determine whether we have indeed married into royalty—however we define it—or are simply stuck kissing, cooking for, and sleeping with a toad.

Innocence and Naïveté: Prey for the Predator

In recent years innocence and naïveté have come under fire. We've been chastised for not knowing better if we fall prey to the tricks of a predator, as if we had X-ray vision and could predict his true motives within minutes. In my estimation it's simply another clever way to blame women for getting into destructive situations. Besides, as clinical psychologist Dr. Martha Stout succinctly states in her book *The Sociopath Next Door:* "Apart from knowing someone well for many years, there is no foolproof decision rule or litmus test for trustworthiness . . . unnerving though it may be."

The Lesson of the Fruit Flies

Award-winning journalist Dianne Hales offers an interesting way to look at this issue in her book *Just Like a Woman: How Gender Science Is Redefining What Makes Us Female*. She relays the research of William Rice, an evolutionary geneticist at the University of California–Santa Cruz, who "...observed several generations of fruit flies as they refined complex offensive and defensive sexual strategies. In essence, the male fruit flies tried various methods to attract and distract the female fruit flies in an effort to mate. Even with such skillful maneuvers, Ms. Hales writes: "If she'd already mated, he'd try to entice her to mate again. But again and again, females countered such seductive moves, even to the extent of producing contraceptive chemicals that blocked fertilization." Genetically, the experiments showed, each new generation of fruit flies seemed to be born with an innate knowledge of their parents' sexual offensives and counteroffensives and "managed to come up with new tactics." Yet here's where it really gets interesting.

> *What would happen, Rice wondered, if only one sex got to put this legacy to use? He allowed forty-one generations of one group of males to mate with certain females and then introduced them to a new, less experienced group of potential partners . . . The insect ingénues fell for every trick . . . But the males' sexual aggression took an unexpectedly harsh toll on the females. It literally killed them . . . While such a scenario is chilling, it underscores a brighter reality: ". . . in nonexperimental conditions, females can hold their own."*

First of all, I'm surprised that the researchers didn't expect such aggression, sexual or otherwise, *not* to take such a dramatic toll. Mitigating male aggression by being hypervigilant is exhausting—and hardly the basis for a relationship. Though, realistically, to remain naive isn't smart; nor, in many situations, is it optimal. Second, yes, it's true: Women *can* develop, and *should* develop, remedies to counter such predatory approaches. Certainly it's in our best interest—and for this reason we'll explore some meaningful ways to heighten our awareness later in the book. Yet it can take time to become savvy to a predator's ploys, especially when he, just like the male fruit flies, is constantly developing new strategies to confuse and control in order to successfully achieve his goals. Unlike our fruit fly brethren's strategies, however, human predators are relatively complex in the sense that they, unlike insects, employ emotional hooks ("I love you . . . I need you . . . I want to be with you . . ."), mind games ("If you loved me you'd . . . I can't believe you won't let me do such and such, I thought you loved me . . .") and play on our fears, loneliness, and insecurities . . . our basic need for love, family and companionship; aspects of bonding that, at least to our knowledge, fruit flies don't much concern themselves with. Yet, as Drs. Paul Babiak and Robert Hare attest in their book *Snakes in Suits*:

> *This psychological bond capitalizes on your inner personality, holding the promise of greater depth and possible intimacy, and offering a relationship that is special, unique, equal—forever . . . the psychopath exerts noble effort communicating that he or she is exactly the person you have been looking for . . . The psychopath's message is: I am the perfect friend . . . lover . . . partner . . . for you.*

Who doesn't want that?!

Our involvement in toxic relationships doesn't happen because we're not smart enough to make better, more informed choices, but because:

- We do not think like a predator and therefore do not comprehend the predatory mentality.
- We may have been raised with or developed learned helplessness and overly submissive standards of behavior.
- We come to identify with the destructive individual (known as the Stockholm syndrome in psychological and medical circles).
- We are often conditioned to be respondaholics whenever men approach us.
- In an effort to make girls "nice," we are taught to be prey to the predator.

While there are remedies for all of these scenarios—such as learning to better trust our instincts, to better identify red flags, to set firmer boundaries, and to hold what I like to call the Divine Dichotomy of good and evil—in all likelihood we were not born with these skills. Nor have most of us developed all of them as part of a sophisticated protective gestalt that acts as second nature whenever we are approached by someone who's no good for us. In chapter 11 we'll discuss these potential remedies and the ways in which they can be used as powerful and effective tools for our safety and protection when it comes to dealing with a destructive individual. For now, let's look at the qualities that make us susceptible. . . . prey to the predator.

The Predator Mentality

"Is the predator smarter than me?" women ask all the time. In some instances the answer is yes, but more often than not he simply thinks differently, and to compare intelligence is a futile endeavor. Remember the description in chapter 2 put forth by Martha Stout, Ph.D.? Psychopaths lack conscience; they lack remorse and are genuinely incapable of empathizing with others or feeling guilt despite their pathological lying, deception, and abuse of others. Yet on the surface they appear quite normal, engaging, and in control. As Hervey

Cleckley, M.D., a psychiatrist and author of *Without Conscience: The Disturbing World of Psychopaths Among Us*, puts it: "[the] psychopath presents a technical appearance of sanity, often one of high intellectual capacities, and not infrequently succeeds in business or professional activities."

Not all predators are the horrific criminals we hear about in the news, and some are even quite likable in a superficial way, "not hurting people in ways that attract attention, but causing problems nonetheless in hidden economic, psychological, and emotionally abusive ways." But don't think for one moment that their ploys aren't systematic and deliberate. They spend a lot of time convincing us that their persona is real when, in fact, it is a facade designed to ensnare us. While we wake up in the morning concerned about attending our child's play, reminding ourselves not to forget the grocery list, and planning for our presentation to stockholders, the predator is scheming . . . and I can assure you, he has no one's best interest in mind except his own.

Remember, the predator's goal is control. Chances are we're just trying to cultivate a relationship and may unwittingly, in our innocence and naïveté, play right into his hand. No, not because we're lacking in brain power. On the contrary, it's because we have a conscience, abide by moral standards, and expect some level of genuine emotional interaction. Wrap your mind around that one!

Learned Helplessness and Overly Submissive Behavior

Remember the story from chapter 1 about the laboratory rats that were shocked repeatedly and, knowing they could not escape the cage, grew more and more complacent? ". . . The rats that were placed in inescapable pain-inflicting situations failed to learn how to flee. Indeed, after repeated exposures to the inevitable shock, this group of rats made no attempt to leave their cages, even after the shocks were no longer administered. They had learned to be helpless." Psychologist Martin Seligman also conducted similar experiments with dogs and found that even when the doors were opened, the dogs stopped leaving their

"People who feel trapped in abusive situations become depressed and anxious and begin to doubt their own abilities. Learned helplessness undercuts their motivation to leave."

cages. Like the rats, it took time for the dogs to overcome the effects of learned helplessness. Fortunately, when the canine subjects were "taught to respond appropriately . . . the helplessness was eradicated." Sadly, though these experiments were performed on our four-legged friends, the findings continue to be highly applicable to the behavior in their human counterparts. Susan Weitzman, Ph.D., puts it this way:

In humans, it is not just behavior that is limited and compromised. People who feel trapped in abusive situations become depressed and anxious and begin to doubt their own abilities. Learned helplessness undercuts their motivation to leave the . . . situation. Learned helplessness can befall all types of women—even independent, successful professionals—partly owing to the power imbalance inherent in male–female relationships, which often contributes to a woman's feeling of powerlessness. Change occurs when the abused woman is helped to see that she has safer and less painful options than staying with the abuser.

Those of us raised in a household where men were given preferential treatment, the double standard reigned supreme, Father was the indisputable authority, and we were taught to always say, sweetly, "Pretty please" whenever we wanted anything, knowing our requests would be met, or not, depending on the whim of others, often learned to be overly submissive. While we may not be helpless, we learned to act that way so as not to threaten those around us. We learned to play the innocent and as a result, we may have underdeveloped life skills, especially when it comes to asserting our boundaries and personal power—again, making us vulnerable to the predator.

Identifying with the Destructive Individual: The Stockholm Syndrome

As strange as it may seem, some women come to identify with the destructive individual in the same way hostages come to identify with their captors regardless of the torture, abuse, and torment they may endure at their hands. Those of us who have become attached to the problem person in this way often hear ourselves defending him with others: "He had a traumatic childhood." "He didn't mean to be so harsh with me." "No one else loves him but me. It would be cruel to leave." In an attempt to withstand such a psychologically dominating and emotionally destructive relationship, we may use this method as a way to get along instead of fighting a losing battle. After all, we're probably exhausted—mentally and physically—and our world is turned upside down; like a Fellini film, top is bottom, logic is illogical, and very little makes sense. Dr. Jill Murray, author of *But He Never Hit Me*, writes: "She has been so emotionally brainwashed that not only does she believe what she is told, but she also identifies closely with him as a person, with his plans and his goals. She hopes to be worthy enough to help him with his plan (which, unbeknownst to her, is her total emotional devastation)."

I heard of one woman whose life read like a textbook case of the Stockholm syndrome. As told to me by her neighbor, "She was a computer programmer in her thirties, a very bright girl who lived in one of the apartments in my complex. She kept telling me about her boyfriend eighty miles south in L.A. who had been unfairly treated by his ex-wife, his two daughters, and all his friends. I didn't think much of it until he came to stay with her and in no time at all, I could hear him verbally battering her when I'd pass her apartment on my way to work every morning. Then he zeroed in on me, making passes to get my attention when she was standing right next to him. When I didn't respond, he became angry and convinced her that *I* was the enemy. Next thing I knew, he had *her* making false reports against me to the apartment manager. She dutifully did everything he said without objection no matter how ridiculous or unfounded. And when he decided controlling her wasn't enough, he talked her into telling other people, including the apartment manager, what they could and could not do. Instead of questioning his insane requests, she merely carried them out. It was amazing to observe the change in her!"

We often see this sort of pattern occurring when the man takes on a second (or third, or fourth) wife. All too often these women naively collude with the man, willingly joining him in his campaign to destroy the ex, justifying her actions on the basis of his claims— which she buys into hook, line, and sinker—that his ex was "insane," "unreasonable," or "abusive." Of course, this second wife may eventually find herself to be victimized by the man in precisely the same way: She becomes the target of the campaign he launches against her with his *next* partner.

Respondaholism

In the case of predators, behavior that seems innocent enough— simply being nice and friendly—can set us up to be readily taken advantage of. In *The Gift of Fear: Survival Signs That Protect Us from Violence*, the author, prosecuting attorney and presidential appointee Gavin de Becker, contends:

> *A woman is expected, first and foremost, to respond to every communication from a man. And the response is expected to be one of willingness and attentiveness. It is considered attractive if she is a bit uncertain (the opposite of explicit). Women are expected to be warm and open, and in the context of approaches from male strangers, warmth lengthens the encounter, raises his expectations, increases his investment, and, at best, wastes time. At worst, it serves the man who has sinister intent by providing much of the information he will need to evaluate and then control his prospective victim.*

In other words, responding in the way that most of us were programmed to behave can be to our detriment.

Be Nice!

In *Women Who Run with the Wolves*, psychologist and storyteller Clarissa Pinkola Estes examines the early training women receive that puts them at great risk when it comes to the wiles of the predator. She writes: "They are taught to not see, and instead to 'make pretty' all manner of grotesqueries whether they are lovely or not . . . This early training to 'be nice' causes women to override their intuitions. In that sense, they are actually purposefully taught to submit to the predator." What's interesting is that this early training isn't exclusively coming from men. It can be passed down if the mother is asleep or naive or hasn't been taught the ways of the world by her own mother, or if her mother's in collusion because she was mothered by an unmothered woman.

One of my clients, Melinda, was a brave soul who recognized her mother's early wounding and decided not to be beholden to the legacy: "My mother was molested by her stepfather and though she later became a feminist and touted independence, it was clear that she still was victimized by earlier training, to submit and 'be nice.' When I left my abusive husband, she chastised me, ignoring and denying his brutality and instead, in some strange way, encouraged me to make it all good, make it nice, so everything would be okay. It was then I realized how deeply these messages go and how easily they are perpetuated. Despite her bold feminist 'self-empowerment' rhetoric, she wanted to align herself with a power system that mistreated women." Or what about the women who, instead of having their daughters' backs, tell them in so many words, "That's the way it is. Suffer with it. It's our lot. At least he's a good provider." Sounds crazy, yes? Yet it's more common than most of us would like to believe.

If we've fallen prey to a predator and are asking ourselves: *How did I get here?* the answer is threefold: *I didn't see it coming; I sensed something wasn't quite right but I wasn't sure what;* or *I knew something was wrong, but in my desperation, youthful exuberance, confusion, lack of confidence . . .* fill in the blank . . . *I chose to ignore my internal warning signs and am now paying the price.* Regardless, far too many of these men have shifting identities and, simply put, are professional manipulators. Often quite skillful, the predator instinctually exploits our weaknesses—and we all have them—in order to take advantage of our good looks, our good heart, our bank account, and the refuge of our home. What do we receive in return? The illusion of a meaningful relationship as we become pawns in his destructive games.

The Hungry Heart: Filling the Empty Well

A good friend of mine who's a child psychiatrist in San Francisco once told me that half of the children who show up in his office wouldn't be there if their parents witnessed who they are. Simply put, they were not seen and heard for who they actually are, and that one factor in and of itself created all kinds of emotional and psychological problems.

Certainly there are plenty of examples of households where the emotional, psychological, and spiritual needs of the children were left unmet. Homes plagued by parental alcoholism, whether of the high-functioning or the fall-down-drunk variety; by emotionally distant and unresponsive parents; or even by despondent parents suffering from chronic depression and unhappy marriages—all are scenarios ripe for leaving holes in a child's heart. Yet even caring families may not be able to meet the inner needs of their children; depending on the parents' own emotional development and maturity, hungry hearts may result.

> Our parents may have done things for us, but did they actually relate to us?

Many of us grew up with material comforts, with parents who drove us to and from soccer practice and sat down regularly for family dinners. Yet coming from a good home isn't always enough. Our parents may have done things for us, but did they actually relate *to* us? Were they on automatic pilot, often too preoccupied with work or other obligations, and therefore simply not present? Did they have trouble "getting" us and, instead of taking the time to find out our individual identities, demand that we conform? Certainly I would contend that the majority of parents love their children, are well meaning, and are doing their best. Nevertheless, that may not fulfill the needs of the individual child. For this reason, I have always encouraged the parents I work with to learn who their children are as unique beings in and of themselves. In my book *Creating Balance in Your Child's Life*, I purposefully added a section on temperament in order to open parents' eyes to a number of systems that help to identify various qualities, strengths, weaknesses, and personality traits as a way to get them thinking about their own children—not as extensions of themselves but as truly unique individuals who have their own preferences, tastes, and ways of feeling, expressing, and doing things.

Whether we came from a neglectful family of origin, an attentive one, or a home that fell somewhere in between, we still may crave love . . . love we never had, love we didn't get enough of, or love that doesn't come with complications. It's not a stretch to see how we can become entangled in a relationship when a destructive individual offers love, affection, and companionship to fulfill our internal longings, even if it isn't ultimately sincere or comes with a hidden nasty side. Out of our deep need for true love, we may have settled for the first man who came along. Perhaps we were carried away with loving overtures that, for reasons related to his own psychological and emotional wounding, he couldn't sustain, and that gave way to the undermining behaviors so common to these types of relationships.

A gifted painter in Europe once told me that her husband would chastise her for wanting to be held. "He knew I craved loving attention and the best way to control me and make himself feel powerful was to refuse my requests whether romantic overtures, loving gestures, or affectionate embraces." He isolated her emotionally and then contemptuously accused her of "being needy" when she expressed a need to be touched, kissed, and made love to. "He wanted to love me," she confided, "but he was too selfish in the end; too emotionally cut off—and he blamed me for his fear of intimacy and emotional unavailability."

While her husband had issues of his own, her hungry heart, she admitted, often compelled her to ask for more love than anyone could possibly give. "In the end," she told me, "I'm responsible for filling up the empty well so I can more reasonably set my expectations and not demand that others fix something inside of me." She had come to a place of self-compassion for all that

A hungry heart can compel us to stay in destructive relationships.

she had been deprived of by her family or that she felt deprived of, and could now begin to move toward self-love. Fortunately, after three devastating experiences with troubled men, she was open to healing her heart so she would be better able to engage in a healthy union sometime in the future—and in the meantime could stop looking for love in all the wrong places.

"Hooked": Addictive Relationships

All of us can get our chains yanked in a variety of ways. Friends bait us with ludicrous statements they know we'll react to; our teenager playfully challenges us and, instead of laughing, we're all too ready to recite the rules. We get hooked, reacting with automatic patterns of behavior instead of responding *in* the moment, *to* the actual scenario in front of us. When I think of hooks in destructive relationships, I think of (1) *reacting to* current scenarios instead of *responding* to them, and (2) reacting *in the hope of* gaining something.

While it's common to be hooked by a destructive individual who overwhelms us with an onslaught of deliberate mind games, we often forget about the less common hook, which is *hope* or, more accurately, *false hope*. This is the aspect of toxic unions that resembles Russian roulette. Although he has deceived us numerous times, the one time he tells the truth we're ecstatic and quickly erase the past. He regularly dispenses verbal cruelty, yet if he arrives home with flowers, in our mind we immediately jump to *He really does love me, deep down.* If we really take a tally to compare the number of times he's kind with the number of times he's pure trouble, I can promise that the numbers won't weigh in heavily in favor of the "I should stay and work this out" category. To the contrary. Nevertheless, we hang in there for the potential reward. "I waited around for bread crumbs and when I got them I pretended they were cake," a TV anchor once told me, "and as long as I kept myself wanting the next piece of cake, I was stuck. I couldn't break away. I eagerly waited for the next goody, stringing them together in my mind as though our relationship was actually comprised of them." Simply put, we're hooked.

> When the negative behaviors of the destructive individual are interspersed with warm and loving behavior, it is easy to get hooked.

In psychological terminology this phenomenon is called traumatic bonding, and it commonly occurs in destructive relationships. Studies conducted by psychobiologists Harry and Clara Harlow showed that "the attachment proved most powerful when the negative behaviors were interspersed with warm and friendly contact." Like an addiction, the situation progressively gets worse, yet we continue on in the relationship, hoping: *He'll be attentive to me this time, won't he? Will he treat me like I mean something to him at* this *holiday dinner?* Our thoughts and feelings circle around the promise of something good and meaningful happening, just around the corner, and so we keep coming back for more. Dr. Susan Weitzman, a clinical psychologist who works with abused affluent women, puts it like this:

> *People will usually stick with a situation even when it seems self-defeating, so long as there is a chance of a reward or payoff. In this type of addictive attachment to a bad situation, which I call slot machine*

love, the woman has already invested much time, energy, and emotion in the relationship, and it intermittently pays off when her husband responds to her in a loving way. This keeps her ever ready, ever hungry for the moment she can hit the jackpot with him again.

The problem with getting hooked is that if we're not careful, we could gamble away our life, forever hoping for a payoff that rarely materializes.

Love Is Not Enough: I May Love Him but It Won't Fix the Problem

Love conquers all. Well, at least in the movies, it does. Then again, the actors only have to be in each other's company for two hours and off they go. Ahh, celluloid love! The curtains close before we have a chance to see what happens behind closed doors. But even real love, though it's one of the strongest forces in the universe, cannot be used to fix another person. When it comes to destructive relationships, love is not enough. It can't fix our problems and it can't fix our problem person. But why should we let that stop us? We try to love harder, to be kinder, to be more understanding and more patient, often bending ourselves into elaborate contortions to take up the slack and, hopefully, achieve a more harmonious relationship. Unfortunately, all the qualities that define love prove to be futile instruments for change. More often than not, they simply add to our stress and make us more anxious to please in an effort to demonstrate our undying devotion. We overcompensate. Meanwhile, he keeps on doing what he's doing.

The truth is, none of us can force another person to change, not even if our intentions are noble. And though love can transform, when it comes to toxic men we can't love them strong enough or hard

> The truth is, none of us can force another person to change, not even if our intentions are noble.

enough. We can't heal them and make them into someone better. We can't fill the holes in their heart and the pain of their childhood. Recommitting ourselves daily to be a better wife—or a better girl-friend—hoping to fill in the gaps so all will be well is simply unrealistic and, sadly, an exercise in futility. "Women involved with abusive men are usually exhausted. They overcompensate as if trying to supply all the love needed to sustain the relationship. They try to do the loving of two people," is how a seasoned counselor once described it to me. It gets us nowhere.

Comedian Bob Hope once joked: "People who throw kisses are hopelessly lazy." As relational overachievers, I seriously doubt any of us are in danger of not holding up our end! Love with detachment. Love with wisdom, but don't love with the intention to change someone else. It never works.

Desperation: "I Have to be in a Relationship"

We've all heard the old adage: "Desperate times call for desperate measures." But what if the desperation is inside of us? Conscious or unconscious, what if a sense of desperation is driving our actions? Desperation can make us vulnerable to destructive relationships. Why? Well, for one thing, it clouds our judgment. For example, we may have seen some red flags while we were dating our current boyfriend, yet because we were worrying excessively about making our mortgage payments, in a moment of panic we said yes and let him move in.

> "I felt like something was wrong with me if I wasn't attached to a man."

Second, we can be desperate about being in a relationship. We feel incomplete without one and are chronically getting involved with one man or another. As a graduate professor expressed it: "I went through men like I went through quarts of ice cream—compulsively.

It wasn't the sex. It was an emotional and psychological craving . . . I felt like something was wrong with me if I wasn't attached to a man—and preferably a handsome one. In some weird way I believed it defined me and made me a better person."

In my life coaching practice, I see this dynamic being played out in a variety of ways. The following scenario is quite common among those in their thirties—not surprising since the looming threat of the biological clock is hanging overhead. Picture this: You just turned thirty-five. Instead of celebrating your birthday, your anxiety about your dreams for the future gets the best of you and there you are, sitting with leftover birthday cake childless and unmarried. The clock's ticking, the internal discomfort's unbearable, and so you go against your better instincts, call your "on again–off again" lover, and impulsively declare: "I want to get married!" and he says, "Let's do it!" And now you're really livin' the dream!

Another version of the desperation to be attached goes like this: "I thought he would save me and provide the relationship with qualities I felt I lacked." When we initially fell in love with and then became involved with the destructive individual, we could see his good traits (some may have ended up being a ruse while others were quite authentic), and in our state of mind we imagined that he would supply things we couldn't; he would behave in ways we couldn't. Thus his strengths would even out our weaknesses, and our ultimate hope was that we'd complement each other. It's not an unreasonable thought. Most people who marry or commit to a relationship anticipate growing together as an effective and loving team. Yet for a destructive individual, power and control are paramount, and in our haste we probably misread what he would actually provide—and we certainly didn't think about what he would take away from our lives.

Our concerns about money are often real, especially if we have children to support. Our hopes for the future are undeniable; we may truly hate to be alone and feel overwhelmed as a single person or single parent. Nevertheless, we must be careful. Latching on to a bad or badly formed relationship and expecting it not to get worse, given these kinds of pressures—and this type of man—is undoubtedly the act of a desperate woman. Now it's up to you to undo the damage. "If we want to feel desperate about something, we should feel desperate to change," were the words of a wise woman who slowly stabilized her finances, her family life, and her "inner insanity"—as she liked to call it—so she could respond to life rather than react out of desperation.

Isn't This Normal? Recycling Our Past Instead of Moving Beyond It

The tendency to gravitate toward the familiar is universal. Most of us are attracted to what we know—for better or worse. Old habits are hard to break, and when it comes to destructive relationships, it can feel almost impossible to do so. Those of us raised in chaotic households may be attracted to drama. Even if we vow that we'll do it differently, we may still find ourselves up to our eyeballs in crisis, staring blankly, asking ourselves the question, *How did this happen?*

The truth is, the situation we're in doesn't feel good, but chances are it feels familiar. According to some of the most common psychological theories, we reenact our past, often unconsciously. So if we came from an alcoholic family, the likelihood of becoming involved with an alcoholic, even a dry drunk (someone who exhibits all the behaviors of an alcoholic without necessarily having a drinking problem per se), is greatly increased. The same holds true for any type of dysfunction.

The determination to change is not enough. As odd as it may sound, the desire to "do it differently" and "*not* follow in my family's footsteps" is trumped by subconscious influences that shape our current circumstances. In other words, a destructive relationship feels so familiar that to be placed in a healthier but unfamiliar emotional environment would make us feel uncomfortable and anxious, inevitably propelling us toward a re-creation of an earlier dysfunctional state. Now, don't get me wrong. It's not that we enjoy being in painful situations. It's just that we may feel more at home in one that's similar to what we've become accustomed to . . . and this pattern can keep us locked in a vicious cycle until we unearth the hidden reasons for "ending up like this."

Those of us raised in chaotic households may be attracted to drama. The situation we're in doesn't feel good, but chances are it feels familiar.

Many schools of psychodynamic theory and therapy, including Hendrix's Imago Relationship Therapy, maintain that adulthood intimate relationships are essentially reenactments of our relationship with our parents. This is especially true for those of us who grew up in a dysfunctional home. In other words, according to this school of thought, we seek out a partner with whom we can replay both the good *and* the bad, the hurtful *and* helpful interactions we had with our parents who, according to the unconscious, childlike portion of our psyche, were our "first lovers." So even though our relationship with a destructive man may be exceedingly painful, we keep going back for more, hoping against all hope that this time, the results will be different—that we will finally get, from this man, the love we need. We're usually wrong.

Happily, there are many ways to create change. I've worked with many women who, as they learn more effective life skills and to take better care of themselves, actually have less tolerance for emotionally and psychologically painful situations. Understanding *what's* keeping us hooked, *what*, internally, is perpetuating our misery, is a powerful first step. As we replace the messages of others with our own knowledge of what's good for us, we begin to shift away from the conditioning of our childhood and move toward greater awareness, and thus greater wholeness. Dr. Susan Weitzman writes:

> *Change occurs when an abused woman gains insight into internal conflicts that would influence her to remain with an abuser and to repeat dysfunctional patterns. Interpretation and insight are essential*

in order for the woman to free herself from the unconscious ideas that determine her self-defeating actions. With insight, the primitive mental and emotional states can lose their strength, and she can choose healthier attachments or leave the abusive relationship.

I would add the following words of wisdom found in the ancient Talmud: "Every blade of grass has its own angel that whispers, 'Grow, grow, grow.'" Making contact with our authentic self helps to cut through harmful voices we've internalized so we can disentangle from negative patterns and start anew.

■ ■ ■ ■ ■

How did I get here? is a good question to ask . . . and an even better one to answer. Then we must ask a more difficult and, eventually, a more important one: "What do I want to do about it?"

| 7 |

The Five Reasons We Stay

Change occurs only after we recognize the destructive nature of our relationship, then put this awareness into action to break our connection to it—and to the toxic individual. In my private practice I serve as a guide, helping women to navigate the nitty-gritty details involved in emotionally moving on—and, if they decide, physically moving out. In this context I will have to paint broader strokes, yet keep in mind that many of the strategies are the same regardless of the ultimate day of departure. Most women I work with choose to leave since continued interactions with the destructive individual are simply too toxic and, like secondhand smoke, nearly impossible to avoid in close proximity. Yet, even in cases where the women stay until an exit is more timely, it's essential to find meaningful ways to break the emotional connection to the abuse *and* to the destructive individual so we don't remain stuck.

In the previous chapters we've taken a look at destructive behaviors that, without question, can and do wear us down over time—and if we're not careful can leave us without enough self-esteem to make an effective exit plan. It's a painful place to be. But remember, help is out there. Resources exist, both personal and professional. Reaching out, we'll find many others who easily recognize our predicament and understand what it takes to make the break. Don't do it alone. With the wisdom, experience, and collaboration of others, the unique configuration of our individual lives can be taken into consideration and different options weighed so that, no matter which direction we go, we feel we've made an informed choice.

For years psychologists, academics, and physicians have pondered the question, *Why do women stay?* In my estimation, there are myriad reasons. We may stay because we believe we're financially incapable of providing for ourselves and our children; even if we expect to be able to secure a well-paying job and ignite our professional career, we may worry that our children are too young to be away from us for so much time during the day. Perhaps we stay because there's too much to lose in terms of lifestyle, status, and economic advantages. Some of us may feel so run-down that we can't see starting over. After all, who would want to be with us? Who could love us in this condition?—forgetting that healing might be just on the other side of the darkness we now feel. In some instances we can't let go of the idea that our partner could suddenly see the light, turning everything around. Undoubtedly we have much to think about, not only in terms of our immediate safety—and if we have them, our children's safety—but also in terms of financial losses, custody of our children, finding a place to live, severing emotional ties, possibly losing status, our standard of living, and support of people we thought were friends. But in the end, only you can determine, within yourself, if it's wiser to make the break or continue to live in a destructive scenario. Only *you* can decide.

In the end, only you can determine, within yourself, if it's wiser to make the break or continue to live in a destructive scenario. Only you can decide.

Fear of His Anger

Destructive men don't want us to leave them, and they become quite angry when we do. No small surprise, then, that deciding whether to leave a destructive situation takes some serious consideration, especially if we're deeply enmeshed. While staying in the relationship may not be the answer, the idea of breaking away can seem daunting both emotionally and financially. Undoubtedly, during the course of our time together, we've invented all kinds of neat tricks to avoid upsetting him ... although the truth is, it's unavoidable. One way or another we're going to make him mad and the toxic behaviors will be showered upon us, whether in condescending remarks, menacing looks, or more inspired psychological warfare. So leaving him ... talk about making him angry! A police officer summed it up nicely when he remarked, "Leaving these guys is the ultimate threat to their control." Small in stature though large of spirit, Madeline, a college librarian, put it this way: "Fear of his anger kept me in line, and when he saw that I had overcome enough of my fear to choose to leave, he was furious, beyond furious."

Influence Has to Go Both Ways

John Gottman, Ph.D., is a psychologist, researcher, and the author of numerous books about relationship dynamics. His seminal work describing the elements of toxic relationships includes the finding that men who batter women "were unable to accept any influence from women, no matter how reasonable and gentle the influence attempt was." Further, Gottman has repeatedly observed that success in marriage hinges on the man's willingness to accept influence from his partner.

Separation Violence: Real Danger

Separation violence is very real. Toxic men who have no history of physical violence may resort to it at this time if they feel desperate enough. Even in cases when we haven't been involved with the problem person for a long period of time, he may not want to let go without a fight. As Gavin de Becker, author of *The Gift of Fear: Survival*

Signals That Protect Us from Violence, writes: "Men of all ages and in all parts of the world are more violent than women," and attempts to be amicable may be met with hostility and aggression. Sarah Buel is an abused housewife who fled her marriage then went on to earn her degree at Harvard Law School; formerly a district attorney for the state of Massachusetts, she's currently a clinical professor at the University of Texas School of Law and the co-director of the university's Domestic Violence Clinic. She explained in a *Psychology Today* article that "one of the biggest reasons women stay . . . is that they are most vulnerable when they leave. That's when abusers desperately escalate tactics of control."

For these men, the thought of losing the upper hand is unbearable. However, the responses vary in severity and style. While some destructive individuals use threats, others resort to physical intimidation; still others choose to amplify our shortcomings in an attempt to deflate our confidence. Some do all of the above.

"We don't have much in the bank, how do you think you're going to support yourself?" they ask. "Don't you care about me and the children?" Some pour on the charm and apologize profusely, insisting that they'll change in an effort to generate second thoughts, so we're convinced that *this* time they really mean it. And some act as though they understand and "want to be respectful of our choice" when in actuality they're engaged in a lockdown. We think, *Gee, he's taking it really well; maybe he's finally come around.* Not! It's another deception. He's busy changing passwords on our accounts, contacting attorneys, hiding cash, hiring detectives, and locking up valuables so that when we leave, we take little more than the clothes on our backs.

Most people have no idea how difficult it is for a woman to obtain legal protections for herself and her children. Few know anything about the family court system's dirty little secrets unless they, or someone close to them, have gone through it. Based on what I've learned from women across the country, the only thing this system does a good job at is enabling abusive and controlling men to continue abusing or controlling their ex-partners. In most cases, it seems,

Calling the Shots

Faced with his girlfriend moving out, one man rushed to the court-house to get an order preventing her from taking the pets with her—pets she'd adopted from the shelter, who were registered exclusively in her name! "He claimed that the pets were a danger to our chil-dren," she said. "He was granted an emergency hearing, and the judge forbid me to have them 'until further evaluations could take place to determine what was in the best interest of the children.' The judge bought into his lies and his feigned concern for the children. It was ludicrous—and an effective way to control what I could and couldn't do." Six months and $1,500 in attorney's fees later, she was finally able to retrieve her beloved "furry children."

"I'm out of the house and he's still calling the shots," she told me. She had to use up her sick days to appear at hearings and a court-appointed psychologist's office. "Like cutting different threads that kept us connected, this turned out to be one of many I had to sever. He kept coming up with games like this to tie up my time and my energy."

a woman who shares biological children with a toxic individual is forced to engage with him repeatedly through legally mandated pro-cesses, no matter how severely he has abused her, or the children, prior to the separation. She may have to deliver the children to the house for unsupervised visitation, meanwhile worrying constantly about her children's well-being while they are in his care. She may also be compelled to show up for numerous court hearings where she encounters her ex-partner face-to-face, over and over again. Depending on how long he persists in filing motions, this might go on for years, even up until the day their last child turns eighteen! In these cases, instead of a woman gaining the independence, dignity, and freedom she is seeking, she may end up being forced, by court order, to keep him in her life—and though not under the same roof, he continues to control many aspects of her life.

Not only do we have to psyche ourselves up for the initial departure, but we also have to be psychologically and emotionally prepared to weather his ongoing wrath. One way or another, it will come. After all, leaving is the ultimate betrayal. In the minds of men such as these, there is no real reason for us to be dissatisfied—with them or the situation— and our compliance is mandatory. Granted, for more passive-aggressive types or those who pride themselves on being nice guys, the tactics may lean more toward routinely checking up on us at work by showing up unannounced; driving by our house to see if we're home; or finding

> **After all, leaving is the ultimate betrayal.**

ridiculous ways to stay connected: "I left you all the DVDs so I'll need to come by to copy them for my collection" is a classic example. Yet if we say, "No, you chose to give them to me so you can go ahead and replace them," they may bad-mouth us around town in response to our uncustomary boundary setting. After all, he was so kind to let us have the "joint" DVDs; doesn't that give him the right to invade our privacy and call the shots when it comes to personal contact? The answer is no, but destructive men don't like that word, especially when it comes from our lips.

Said Margory, a recently separated young professional, "I also tell women to be careful of begging and profuse apologies because these can also be tactics used to get us back—and if we return, it doesn't take long before we are punished for our temporary escape. And then we are right back where we started."

Evan Stark, Ph.D., uses the term *coercive control* to encapsulate the myriad means and methods used by men to control their partner—a term that he used for the title of his most recent book. I agree, and I would add my own observation that whether a man uses physical, verbal, sexual, social, or financial forms of partner abuse, the effects on the woman are the same: She feels anxious, fearful, and apprehensive; she becomes depleted and exhausted; and her self-esteem, optimism, and hope for the future plummet—unless, and until, she escapes.

If you're concerned about any kind of physical violence, verbal battery, or harassment, take action immediately to have a restraining order put into place. But keep in mind that the authorities cannot completely guarantee protection. (Nor can a full-time bodyguard!) Be smart. Keep your eyes open. Set boundaries. Take back your power. Stay out of denial. Don't give him the benefit of the doubt—and don't count on him changing now that you're gone. It can take months or even years for him to settle down and turn his attention elsewhere. Don't expect his forgiveness; don't expect him to see the sense in the split. You will need support, safety, financial resources, and endurance to get through this phase. Keep the faith. No matter how much time it takes, if you take things a step at a time and enlist the help of others, things will improve.

Some things to keep in mind if you leave:

- Take actions for your safety, if needed—and for the safety of your children.
- Surround yourself with friends, counselors, and/or professionals who can help you to keep a perspective and stay strong in your resolve to leave him behind and *not* go back.
- Be mindful of dirty tricks, manipulations, and false promises—any emotional or psychological hooks that you tend to be particularly susceptible to.
- Take friends with you to retrieve your belongings or have friends or a police escort present when he comes to retrieve his things.
- Learn how to *not* be afraid of him so you get better at thinking first, instead of reacting.
- Emotionally detach and treat interactions like business deals, knowing that he will test you; he will try to play you; and he will attempt to intimidate you and, possibly, try to get you back where he wants you—with him!

■ It may not come fast enough for your taste, but this, too, shall pass . . .

Money: A Key Tool of Control

Money is one of the key tools of control. When it comes to leaving a man who's no good for us, it's essential to face financial facts. Except in rare instances when a trust fund or other more secure financial arrangements are involved, money is going to be an issue. These types of men are notorious for controlling the finances and withdrawing financial support to prevent us from leaving. If we do choose to leave, the odds that they will use money to undermine our efforts to get ahead and care for our children are quite good. If we're thinking about moving on by moving out, money is going to have to be one of our main concerns.

"Six months into our marriage," one woman told me, "Ron started to 'joke' with me about never being able to leave him because so much of our financial security was based on his inheritance. In Canada, just like in the States, I couldn't make any claim to the passive income that had partially supported us regardless of the fact that my small inheritance had been spent to buy private school educations for our children. Ron had refused to contribute. It's so unfair. I made a choice in favor of my children that, in the long run, impacted the timing of my departure. I had to wait until I'd saved up enough to afford to leave. It took me twenty years."

The painful reality is that antiquated attitudes still prevail. Marriage continues to be viewed as a union of separate spheres. This contends that mothers' caring contributions are not economic in nature and therefore, do not entitle us to any economic consideration or compensation. As Pulitzer Prize–contending author and *New York Times* reporter Ann Crittenden writes in *The Price of Motherhood: Why the Most Important Job in the World Is Still the Least Valued*: "Your work on behalf of other family members is a labor of love, and we all know that love is its own reward."

What happens when attitudes such as these extend into applications of the law? Categorizing "women's work" as entirely outside the economic realm works to keep married women in a subservient position. In essence, our currencies are worthless when it comes to monetary compensation; to deprive us of a portion of the family's financial assets is, in some cases, by some courts, perfectly justifiable. "It's institutionalized discrimination," a district attorney once confided. Ann Laquer Estin, a professor at the University of Colorado School of Law, has put it this way: "Within the law, there is a remarkable disregard for caregiving—the norms of nurturance, altruism, and mutual responsibility that are usually thought to characterize family life . . . [are] almost entirely irrelevant when courts resolve the financial incidents of divorce. The current statutes suggest that ultimately self-interest and autonomy matter more than connection and interdependence." Current divorce practices play neatly into the hands of destructive men who are much less interested in relating than in controlling. I remember one particular mother who came to visit me on the Hill when I worked for Congress. Through tears she told me that she had dedicated her entire life to her family and her husband's military career, but their marriage ended in divorce: "We were a team, or so I thought. But during the divorce proceedings it became abundantly clear that somewhere along the line *our* dreams became *his* dream and he was entitled to most of the assets. At age sixty-five I was deprived of all pension benefits."

The lesson? Have a plan well in advance—particularly if children are involved. Once a decision has been made to break away, find ways to build up your own financial reserves, and your own streams of income, preferably without his knowledge. Take Elizabeth: "It was a painful and arduous journey, but it worked out in the end. A year

> Current divorce practices play neatly into the hands of destructive men who are much less interested in relating than in controlling.

before I left, I authored a book. I placed the advance in a separate account and used $1,500 of it to secure an apartment. Then, upon receipt of my first royalty check of $35,000 (my book had record sales in its first six months of release), I moved out with my five-year-old son. Later I learned that my husband was entitled to an automatic fifty–fifty split of my royalties whereas I had little claim on his business, and so I had to trade off spousal support in order to keep any future earnings from my book. We got a new start but I had to continue writing, speaking, and consulting part-time for high tech companies to make it all work—not because my son and I had an extravagant lifestyle, but because I had to hire an attorney to deal with the complexity of my case. I was wrapped up in litigation for over ten years, and it probably cost my parents and me about $1.5 million in total. It was difficult, but it worked, and here we are eighteen years later. My son and I are extremely close."

In the past women were viewed as the primary caretakers of children and in need of continued financial support in the case of divorce. It's not that women's currency was valued in monetary terms and the duties carried out in the marriage—as a supportive wife and, if we had children, as a mother—were seen as direct economic contributions. Generally speaking, however, there was an obligation to "care for women and children" under traditional gender roles. As a result, alimony was easier to obtain. Granted, in cases where we worked outside the home in order to put our husband through law school, medical school, seminary, or military training, the assets—namely, investments in our spouse—would probably never be retrievable upon separation unless we received an extremely generous alimony settlement. But overall, alimony was given serious consideration. Nowadays we can no longer depend on more chivalrous attitudes or proof of wrongdoing; the focus is on getting women to be "independent" as quickly as possible regardless of where they end up on the economic scale, not because it's in women's best interest, and definitely not because it's in the best interest of the children, but because it gets the soon-to-be-ex-husband out from under many basic financial

| 117 |

responsibilities and protects him from having to share any assets or income once the marriage is over. Oddly enough, while the notion of alimony was being eliminated for women, for the first time in modern history men became eligible for alimony, providing they were in financial need, after the Supreme Court decision in *Orr v. Orr*. If all were truly equal, this arrangement might make sense, but considering the fact that women, regardless of the court-ordered custody agreement, are much more likely to be responsible for the children's care and well-being, it's simply another tactic to place more power in the hands of men . . . and when we're dealing with a destructive individual, chances are, he'll take full advantage of the inequitable interpretations of the law.

The truth is, with the advent of no-fault divorce, we lost our bargaining power. As Karen Winner, an attorney and the author of *Divorced from Justice: The Abuse of Women and Children by Divorce Lawyers and Judges*, points out: "Marital misconduct was no longer legally relevant as an issue in the divorce." As a result, women's economic leverage was eradicated whereas in the past, "Linking property awards to fault, such as cruelty, had some important consequences, giving 'the innocent party' a decided economic advantage." In other words, alimony, now referred to as spousal support, is not automatically rewarded and cannot be tied to a man's conduct during the marriage. And in terms of the marital assets, new laws put the burden on women to prove their claims through discovery—a process laden with problems. Karen Winner writes:

> *If a woman's husband chooses to conceal assets, the discovery process can be dragged out for years, her lawyer charging fees every step of the way, in the effort to collect and assess financial information from her husband and his lawyers. The legal burden is on the woman to prove the assets she already theoretically owns as a partner in the marriage. She must pursue discovery or forfeit her rights. The abuses in discovery are a well-documented problem throughout the civil court system.*

I'm not going to sugarcoat the potential financial hazards of divorce. In the current climate, certainty of a judge's rulings in our favor cannot be counted on, and we need to weigh the possible outcomes

Spousal support is not automatically rewarded and cannot be tied to a man's conduct during the marriage.

should things turn in our partner's favor. I can say, however, that there are some adept attorneys, fair-minded district attorneys, and sane court-appointed psychologists—though in my opinion they are in the minority. In the end it's a risk we must decide to take if we are legally bound to the destructive individual or must disentangle financially in such a way that requires legal assistance. No, it's not a pretty picture . . . but neither is the alternative. We may feel stuck, yet once a decision is made—either way—we'll feel some relief. "You can get on with your life anytime and in many different ways," a twenty-year Al-Anon veteran once told me. "Just learn to believe in yourself so you can handle what's thrown at you, love your children despite hardships, and have fun even in the midst of other people's insanity."

Getting Control of the Financial Tool

Yes, there are many ways for a destructive person to use finances as a method of control. Luckily, there are a variety of countermeasures that can be taken. If you are planning to leave, it's essential that you secure independent funds for yourself and your children *before* your departure. If at all possible, line up a well-paying and flexible job—okay, in some cases a starter job or any job—and a support system to keep you buoyant and ensure that others you trust are available to care for your children. At the very least, make certain you have comprehensive and up-to-date financial records: bank statements, stock portfolios, credit card statements, pension plans, annuities, IRAs, life insurance policies, insurance statements, HSA accounts, deeds, trusts, contracts, and the like. That way, should he deny the possession of any accounts and financial assets, you already have the proof—and, hopefully, this will prevent drawn-out discovery shenanigans. It's also important to find out whether leaving your home could put you in jeopardy of losing any rights when it comes to property claims. Know the facts.

At the very least, make certain you have comprehensive and up-to-date financial records.

Once separated, beware! He can file frivolous lawsuits. To defend ourselves, our children, or our assets costs money and can keep us engaged. If our problem person is more interested in acting out his narcissistic rage than maintaining a bank account, we may have to work extremely hard to sever any ties that bind and gag—and hope he develops other hobbies! On the other hand, if he places a higher value on keeping "what's his, his," then negotiating our own written financial agreement without attorneys is probably a better way to go. Just be sure to file the signed document with the court. "The sooner you can become financially independent, the better off you'll be," a district attorney once told me. "Just don't make so much money that he's tempted to approach the courts for spousal support. It happens more than most women think. Even if the courts don't award him anything, legal bills can drain your funds."

Granted, every scenario is different, and working out the details can be like having a tiger by the tail. Still, here are some strategies women often use:

- Build your own income streams.
- Separate finances so you always have money in an account you can access.
- Copy all financial records and keep them in a safe place.
- Make sure your name is on all savings and checking accounts.
- Arrange for a signature card to be held at the bank so both signatures are required for a withdrawal of funds exceeding $100 (or whatever amount you decide is acceptable).
- Order credit reports to make sure they are free from unilateral

debts assigned to your name, unpaid bills, and bankruptcies.

- Copy all tax returns and have them reviewed by an accountant or tax attorney to see if any fraudulent claims or illegal omissions have occurred.
- If you suspect your husband has been involved in illegal activities, hire a reputable private investigator to search for multiple Social Security numbers, aliases, and any history of criminal charges brought against him.
- Consult an attorney or financial adviser—ask for an hourly rate— or check out www.nolo.com for legal information.
- Draft, sign, and notarize a prenuptial or postnuptial agreement.
- Create a separate business entity, whether it's a home-based business or not.
- Hide income and tuck away any unused portion of your weekly allowance.
- Borrow from family and friends.
- Ask parents for an early inheritance or partial inheritance.
- If your parents can afford to give you an annual gift of $24,000 (the maximum annual amount allowed as a tax-free gift) have them do so.
- Borrow from pension funds with low interest rates and reasonable repayment plans.
- Create a home-based business (this can also eradicate the need for child care).
- Choose your battles carefully.
- Don't let vindictiveness drive your decisions.
- Calculate the worth of your time and energy and then balance it against the possible monetary gains before you file any motions with the court.
- Let him have the upper hand or at least the illusion of it if it doesn't cost you anything important.
- If you have children, save your time, energy, and money for them—or for battles on their behalf.
- Rest, relax, rejuvenate when you can—make time.

Certainly the issues surrounding money and divorce are complex and exceed the scope of this book. I highly recommend you take a look at various resources, including those offered at the back, to get a realistic sense of the challenges you might face. The truth is, if you are younger (under forty) and have maintained a career path or gainful employment and are without children, in terms of generating income and recovering financially, you are more likely to have an eas-ier time of it. But don't kid yourself.

Many solutions exist. Find the one that's best for you.

Despite all kinds of progress for women, when it comes to divorce rights we've taken a step backward in the past twenty years. Plan your escape, talk to other women who've had similar experiences, and create some kind of plan, elaborate or not. Like it or not, self-determination and true independence are inseparable from economic realities. Many solutions exist. Find the one that's best for you.

The legal Pandora's box that faces most women who are sepa-rating or divorcing from a blatantly destructive man has become, unfortunately, more the rule than the exception, at least in most parts of the United States. For the average woman, this box may contain any number of legal, financial, and emotional dilemmas, especially for women with children. It simply is no longer true, if it ever was, that as far as the legal system is concerned mothers have an edge over fathers. Therefore, I would strongly advise women who wish to leave a toxic man to think things through, slowly and carefully, ahead of time. Look before you leap into the legal system: Find out the track record of any lawyer you're thinking of hiring. Ask the lawyer to put you in contact with previous female clients. Talk to them about their experiences with the lawyer, how he or she performed on their cases, and how he or she treated them. Consult with others who have already gone through divorce or custody liti-gation in your locality. Equally important, take exceptionally good care of your physical and mental health during this period. Lean on family, friends, allies, and confidants for support, as this is the time you're most likely to need it. Never go to court alone; always take someone with you. Learn all you can about the legal realities facing today's separating or divorcing women. Go online to discover the many Web sites and organizations helping women go through these processes successfully.

Image: What Will People Think?

What will they think? It's a question that crosses all of our minds. We wish we didn't care, but we do. Peer pressure is not a thing of the past. Graduating from high school didn't make it go away. For many of us the embarrassment and shame of leaving—especially when it comes to other people's responses—are quite real. The sense of personal failure is devastating, and anticipation of public judgment can be equally difficult to process emotionally. Those of us in high-profile professions feel the gaze upon us since privacy is difficult to secure, and once our divorce becomes "community property" others may feel that everyone has a right to their opinion when it comes to the details of *our* lives. Always a high achiever, Gracie, a television anchor, confided, "I felt as though I'd fallen from grace. Other people seemed disappointed in me. Some even avoided me. It only added to the pain I felt."

Even if we're not in a highly visible profession, we may worry that our relationships—with his parents, our neighbors, and our mutual friends—will be negatively affected, especially if he twists the facts and plays on others' sympathies. Be prepared. He may not flatly bad-mouth you. He may choose, instead, to play up the unfairness of your actions . . . and lie: "I wish she'd told me she was unhappy. I offered to go into counseling but she refused. What was I supposed to do?" In no time at all, he looks like the nice man who has been treated unfairly by an uncaring woman. Remember, a destructive man is usually adept at getting others to feel sorry for him and can skillfully manipulate them such that he comes out the victim. In other words, don't expect

Remember, a destructive man is adept at getting others to feel sorry for him and can skillfully manipulate them such that he comes out the victim.

this type of man to tell the truth. To do so would mean admitting to his abusive behavior. It's not going to happen—unless, of course, pigs are flying!

Fear of rejection after separation can be justified. If we belong to a tight-knit or religious community or are closely associated with a specific social class, we may be shunned and ostracized from the group. In some cases it's because we are threatening the status quo. In other instances women who want to leave, but choose not to because they feel they can't, resent our courage since it's in stark contrast with their being stuck. Sandra, a minister's wife, came to see me for a session as she was preparing to leave her toxic husband. "When the other women in our congregation learned that I had filed for divorce, they were furious with me. Their cold stares and contemptuous behavior were hard to take. Then one Sunday after the service, the choral director's wife approached me in secret and whispered, 'I wish I was you,' and then she walked away. My heart ached for her. It ached for all of us. I knew how trapped she felt in an unloving marriage; one that outsiders perceived as being so nice."

If the destructive man in our life is good at image management—and most are—then co-workers, neighbors, schoolteachers, and the like will perceive him as a charming, generous, good all-around guy and call our perceptions into doubt as though they are mean-spirited distortions. Unless they are privy to the facts, are perceptive people who know these kinds of men, or have been involved with them in the past, then the chances of convincing others of our side of the story—or that there is another side to the story—are slim. This is a good time to put the slogan "Choose your battles carefully" into practice. Spending your time and energy justifying yourself and your actions is, after a point, a waste. If we want to persuade anyone of the validity of our story, we must convince ourselves—and a judge if necessary. It will keep us strong in the face of any adversity we may encounter.

Fortunately, there are those who get it and will offer their love and support. They can be family members who have caught on to him, children who've witnessed put-downs and public humiliations disguised as jokes, friends who have seen uncharacteristic changes in our behavior and believe us when we tell them that he's been the main cause, and those women who have found themselves in similar scenarios. Find those who provide the support you need to act in self-protective ways and take actions that are in your best interest. As Tamela, a talented sculptor, put it: "They were my angels. They helped me to see that taking care of myself was not the same as being selfish. They gave me permission to love myself again."

Changes in Self-Image

One of the common consequences of being in a destructive relationship is that we become convinced that we are unattractive and unlovable; that "something's wrong with us." If our self-image has slipped too far, we may believe that our appearance is so displeasing that another man would never want us. We project so far into the future . . . but what are we projecting? We're projecting the current state of affairs. It's essential if we are falling into despair over our self-image that we take action to gain a more realistic perspective. Shanika, a guidance counselor for unwed mothers, often used to joke, "Girls, I wasn't that good looking in the first place, so there wasn't much he could do to make me insecure about my appearance! But when I began to feel ugly toward myself inside, then I knew something had to be done. He wasn't worth the loss of my integrity and self-esteem."

It's true. The combination of others' disdain, gossip, disapproving

> One of the common consequences of being in a destructive relationship is that we become convinced that we are unattractive and unlovable.

stares, and an already battered self-image can be difficult to endure. We may need to cry, often, as we come to terms with the blatant cruelty, the insensitivity, and the ignorance of those who are fooled by his lies. It's not easy, but when we think about it, there are probably bigger fish that need frying. Get a perspective. Do what makes you feel good inside and administer a little self-care. As my friend's mother used to say, "It's nothing a new dress and a pedicure can't fix!" Now may be one of those times.

Changes in Status and Standard of Living

Studies show that upon divorce, women's economic status decreases by 37 percent while men's increases by 15 percent, and recent research concludes that having children is the number one cause of bankruptcy for women. Sylvia Ann Hewlett, an economist and author of *When the Bough Breaks*, explains:

> Not only is the typical divorcée faced with the lower wages typical of women's jobs (and year-round, full-time women workers still earn only 71 percent of the male wage) but often she is returning to the labor force after years of being a full-time homemaker . . . Add to this the fact that 52 percent of divorced women have custody of minor children. Inadequate and expensive child care provides a further constraint on the kind of employment a divorcée can get or accept.

Some losses we can predict; others may come as a painful and shocking surprise. We've all read about high-profile divorces where the couple amassed around $100 million and regardless of the fact that the wife relinquished coveted professional positions to be the faithful executive's wife while he climbed the social ladder, once the verdict comes down jaws drop. The fifty–fifty split went right out the window; she walked away with three children and, maybe, $10 million. Granted, some of us might be saying to ourselves, "I'd be happy with one million!" Reconsider the math. She invested twenty-five to thirty-five years of her life, gave up many opportunities to make her own millions for the sake of her family and maintaining her husband's status—and received less than 10 percent of the assets. We don't have to be math geniuses to figure out that those numbers don't compute.

Some of us, though not all, will suffer a loss of status simply because we can no longer support the lifestyle. It can be devastating and yet may be something we'll have to count toward the cost of freedom. Joan, an investment banker's former wife, offered this wisdom: "I learned that I missed some of the trappings of my old life. I also learned that I could be content without them and could more readily place feelings of deprivation in their proper place. It wasn't fair. I couldn't change my drop in status. What I could do was to find a new kind of happiness and add more meaningful activities to my calendar. Did I tell you I've joined an activist group to reform family law!"

By some measurements Joan had fallen in stature because of her loss of status. But by others, she had risen simply by aligning herself with a different social sphere; one more concerned with her talents than her bank account.

> Some of us, though not all, will suffer a loss of status simply because we can no longer support the lifestyle. It can be devastating and yet may be something we'll have to count toward the cost of freedom.

Do I tell you these things to discourage you? No. I simply want you to know what you may be up against if you choose to leave. I can assure you that despite the economic odds, and the likelihood of unfair rulings in family court, millions of women have built a better life once outside of a destructive relationship. Although statistically leaving looks like a daunting task, many women find their energy, sanity, and hope renewed after they're out from under the tyranny of a toxic man, making them better able to come up with creative alternatives should income be an issue.

What About the Children?

It's funny. We are such relational creatures that to place ourselves in the equation can seem selfish. But now is the time to do exactly that . . . not only for our sake but for our children's sake as well. If we're miserable in our current situation and cannot foresee a way to improve things at home, we'd be mistaken to think our moods won't affect our children and color their home life experience. On the other hand, if getting away from the destructive individual will only further exacerbate our difficulties by making them more complex, especially in terms of survival issues, then we must seriously consider the impact.

Leslie, a mother of two children, one with autism, looked at it this way: "What kind of mother would I be if I leave and our standard of living goes down and I'm forced to work more hours outside the home? And if I stay and continue to be anxious, unhappy, and on edge, what kind of mother will I be then?" Most of us have to be convinced that we'll be able to function as better mothers once outside our toxic union if we're going to make the break. It can feel like being between a rock and a hard place, and there is no perfect solution. So it's important to ask ourselves, *What is the* best *solution for the children and me?* Then we can weigh out probable scenarios, having faith that what we choose will work out in the grander scheme of things. Frankly, though we all ask *Am I being selfish?* it's the wrong question. After all, if it was all about us, then we wouldn't stop to ponder, we'd just act on our own behalf. Structuring our lives so that our children's and *our own* happiness are best served benefits everyone in the end.

Am I being selfish? is the wrong question.

Will I Lose My Children?

Once upon a time, the importance of a mother's nurturing, especially in the early years, was considered common knowledge. Even in cases where custody is joint, the time sharing is often weighed in favor of the mother so she can continue caring for her children unless, for some reason, she decided to relinquish her rights. And now for the bad news . . . according to Karen Winner in *Divorced from Justice*, studies show that 70 percent of men who file for custody actually are awarded either sole or joint custody. With concerns such as these looming, it only makes sense to be nervous about losing our children.

The truth is, if we love our children and want them with us, we are vulnerable. Destructive men know that the better a mother is as a parent, the less likely she is to engage in a custody battle because of the emotional and psychological impact on the children. Accustomed to manipulating our fears to keep us in line, destructive individuals count on our loyalty to our children to get a leg up. They may threaten a custody battle to coerce us into accepting a less-than-equitable financial settlement. Economic incentives can and often do bring out the worst in others. Yet for the destructive individual, treatment such as this is par for the course. He's been acting as if you were an adversary throughout the course of your relationship, since control is his first concern. Divorce court is simply a continuation of these behaviors in a different arena—one with very high stakes. Should he decide that economic control is not enough, he may attempt to get more control over the children. In cases where the father requests more time and pleads with the judge for greater involvement in his children's lives, regardless whether he actually interacts with them or turns them over to nannies, babysitters, or relatives, more and more courts are likely to take him seriously due to the efforts of father's rights and other so-called men's rights groups.

Again, I'm not informing you about the climate of today's divorce courts to deter you from your goals. Rather, I want you to be prepared. I want you to plan ahead. I want you to figure out the best approach to keeping your children safe, secure, and surrounded by your love.

Can I Support Them?

The importance of being able to support our children financially cannot be overstated. To know the facts, it's best to consult with an accountant, an attorney, or a trusted financial adviser. The numbers may not tell the whole story, but they will provide an idea of what we can and cannot do until additional income enters the picture.

Equally important is the other side of support: emotional support. It is a critical aspect of parenting. If you are working long hours, always tired and irritable, you will have little left for your children. In some cases they'll have rough spots when you might not be as emotionally available, yet that may not be the norm . . . ebb and flow of time and energy is essential and will feel like a much more workable scenario once you move out. And keep in mind that it's not entirely up to you. Having loving family members nearby, reliable neighbors to exchange favors with, and friends who simply enjoy your children and are happy to serve as "aunties" and "uncles" can provide you with rest, reprieve, and other vital resources.

Will They Be Okay?

"Living with a man like this lets me know that there is a limit to my reach. I can't control him, and I can't protect my children from all of his destructive behaviors no matter how hard I try. I don't take kindly to feeling helpless, especially where my children are concerned." Joyce's words echo all of our feelings. As unnerving as it is, there are no guarantees in life, especially when it comes to raising children with a destructive individual in the picture. That said, having a loving connection, being a positive role model, taking genuine interest, and keeping communication lines open undoubtedly contribute to our children's well-being and eventual success. In other words, we can't control all the variables and influences on our children, yet we can certainly provide them with many counterbalances, increasing the probability of healthy relationships with themselves and others.

Children are resilient. Some are even "transcenders," people who flourish despite a tumultuous and unhealthy past. Being cognizant of and sensitive to each child's temperament, age, and level of development can help you to decide if you leave and when. Timing is very important when it comes to children. A number of my clients chose to leave before the teen years hit so they could have time to get the children on more solid footing before adolescence. With their energy now freed up from deflecting barbs and caustic statements couched in jokes, they found there was so much more to offer their children—they simply felt better.

Timing is very important when it comes to children.

I have a number of other clients who waited until the last child was out of the house because they were more frightened about the potential ramifications for arranged visitations, particularly unsupervised, than countering destructive behaviors under the same roof. In other words, when agonizing over the decision of whether or not to leave a toxic husband, many mothers are forced to choose between the likely damage their husbands will inflict on the children during unsupervised visitations and the abuse she will continue to endure if she stays married to him.

Many father's rights proponents cite research to claim that, after parents divorce, children who are deprived of contact with their biological father inevitably suffer psychological harm. The research, in fact, says nothing of the sort. Indeed, if alcoholism, drug addiction, and physical violence are involved, there is much research on their contribution to the cycle of violence as well as the physical and psychological safety of the children. These days, most children do maintain some form of contact with their noncustodial father. In the majority of cases, this seems appropriate—but only when both parents are able to interact, as co-parents, with civility and camaraderie. This is not the case when the man is destructive, whether toward the mother, the children, or both.

While there's research that warns against depriving contact with either parent, in my experience few of these studies take into account the personality types described in this book—and a more individualized approach should be taken. More often than not, mental health professionals, in an attempt to remain neutral, assume that both parents are equally concerned about and responsive to their children's well-being. Pathological lying, charming manipulations, twisting of the facts are often overlooked by those who are less perceptive or are simply unwilling to probe further to discover the possible ulterior motives driving some parents' attempts to gain custody of or unfettered access to their children. Like many of us, they give these men the benefit of the doubt without fully checking things out.

Again, we all have our issues. There is no perfect parent. But if we do seek out a professional to help our children cope with changes and deal more effectively with toxic behaviors, it's essential to make sure he or she really gets it before we sign on. Otherwise we'll find ourselves working hard to convince yet another person of the validity of our claims and the truth of our experience. They can't help us or our kids if they don't really know what's going on, are in denial about it, or are minimizing the impact. Pay for your children's education—not the education of a professional who is supposed to be helping you to lessen the effects of destructive behaviors so your children have the best chance possible to triumph in life.

If you enlist professional assistance for your children—counselors, psychologists, or other mental health professionals—it's essential to find someone who understands how to deal with a destructive individual.

Hope and False Hope

We all want to believe that the destructive man in our life is capable of change, and that if he really loved us, he'd do things differently. He'd stop drinking. He'd go into counseling and actually reveal the truth about himself and his past. He'd admit his problems so the sky would break open, a chorus of angels would bellow forth from the heavens, and he'd be a new man. Why do so many of us cling to this dream? We love our man and would like nothing more than to have our relationship work out.

Sadly, change is not something to bank on. If we're at the point where we're seriously considering leaving the relationship, we've probably already been lied to, deceived, and given more empty promises—or empty apologies—than we care to count. We're living on false hope. So basing our decision to leave on his ability to change is, in any market, a lousy investment. Besides, if genuine change does occur, he may not choose to continue the relationship anyway. Positive personal growth does not automatically translate into a saved marriage. If we're waiting for him to get better before we make a choice about our own lives then, basically, we're allowing his well-being or lack thereof to control our destiny.

> Continually changing ourselves to compensate for his shortcomings and demeaning behaviors is simply self-abuse.

We'd better think twice about turning over so much power to someone who is incapable of having our best interests in mind.

I once heard a beautiful woman say, "The harder I tried to be what I thought he wanted me to be, the less I saw of myself in his eyes." Continually changing ourselves to compensate for his shortcomings and demeaning behaviors is simply self-abuse. We're holding on to a fragile hope, a false hope that making ourselves friendlier, more upbeat, more attractive, more humorous, more understanding, more sympathetic . . . more, more, more . . . will somehow transform him and the situation. It's an illusion. It's an act of desperation—and it's an assumption that we're not good enough as we are. As frustrating and painful as it is to accept, we cannot control a problem person or the problems he creates. We cannot fix things by attempting to be more pleasing, because this is in actuality a veiled attempt at controlling him—and if we've learned anything so far, it's that *he* likes to be in charge. Even if our intentions are good and we think it will help him if we're a better person (however we define that), it won't work. Ultimately, why he acts the way he does, why he treats us the way he does, has little to nothing to do with us. Like it or not, we're not powerful enough to restore him or the situation to sanity. If we're going to make changes, it's best to make them for ourselves. Others will benefit, not because we're being everything they want—or we think they want—but because we'll have more of ourselves to give.

Like it or not, we're not powerful enough to restore him or the situation to sanity.

| 8 |

The Quicksand of Depression and Fear

Anger turned inward, denial of our feelings, self-blame—all of these things can lead to depression. Like a heavy, damp blanket, depression affects everything: our moods, our thoughts, our attitudes, our interactions, and our bodies. Chances are, if we've been enmeshed with a destructive individual, we're going to experience some level of melancholy. We just don't feel quite like ourselves because, in actuality, we're being altered by the destructive situation—and by him. Remember earlier in the book when I talked about toxic people having an impact on us—like an emotional cold or flu? Well, regular involvement with a destructive man can negatively alter our physiology just as any stressful situation can.

Ramona, a client who bravely ended a twenty-eight-year marriage after contracting numerous STDs as a result of her husband's sex addiction (he had multiple affairs spawned from hookups on the Internet), told me: "I went in and out of depression because I felt so discouraged. None of the strategies I was using—therapy, introspection about my own issues, and actively developing better communication skills—was working, and it's no wonder, I didn't really understand what or who I was dealing with and neither did the professionals I'd consulted. I thought our problems were entirely my fault."

Ramona's not alone. Many of us spend way too much time "working on ourselves" or "working on the relationship," which only serves to keep the attention on us and away from tricks used by the destructive individual. The result? Depression. Why? Because we're putting the entire responsibility for the relationship squarely on our own shoulders, convinced that we can handle it, we can fix it—or at least we're going to try. But the fact is that although the situation isn't working for you, it *is* working for the destructive individual.

> **Although the situation isn't working for you, it is working for the destructive individual.**

Why would he be motivated to change it? Sure, he may tell you that he wants to be closer. He wants to learn how to get along better. He wants you to be happier, yet his words are anything but sincere. You want to believe him, but unless the clouds part and a miracle occurs, change isn't really what he wants—and that can make you feel hopeless and helpless.

Being involved with a man who's no good for us affects our well-being. Our spirits are corroded by living in an atmosphere of revolving contention and disguised hostility. And a man who regularly approaches us in an adversarial state of mind puts us on edge and incites all manner of worrying. Author, Harvard professor, and behavioral and brain sciences reporter for *The New York Times* Daniel Goleman writes in *Emotional Intelligence*: "Indeed, one of the main determinants of whether a depressed mood will persist or lift is the degree to which people ruminate. Worrying about what's depressing us, it seems, makes the depression all the more intense and prolonged . . . Typically none of this reflection is accompanied by any concrete course of action that might alleviate the problem." In other words, if we don't take action, we can get caught up in a cycle of worry and depression. But what prevents us from taking action? Usually it's fear. Fear of change. Fear of the unknown. Fear of loss. Fear of standing up for ourselves and rocking the boat. Together depression and fear are a deadly combination that can be immobilizing.

Thankfully, we can take action. We can decide to leave our relationship. We can decide to stay and find out how to best navigate the destructive behaviors with the help of a therapist (one who understands the anatomy of a destructive relationship and can see through the tactics of a destructive individual), a 12-step program, DBT (Dialectic Behavioral Therapy), a DBT support group, self-help books, or forging a new group of our own.

If we do decide to seek out medical advice to quell the depression and accompanying anxiety—an outward display of fear—then it's important to find a psychiatrist who is well versed in pharmacology and can take our scenario into account. Antidepressants that are prescribed for situational depression—in other words, depression that occurs primarily because of a situation we're in as opposed to an inherent physiological imbalance—can be used as a tool to get us from point A to B. They need not be continued as ongoing medication once we regain our balance. As research has shown, the farther removed we are from the toxic individual in our lives, the more easily we can clear the confusion in our minds and come back home to ourselves.

Now, if we've already left and are experiencing depression, it's quite possible that we're experiencing a mixture of unexpressed anger, residual rage, and grief. Just because he's no good for us doesn't mean we don't love him—or didn't love him. We're going to feel some loss. We're going to miss the good things about him and the good times. If the sadness persists, take action. Join a support group dealing with grief and loss. Consult your physician. Improve your diet. Exercise. Go to the movies; out with friends. Get professional help if necessary. Take care of yourself . . . so you can continue moving on.

In sum, when our sadness gets sadder, it's best to take action and do something about it before it gets worse so we can right what's feeling wrong inside of us.

Doing the Same Things Harder Instead of Doing Them Differently

Ever hear someone say that doing the same thing over and over and expecting different results is called insanity? Well, they're right. Doing the same things harder doesn't make sense. But does that stop us? No. When we're feeling desperate and defensive, we often rely on outmoded coping devices because we're just not sure what else to do. But can we expect things to turn out differently when we're putting effort into a plan that didn't work before as though it's going to work now? Of course not. It's simply the wrong approach. Like it or not, we have to learn how to do things differently. If ever there was a time for a Plan B, it's now.

We have to change if we want to create change. For some of us, change will mean moving on and moving out. Others will stay and attempt to come up with a new game plan. Yet all of us need to heed this sage advice: "Begin to put the focus on yourself. Learn more about what, and who, exactly, you're dealing with in order to put your problems in their proper perspective and then make the necessary changes."

If you are missing a few life skills in your proverbial tool belt or never loaded up on the ones appropriate to the current situation, now's the time to expand your repertoire.

Our situation is not going to change unless we do. So pay attention to your coping strategies. How far have they gotten you in the past? Which ones clearly have to go? Which ones can be modified? Where can new problem-solving tools more apropos to our situation be found? Ask yourself, *Am I committed to putting them into action?*

If you are missing a few life skills in your proverbial tool belt or never loaded up on the ones appropriate to the current situation, now's the time to expand your repertoire. Self-help books, counselors specializing in destructive relationships, Al-Anon meetings, DBT training . . . even watching *Dr. Phil* . . . can open your eyes to more effective approaches for dealing with bad-news individuals and the problems they bring. If developing better strategies for self-care, self-respect, and healing feels overwhelming, just remember the words of Carlos Castaneda: "We either make ourselves miserable, or we make ourselves strong. The amount of work is the same."

Even in the midst of breaking off a clearly toxic relationship, many women have a hard time dropping the habit of focusing on their male partner instead of themselves. Even when a man has treated us badly, cheated on us, verbally abused us, or simply been a really lousy partner, we continue to obsess, for too long, over how he feels, what he's doing, whom he's with, what he wants. We can have a tendency to worry about his pain, his needs, and his life rather than our own.

Victim Mentality: The Enemy That Has Outposts in Our Heads

My grandpa used to tell me, "If you think you can't, you probably won't be able to." He was right. The problem is, after being with a man who chips away at our confidence, it's not unusual to discover that a host of negative messages have embedded themselves inside our brain, confusing our thoughts and leaving us unsure about our decision-making abilities. We may have become tentative and jumpy. Walking on eggshells in our home can and often does extend out into the larger world, and so we can find ourselves feeling uncertain; we're not sure what to think. When the disparaging voice of the problem person takes up residence with any other negative programming that's been previously installed, we may no longer be able to distinguish between our authentic voice and the enemies that have outposts in our head. As a result, we feel unsure of ourselves. We may no longer trust ourselves to make the right choice or to express our true feelings. We weren't safe before . . . are we safe now? Do we even know our own mind or are we overwhelmed by self-doubt and second-guessing ourselves?

If we're not careful, we can internalize put-downs and invalidating remarks to the point that they obscure the inner voice and we mistake toxic self-talk for inner guidance—when in reality it's self-sabotage. We may see ourselves as ineffectual and actually come to believe it. If we've grown accustomed to listening to others, giving their opinions more weight, or allowing them to direct our actions and make up our minds for us, we can be especially susceptible to mistaking outside messages for our own thoughts. But they are not. Though certainly we can feel victimized by them, it's up to us to determine whether we will allow them to keep us stuck. Do

We may see ourselves as ineffectual and actually come to believe it.

we want to continue to give up our power to people with intimidating and manipulative personalities? Do we want to take leave of our senses just because we've fallen in love?

Dismantling the enemy that has outposts in our head can take time. One of the first steps is to take a look at the forces in your life that influence you, whether they are institutions such as the church, particular individuals, or something else entirely. Become aware of the obsessive voices that can flap around inside your head. If they're constantly critical or determined to berate you, talk back to them. Are they lies or truths? Can you tell the difference? Strengthen the voice of your own self-authority by keeping company with those who see who you really are; those who truly hear you and are eager to know what you have to say. Talk to those who get your situation instead of those who, in their ignorance or denial, insist that what you think you're experiencing in your relationship couldn't be what you think it is . . . those people have to go. Hang out with the ones who honestly have your best interests in mind. Being surrounded by trusted friends can help you feel safe enough to express the truth, the uncensored truth, even if aspects of it are ugly. Dismantle the enemy.

Contending with a destructive individual—whether in our home, in court, or on the phone as we sort out the breakup—is no doubt challenging. We may feel like a victim—and the destructive individual may repeatedly try to victimize us—but we don't have to act like one. Remember, even tiny steps are steps. If others offer assistance, sound advice, and support, don't refuse them as an excuse to remain in the same predicament. Accept the help and grow from it. Learn to disregard any falsehoods that are designed to keep you down or that play on your insecurities. Build your inner strength and, as clichéd as it may sound, find a way to love yourself. No one can do that for you.

Each of us must decide which voice it is we're going to listen to . . . the one that holds us hostage or the one that enables us to flourish. We do have a choice. We do. Even if we may not feel like it in the moment . . . we just have to be willing to take the first step. A client in France, Eliette, put it beautifully when she said: "I turned away from the enemy and now I can hear the voice of my soul calling out to me. It's like music in my mind. I know who I am once more."

> Each of us must decide which voice it is we're going to listen to . . . the one that holds us hostage or the one that enables us to flourish. We do have a choice.

Surviving Not Thriving: Beaten Down by Crisis

Neuroscience is now the lending authority to what many of us have known all along: Chronic stress can seriously affect our health and well-being. When we're in a continual state of disease, we are more prone to physical ailments, psychological disturbances, and emotional instability. Our system is out of whack, and as with any other imbalance we must have some recovery time. But do we get it? Probably not. Destructive individuals are known for being relentless. Even if subtle, they keep the pressure on and they make sure to pull the rug out from under us, since it secures their one-up position. In destructive relationships the problem person often instinctually senses when we are attempting to regroup and engages us in ridiculous mind games to keep us off-balance. It could be a squabble over who cleans out the cat box or a series of subtle comments about our weight or strange insinuations that have us guessing: *What did he mean by that?* Even if we do manage to get away for a weekend at the spa or drive a few hours to visit a friend, our troubles seem to go with us and we either talk about them with others, hoping to figure out what the heck is wrong, or persevere, rolling the same thoughts over and over again, as if a solution will pop out of nowhere so we can finally relax.

If we're still vacillating, moving in and out of denial, or haven't been able to completely wrap our mind around the nature of our problem, then the best thing we can do for ourselves is to surrender to the truth, as painful as it is. Allowing yourself to hit bottom and begin to accept the reality of your situation may feel uncomfortable, yet it's also an opportunity ripe for change. In your beaten-down state, you may feel too exhausted to talk yourself out of what you are experiencing and can more readily admit that your relationship isn't working. You can tell a trusted friend, "I'm not happy. I want out."

> Allowing yourself to hit bottom and begin to accept the reality of your situation may feel uncomfortable, yet it's also an opportunity ripe for change.

Though we may have had little say about being pushed into a survival mode—after all, it probably occurred gradually—we do have a say now. As strange as it may sound, remaining in a survival mode, succumbing to it, and taking it on as a lifestyle can only happen with our consent. If we keep insisting that we can handle things; if we try doing the same things harder instead of smarter; if we get trapped in becoming a better mother, a better wife, or a better lover in order to rectify the situation—we're only going to perpetuate it. And what happens when we fruitlessly spin our wheels? We become exhausted. We feel beaten down. We simply survive . . . it's not a way to live.

Don't Be Antagonistic to Your Essential Self—He's Already Got That Covered!

Falling into negativity is not uncommon. We all go through it. We may secretly punish ourselves for the difficulties in our situation. We may act out or become self-destructive, not knowing how to express the painful feelings we've stored up inside. "All I wanted was a loving relationship," you may find yourself saying. "How in the world did this happen?" If we're not careful, we can end up being cruel to ourselves simply because, inside, we feel awful. Even if we're the one leaving, we can still feel rejected, betrayed, and unlovable as a result of the tactics used against us by the man who made all kinds of empty promises—empty promises we based our decisions on and created a life around.

As Jennifer Louden, author of *The Woman's Comfort Book*, attests, women are conditioned to meet everyone's needs before their own and believe that the people in their lives will likewise anticipate and meet their needs. "When this does not happen," according to Louden, "we begin to feel we have no right to our needs and desires. What we end up with is women who are experts at nurturing others—until we drop of exhaustion or illness or escape into excessive drinking, shopping, or eating."

> Women are conditioned to meet everyone's needs before their own and believe that the people in their lives will likewise anticipate and meet their needs.

Like the woman who looks in the mirror and sees herself as much larger than she really is, our self-perception becomes distorted. We can't fix an unworkable situation, not realizing that the problem is

Being antagonistic to your essential self can become a habit that perpetuates itself unless you intercede on your own behalf.

bigger than we are. Instead of taking loving action toward ourselves and making healthy choices in our favor, we may perpetuate negative patterns. He blames us, we blame ourselves. Like depression, being antagonistic to your essential self can become a habit that perpetuates itself unless you intercede on your own behalf.

Do we believe we deserve less? Do we think something is wrong with us? Do we feel undeserving of real love? If we answered yes to any of these questions, it's more important than ever to develop or rediscover ways to nourish ourselves, deep in our souls. As my friends in Manhattan always say in their heaviest New Yawk accents: "Enough awlready!"

The destructive man in our life will no doubt continue to be antagonistic. He's got that covered. He knows how to undo us by striking at the heart and hitting us where we live. It's up to us to decide whether we want to carry on this belligerent tradition or find ways to express our essential self despite bad days, bad times, or bad individuals. Don't forget, what happens to us may shape us . . . but it does not define us. We're not what is happening to us. As John Ruskin once said: "The question is not what a man can scorn, or disparage, or find fault with, but what he can love, value, and appreciate." It's not a creed common among destructive individuals, but we can claim it as our own and put it to good use.

| 9 |

If Adam Was Made in God's Image, Whose Image Was I Made In?

Remember the delightful story told by Robert Fulghum, author of *All I Really Need to Know I Learned in Kindergarten*? He talked about being a young minister assigned to a large group of children. It was his job to keep them occupied, so he cleverly devised a game whereby the children could choose to be either giants or dwarfs. As he was dividing them up into their chosen groups, a little girl approached him and asked, "Where do the mermaids stand?" When he informed her that there were no mermaids, she replied, "But I'm a mermaid." Now, this little girl wasn't about to have anyone tell her who she was, and so she held her ground. Luckily, the Reverend Fulghum understood how important it was for her to keep her chosen identity intact, and so he expanded the guidelines of the game to include "mermaids," instead of forcing her into a role that simply didn't take her own unique sense of self into account.

But what happens when society insists on our conformity and doesn't make room for mermaids? What happens when we are told that mermaids or fairy princesses or magical explorers don't exist and, therefore, we couldn't possibly be one? Simple. Our internal identities are invalidated and, just like a destructive relationship, we are told that someone else, someone outside of us, not only knows more about who we are and how we should be, but also has the right to define us, usurping our own self-authority. What happens to our self-esteem? If we fail to find others who honor our individual nature and encourage its expression, it can be devastating. As Mary Pipher points out:

> *Without some help, the loss of wholeness, self-confidence, and self-direction can last well into adulthood . . . Many have tried to be perfect women and failed. Even though they followed the rules and did as they were told, the world has not rewarded them. They feel angry and betrayed. They feel miserable and taken for granted, used rather than loved . . . They struggle with adolescent questions, still unresolved: How important are looks and popularity? How do I care for myself and not be selfish? How can I be honest and still be loved? How can I achieve and not threaten others? How can I be sexual and not a sex object? How can I be responsive but not responsible for everyone?*

The dilemma, once again, is between the self and the other. It's no mistake when we consider the images of womanhood being thrust upon us. Somehow we're supposed to incorporate them as part of our being without squeezing out our essential self. To a certain extent, women are expected to emulate an image rather than discover their true feminine identity. In these instances real women need not apply.

Whose Version of You Are You?

I'll never forget when one of my male colleagues suddenly blurted out, "A woman's identity is always up for grabs, isn't it?" It was as though, from out of nowhere, he had a revelation that abruptly gave him insight into the plight of women. He got why it was so difficult for us to individuate from the pressures of conformity and claim our true selves. I remember thinking that the ramifications of his statement probably exceeded his own understanding of the complex experience of women—yet how refreshing it was to know that he had taken notice, felt the pang of empathy, and spoken it out loud. I felt as though someone understood a deep truth within my psyche that I had often tried to articulate, only to be met with defensive barriers and constant accusations that I didn't possess enough evidence for such claims. It didn't matter that many prominent women had been stating our case for hundreds of years; if someone simply didn't want to hear it, no amount of reasonable "proof" could move them from their stance. But I knew, just as my colleague did in that moment, that our identity, as women, is often treated as though it belongs to everyone but us . . . and others are all too eager to define us, with or without our conscious consent.

> What happens when our identities are up for grabs and defined from external sources, instead of from the truth of who we are?

What happens when our identities are up for grabs and defined from external sources, instead of from the truth of who we are? Our thinking can be plagued by self-doubt, negative self-talk, and invalidating perseverations that keep us off-balance in the same way an unhealthy relationship can. None of us is immune. And dismantling what authors Elizabeth Diane and Andrew Marshall refer to as programming in their book *Listening with Heart 360: Wisdom Women Have Forgotten* can be more challenging than we might think. After all, the full idea of liberation is not clearly and compassionately defined and, in many instances, has been co-opted as a way to confuse and control women. In addition, there's so much disorientation in the female psyche as a result of too many voices vying for our identity. There are too many images of how we should be and who we should be, and as a result, we feel overwhelmed as we decide to reject or embrace each one, trying on conflicting identities as though they were dresses, often forgetting that the answer usually resides within us. Or it used to. More often than not, we've been socialized out of trusting ourselves and readily listening to the still, small voice inside that connects us to our authentic selves.

Mary Pipher, Ph.D., author of *Reviving Ophelia: Saving the Selves of Adolescent Girls*, contends that, around the time of adolescence, girls come under intense pressure to conform to external standards to please others while simultaneously alienating them from themselves: "Adolescence is when girls experience social pressure to put aside their authentic selves and to display only a small portion of their gifts. This pressure disorients and depresses most girls. They sense the pressure to be someone they are not. They fight back, but they are fighting 'a problem with no name.'"

Of course this "problem with no name" is nothing new: Whenever a society glorifies the masculine and devalues the feminine, women's identity and authenticity become warped and constricted. In her groundbreaking 1963 treatise *The Feminine Mystique*, considered by many a launching pad for the women's movement and second-wave feminism, Betty Friedan described the unhappy desperation of many women of her era, particularly women who married and devoted the majority of their lives to homemaking and childrearing. Like the young women of today, these earlier generations suffered in silence while pretending to feel contented and fulfilled in the roles their culture assigned to them.

In *The Feminine Mystique* and other writings, Friedan convincingly argued for women's need for opportunities that extended far beyond homemaking and caretaking. She called for sweeping changes at the personal and political level in order to buck a system that rarely asked us what *we* wanted. Simone de Beauvoir, author of *The Second Sex*, Betty Friedan, Gloria Steinem, and many others constituted the new voice of women sounding out the inequities as well as the very real human cost to the feminine soul.

At the time these authors were writing about feminism, the notion of women's equality was far from new—after all, founding father John Adams's wife, Abigail Adams, made a strong case for recognizing women as equals in the Constitution. Elizabeth Cady Stanton, Matilda Joslyn Gage, and other eighteenth-century suffragists worked tirelessly to include women in the laws and culture of nascent

America after being introduced to the Iroquois and other Native American nations where women participated equally with men. To no avail. Legally, socially, and economically, women still did not have equal representation under the law.

The women's movement attempted to eradicate these inequalities in public spheres as well as more private ones in order to strengthen women's self-esteem and self-respect. Individual sovereignty and self-determination became more than words and intellectual concepts; they became frameworks by which women could refashion themselves, at least in theory, on their own terms. Unfortunately, the sometimes reactionary nature of the movement—as with any pioneering social activism—created pockets of dogma that at times ignored the importance of cultivating equal rights simultaneously with genuine love of what Riane Eisler, Ph.D., calls "The Conscious Feminine": a far truer feminine identity emerging from deep within instead of depending on external forces.

To her credit, Friedan recognized that women, in our urgency to right past wrongs, were in some instances metaphorically trading a smaller cage for a larger one instead of removing themselves from confines and flying. In *The Second Stage* she wrote, "In the first stage our aim was full participation, power, and voice in the mainstream. But we were diverted from our dream. And in our reaction against the feminine mystique, which defined women solely in terms of their relation to men as wives, mothers, and homemakers, we sometimes seemed to fall in a *feminist* mystique which denied that core of women's personhood that is fulfilled through love, nurture, home." The false polarization caught women in an unwinnable bind that we are still wrestling with today.

Friedan was not the only one to caution women about the pitfalls of polarization. In 1986 First Lady Barbara Bush acknowledged the difficulties for women who too closely aligned themselves with a cultural identity that was adopted without question. No matter what the promises, a closer examination of both the real and potential outcomes is always a worthwhile endeavor. During her keynote address to the graduating class at Wellesley College, she reminded the women that while striving to be a CEO before the age of thirty was a worthy goal, it was important to consider whether it was also a personal goal. Did the vision of success belong to them or had it been established by social forces? Blindly adopting an external identity to build a life around might end up sacrificing the uniqueness each woman possessed, Mrs. Bush cautioned, reminding these ambitious women the importance of taking time out to ask themselves, *Who am I? What do I want?* Though on opposite ends of the political spectrum in many regards, both Barbara Bush and Betty Friedan emphasized the importance of women putting their own needs, wants, and desires into the mix, recognizing that this essential ingredient was necessary for genuine success, personal happiness, and accurate self-identification.

From Housewife to Superwoman

Remember the image of the 1950s housewife? Of course you do! No matter that she has been reinvented and now has pithy one-liners, thanks to artist Anne Taintor's comical work. Funny or straight, she's an American staple. About half a century ago, television programming inundated us with the image of Mrs. Ward Cleaver, and this image had an overwhelming impact on women's self-perception and the idea of womanhood. In fact, her image—that of the prototypical suburban housewife—became synonymous with American women, although in actuality it was little more than an icon of deception. As author and sociologist Stephanie Coontz points out in *The Way We Never Were: American Families and the Nostalgia Trap,* June Cleaver never existed:

> Like most visions of a "golden age," the "traditional family" . . . evaporates on closer examination. It is an ahistorical amalgam of structures, values, and behaviors that never co-existed in the same time and place. The notion that traditional families fostered intense intimacy between husbands and wives while creating mothers who were totally available

*to their children, for example, is an idea that combines some character-
istics of the white, middle-class family in the mid–nineteenth century
and some of a rival family ideal first articulated in the 1920s. The
first family revolved emotionally around the mother–child axis, leaving the husband and wife relationship stilted and formal. The second
focused on an eroticized couple relationship, demanding that mothers
curb emotional "overinvestment" in their children. The hybrid idea
that a woman can be fully absorbed with her youngsters while simultaneously maintaining passionate sexual excitement with her husband
was a 1950s invention that drove thousands of women to therapists,
tranquilizers, or alcohol when they actually tried to live up to it.*

Does this ring a bell? It should. The 1950s "hybrid" morphed
into the Superwoman of the new millennium, who not only possesses
the attributes described by Coontz but also remains breezy and self-
assured as she effortlessly holds down a successful career on top of
everything else. As usual, the image touted as desirable effectively
neutralizes our attempts to develop and express our authentic selves.
We find ourselves confronted with a more glamorous repackaging
of the selfless woman, but today she holds a baby, a briefcase, and an
alpha-female job that she claims to love almost as much as her children. Granted, achieving greater
access to the higher echelons of
business, government, art institutions, universities, and so forth
was something to celebrate. However, many of us didn't anticipate
the price we might have to pay
or what, in relational terms, we'd
have to give up out there in the "male world." Superwoman looked
great on paper, but in reality she turned out to be a prescription for
exhaustion.

As a wise Afro-American mentor pointed out while the social
eruptions of the 1960s were taking place: "Honey, you all are striving

> Superwoman looked
> great on paper, but in
> reality she turned out
> to be a prescription for
> exhaustion.

for the right to work. I've always had that right . . . and the right to tend to my household and to raise my children and to care for my ailing mother . . . don't think men are going to suddenly rush home so women can manage the two spheres of their lives. It just isn't going to happen." Turns out, as Arlie Hochschild's groundbreaking study confirmed, she was right. In her book *The Second Shift*, Hochschild found that in only 20 percent of dual-career families do men share housework equally with their wives. While the women in the study revealed that they accepted the inequity in order to keep the peace, they tended to suffer chronic exhaustion, low sex drive, and more frequent illness. In other words, women who ventured outside the home to work discovered that when they returned to the sphere of the family, they simply took on a "second shift." The fact that they were participating equally in bringing in income didn't necessarily translate into a more equitable and balanced division of labor at home.

In 1996 writer and activist Audre Lorde wrote an article for *Ms. Magazine* titled "Holistic Politics: Difference Is Our Strength." She says, "I find I am constantly being encouraged to pluck out some one aspect of myself and present this as a meaningful whole, eclipsing or denying the other parts of self. But this is a destructive and fragmenting way to live." Clearly, Ms. Lorde worked to shape her own identity despite pressures to conform to externally imposed definitions. Yet as she acknowledges, the pressure to conform is very real, and too many of us find ourselves striving to squeeze into roles prescribed by others. Though we perform them well, inside we may feel like female impersonators, uncomfortable exposing our authentic selves—or perhaps we're out of touch with our real selves, mistaking an assigned role for our true identity. After all, sorting through all the roles we're supposed to fulfill to perfection can leave us feeling overwhelmed and compromised: "The Perfect Wife," "The Perfect Mother," "Trophy Wife," "Pinup," "Helper," "Successful Career Woman." Just fill in the blanks.

A thirty-something mother of three described it this way: "By the time I tend to the children, do the books for my husband's business, volunteer for the kindergarten class, walk the dog, feed the cat, phone my parents, and answer phones as a part-time job, I don't have enough energy to relate to myself in order to keep my sense of self intact. Something's got to give, and usually that something is me."

> The pressure to conform is very real and too many of us find ourselves striving to squeeze into roles prescribed by others. Though we perform them well, inside we may feel like female impersonators.

The problem may seem like one of modern day, yet I can assure you it's not. In her timeless classic written in 1955, *Gift from the Sea*, Anne Morrow Lindbergh penned the concerns of her generation, concerns that are perhaps more intense and unrelenting in our time than in hers, but they certainly aren't new: "Woman's life today is tending more and more toward the state William James describes so well in the German word, 'Zerrissenheit—torn-to-pieces-hood.' She cannot live perpetually in 'Zerrissenheit.' On the contrary, she must consciously encourage those pursuits which oppose the centrifugal forces of today." To counter the pull that threatens to split us off from our true selves for the allure of "cultural prescriptions for what is properly female," we must have some sense of who we are. We must be self-directed instead of externally referenced. Otherwise we too easily lose sight of our unique identity and, instead, take on roles that threaten to consume us. A longtime client, Elaine, said it best: "I can bring myself to the various roles in my life, embracing them, stamping them with my individual signature, or I can adopt an assigned role and shape myself to it, knowing I might lose touch with the core essence of my very being. Sure, at first I might feel capable of warding off any intrusions, yet over time the person I know myself to be could fade or be erased. It's a risk I'm not willing to take."

In addition to feeling alienated from our true selves, when allowing outside forces to determine who we are, we not only run the risk of losing touch with our authentic identity but may also be setting ourselves up for failure. By giving ourselves over to cultural definitions of womanhood, we may find ourselves hating who we've become because we feel inauthentic—and we may not be able to live up to unreachable ideals. Under these circumstances, it's not surprising that so many of us suffer from depression and

We can feel as though we are never enough.

self destructive behaviors: overeating, anorexia, alcohol abuse, anxiety, stress, and nervous tension. We can feel as though we are never enough.

Something must be wrong with me . . . , we say to ourselves, forgetting to question the external standards themselves and the authority with which we imbue them.

Indeed, basing our identity on external images creates confusion in the feminine psyche, setting us up for involvement in destructive relationships. Often, starting in adolescence, we are encouraged to conform, and it can be difficult to keep ourselves intact. Instead of asking us who we are, others are all too willing to tell us who we should be. And like a destructive relationship, society's pressures can whittle away at our core sense of self, making it difficult to distinguish where others end and we begin. Our spirit suffers. As Anne Morrow Lindbergh put it:

> *We are aware of our hunger and needs, but still ignorant of what will satisfy them. With our garnered free time, we are more apt to drain our creative springs than to refill them . . . Not knowing how to feed the spirit, we try to muffle its demands in distractions. Instead of stilling the center, the axis of the wheel, we add more centrifugal activities to our lives—which tend to throw us off balance.*

In the extreme, our soul may be starved from sacrificing our true nature, abbreviating our authentic self and replacing what belongs to us with identities that are pleasing to others, yet leave *us* hungry. Clarissa Pinkola Estes writes: "It is typical of the injured inner psyche and culture as well, to not notice the personal distress of the self." That is until our self-destructive behaviors become blatant and obvious . . . and even then those around us may deny them in order to keep us aligned with their agenda. After all, how can a woman be controlled if she is operating from a place of strength? How can she be easily manipulated if she values who she is more than she values the approval of others? Indeed. Placing our personal power in the hands of external forces by allowing them to define us and override our innate sensibilities makes us susceptible to the directives of others— directives that may be completely unconcerned with what is in our best interest as individuals, and as women.

Give Me Liberty or at Least Give Me My Space: Internal and External Boundaries

In recent years the concept of boundaries has flooded the popular vernacular—and with good reason. Every day we must contend with a barrage of information, manufactured images, and alluring purchases vying for our attention and consumer participation. To sift through the plethora of choices, we erect mental boundaries that act as a gatekeeper, allowing some things into our thoughts while dispensing with others.

When it comes to relationships, boundaries are essential to our well-being. They help us to define where we end and another person begins. Simple, right? Not always. If we don't have a strong sense of self and healthy internal parameters, personal boundaries can be difficult to define—and if they're difficult to define, they're almost impossible to enforce. After all, boundaries act as a good defense against unacceptable behavior, and they also prevent others from imposing their beliefs, actions, and preferences on us. If we haven't taken ownership of our comfort zones and don't have a clear understanding of our values, our boundaries can be blurred, making it easy for others to bend them to their will or violate them without compunction.

Boundaries are essential to our well-being. They help us to define where we end and another person begins. Simple, right? Not always. In truth, we have to love and respect ourselves enough to firmly set limits that are designed to keep our integrity and our well-being intact. Yet even if we have positive self-regard, we may experience some confusion about boundaries, since most of us were encouraged to be nice regardless of another's intentions. As Gavin de Becker writes in *The Gift of Fear: Survival Signals That Protect Us From Violence:*

> *I encourage women to rebuff unwanted approaches, but I know it is difficult to do. Just as rapport building has a good reputation, explicitness applied by women in this culture has a terrible reputation. A woman who is clear and precise is viewed as cold, or a bitch, or both. A woman is expected, first and foremost, to respond to every communication from a man. And the response is expected to be one of willingness and attentiveness.*

Granted, we may become much more comfortable halting the advances of a stranger, an unpleasant co-worker, or a telephone solicitor, and in such cases we may not feel uncomfortable acting like an Amazon. But drawing and holding clear boundaries with someone close to us can be more challenging. After all, the reflexive temptation to be nice and accommodating, to be fair and loving, has to be modified in such a way that we come to understand that even someone who loves us—or claims to love us—can cause harm and, therefore, requires firm physical, emotional, psychological, and spiritual boundaries.

Dr. Hannah comments: "I have seen many people, both males and females, with poorly developed boundaries stemming from their upbringing. Boundaries that are too loose or porous, which allow other people to take advantage of you, or boundaries that are overly tight or constricted, which keep others at a distance, may be transmitted by parents who have their own boundary problems and so serve as poor models for their children. Some children learn that being loved and having your boundaries violated are intricately connected, and are in fact one and the same. I've witnessed a number of these children, as middle-aged adults, continuing to allow their now elderly parents to violate their boundaries in the same way they always did. Some parents, tragically, keep doing so until the day they die."

Early life experiences in which people who loved us violated our boundaries can make it difficult to develop boundaries with someone we're in love with. We struggle to maintain some type of connection while protecting our own mental health and well-being. It's a bind. And when we consider the fact that a common denominator among destructive individuals is that they test others' boundaries to see what and how much they can get away with, we often have to learn a broader range of setting limits as well as finding the strength to consistently hold our ground. If it sounds exhausting, it is.

One woman, Elizabeth, described her situation like this: "James was always testing me to see how much I would take of his manipulations and acting out. Like a perpetual and mean-spirited teenager, he would push me, test me, until I would snap . . . and then he'd apologize. But the minute I felt better, he'd start up again. It was as though he got off on oppositional behavior. Luckily, with help from a 12-step recovery program, I learned to detach with love . . . and that helped the mood at our home. But as I developed better boundaries, I learned that loving myself and truly respecting my own needs and sanity meant I only wanted to live with others who didn't confuse antagonistic behavior with relating. I'm much happier now that I don't tolerate verbal and emotional abuse."

While Elizabeth didn't always have to be an Amazon to assert her personal boundaries, simply exercising them, strengthening them, and developing them into more sophisticated self-care tools helped her to find effective ways to respond to difficult people, including her husband. In her words: "I now understand that knowing my boundaries doesn't mean forcing others to change; it means that I know my own limits and take care of myself by respecting them. I have greater ownership of my life."

Keep in mind that it took Elizabeth years to fine-tune her repertoire of boundary setting. At first she, like most of us, was deeply uncomfortable with setting limits because the very act of doing so could create conflict. "Yes," she told me, "I was conflict averse, always thinking there was a nice way to handle things since I dreaded standing up for myself. It felt uncomfortable—and I certainly wasn't accustomed to doing it since I was a people pleaser. Thankfully, I finally figured out that there are positive ways to say no without inciting a riot . . . but that's not just up to you . . . sometimes my husband just wanted to argue and no matter how lovingly I would uphold my boundaries, he would challenge me and try to hook me into a disruptive conflict. I now think of setting boundaries as the ultimate act of self-love."

Internal Boundaries:

- Knowing your value system and trusting its integrity.
- Being cognizant of violations to your value system and personal integrity.
- Trusting your gut, knowing its messages, and feeling you have a right to back it up with choices and actions.
- Knowing you have a right to your feelings, perceptions, ideas, opinions, and dreams.
- Believing your individual limitations are justified and need not be explained and defended repeatedly.
- Valuing self-care and emotional needs—sleep, nutrition, exercise, meditation, prayer, play, friendships, sexuality, intimacy—as essential to your well-being.
- Listening to the still, small voice inside—your intuition—and trusting your self-authority enough to not let others talk you out of what you know to be true for you in the moment.

- Believing you have a right to say "No," "Can I get back to you?" and "Let me think about it" without guilt, shame, or feeling selfish.
- Trusting it's okay to ask for help and receive support.

External Boundaries:
- Saying no when you mean no and saying yes when you mean yes.
- Prioritizing: First things first.
- Making certain your needs and desires are taken into account and put into the equation, daily.
- Expressing your opinion, views, and preferences.
- Standing up for yourself when necessary and finding ways not to get emotionally hooked into mind games, manipulations, and others' dramas.
- Holding your stance in order to avoid being sucked into ridiculous arguments.
- Walking away, getting out of the house, letting others know you're not available at the moment.
- Removing yourself from fruitless discussions in which "processing emotions," blame, and "let me tell you about yourself" tactics are used to violate your boundaries. Examples: "I told you we could talk later, not now." "I agreed to discuss these issues only when we're with a therapist." "You clearly don't want to resolve the issue. You're only interested in wearing me down so I'll give in to your version of the story. I've already told you twice, I'm not willing to go around and around with you."
- Setting clear boundaries with clear consequences.
- Upholding and enforcing consequences consistently.
- Trusting yourself to know when to modify boundaries and make exceptions when circumstances merit it.

Without a doubt, destructive relationships challenge us to develop and uphold our personal boundaries in terms of both physical and inner space. After all, problem people are notorious for intruding on our psychological, emotional, and psychic boundaries while simultaneously preventing us from getting close to theirs which inhibits honesty, vulnerability, and true intimacy. Many of us must overcome early programming that encourages selflessness and being nice to find the courage to incorporate boundaries as part of our self-care regime. This is essential, since problem people often have complete disregard for our needs, leaving it up to us to set limits and demand self-respect.

"Learning how to stand up for myself in a healthy, nonreactive way was one of the best things I'd ever done for myself," Virginia confided. "It took me a while, but I learned to say no without remorse or worrying that I was offending anyone. Do you believe it? I used to be concerned about offending a man who had just verbally abused me and shattered my internal boundaries when I demanded that he stop talking to me like that . . . it's crazy . . . I feel so much more confident now, clearer in my mind. No one has the right to obliterate my boundaries and compromise my safety."

Think about it. Why would we expect a bank account to be brimming with funds if we are forever making withdrawals and seldom making deposits? It makes no sense financially, nor does it make sense physically, emotionally, psychologically, and spiritually. Boundaries help us to regulate the expenditures of our life force energy so we don't deplete ourselves and waste precious personal resources. By the same token, when we honor our boundaries, we don't allow others to take from us that which is not theirs. "In the past I didn't have a very solid sense of myself, and I allowed others to walk all over me, or I overextended myself. Now I can distinguish where I end and another person begins, and it's easier to make choices about how close I will allow them to be in my personal space. It's a really powerful place to be."

Remember the research with the fruit flies? In essence, the female fruit flies with each new generation strategically developed physical boundaries to stave off the sexually aggressive advances of the males. However, when the less genetically sophisticated females weren't so adept at asserting their boundaries, the male fruit flies not only took advantage of them but actually snuffed out their life force —to the point of death. While it may seem extreme, I can guarantee you it is not.

Dr. Caroline Myss, author of *Anatomy of the Spirit: The Seven Stages of Power and Healing* and a well-known medical intuitive and pioneer in energy medicine, tells the story of a woman named Julie who came to see her because she had cancer in both her breasts and her ovaries. Clearly, from the description of her husband's treatment of her, Julie was involved in a toxic relationship. Dr. Myss writes: "Her illness was a symbolic statement of her feelings of rejection as a woman . . . Julie could not see herself as having any personal power because she saw her husband as the source of her security; her biology was constantly receiving 'power-lessness signals.' Julie died within a year."

> By allowing her husband to define her, she bought into the abuse.

By allowing her husband to define her, she bought into the abuse, thinking herself less-than, giving away her personal power. In essence Julie sacrificed her much-needed protection, eventually becoming boundaryless.

An amazing woman in her own right, Eleanor Roosevelt is famous for saying, "No one can make you feel inferior without your consent." While there is much truth to her words, they don't tell the entire story. Saying no (verbally and nonverbally), taking our space, and respecting our individual needs doesn't necessarily mean that those around us are going to like it. In fact, they may perpetually disrespect our boundaries. They may act out more often, test us repeatedly to see if we really mean it, or flat-out reject us if we don't provide whatever they want—or think they want. Just as in any destructive relationship, Eleanor endured humiliation, dishonesty, ridicule, loss, and emotional distancing from her husband, President Franklin Roosevelt. She paid a high price for her individuality and the expression of her personal power. It's no secret that she suffered from serious bouts of depression due to her husband's betrayal and chronic infidelity. Although her mother-in-law forced Franklin to promise that he would relinquish his mistress because of the distress it was causing the family, he never did, and so lies followed more lies, much to Eleanor's emotional, psychological, and spiritual detriment. Not even the great Eleanor Roosevelt in her privileged position could escape the heartache that comes from keeping her dignity despite the actions of those around her.

Because she didn't see her husband as her main source of happiness or individual security, nor did he define her, Eleanor had choices, many that she had to make on her own behalf regardless of the circumstances. By remaining in the marriage, she had to find ways to take care of herself, ways to create her own life—separate but under the same roof—knowing she could not depend on receiving any type of emotional intimacy from the man she loved. Clearly it was heart wrenching, but in the end her spirit remained intact.

Motherhood in Today's World

Talk about external images barraging women! When it comes to motherhood, we have the world *and* the inscriptions of Hallmark greeting cards on our shoulders. Motherhood is one of those institutions that everyone seems to feel they have the right to define for us: the church, the media, the politicians, the men. The married version expects us to be a never-ending abundant source of love, time, and energy for every member of the family. Taking time for ourselves is, well, simply selfish despite the fact that studies on stress clearly illustrate the need for rest and rejuvenation. Even then, the facts can be dismissed by a condescending attitude designed to induce guilt that we have to honor our internal needs for contemplation, relaxation, and self-attunement. It kind of reminds me of a friend who leaned over to comment on the first astronaut landing on the moon: "Watch, now they'll dim the importance of her mystery and make her one big science project."

The catch-22 is that we're also supposed to be sexual creatures, at least with our husbands, despite the emotional and physical expenditures we make as mothers. Under these conditions, Superwoman may not be dead, but she'll soon be dead tired—and stretched too thin.

Now, in all fairness, marriages are changing, but like it or not, images of Donna Reed still lurk in the background, and their influence is far from over. Dalma Heyn, in her controversial book *The Erotic Silence of the American Wife*, describes the pressures on women to conform to an ideal of wife and mother in this way:

> *She is beautiful, smiling, supportive, contented, giving, feminine—she is, in a word, good. "Good" as it applies to the Perfect Wife inevitably modifies and diminishes the word "self"—as in self-sacrifice, self-abnegate, self-restraint, self-denial—the suffix always restraining or containing or constraining in an effort to make that woman's self a little less something. Her virtue exists in direct proportion to how much of herself is whittled away . . . if she is amenable to expunging the self altogether—to be selfless—then she has succeeded in accomplishing the highest goal, attaining what many believe to be woman's best self, often calling it her "true" self, obviously empty of her true self though it is.*

It's this trap that can keep us tied to a destructive man long after we should have left, children or not.

However, once divorced, we may become acutely aware of how prevalent the perceptions of selflessness and virtue really are. Judgments about our character surface along with open hostilities about our role as a mother: "How could she have done that to the children?"

neighbors will say, ignorant of the abuse we've suffered or the toxic marriage we left. If we challenge them, "So you think it's better for children to be in a toxic atmosphere with a destructive man?" they may act as though you're making it up or could have found a better way if only you'd tried hard enough. It's a strange dynamic that exemplifies the pervasiveness of these images of women and when we exit a destructive situation, chances are we'll bump up against them.

Sexuality is another hot button for divorcées. "I thought I was living on the set of *Desperate Housewives* after my divorce. It's as though everyone expected me to seduce their husbands and felt threatened I was single again, yet they also got insulted if I didn't think him 'worthy' of making a pass at—talk about mixed messages!" If we do choose to take on a lover, date a younger man—or any man—or take vacations to exotic ports of call, our competency as a mother may get called into question. "Yep," Jan told me, "he was known for his indiscretions, but when I began having men in my life—dates or friends—I was the one they vehemently criticized." To again quote Dalma Heyn, "With every new sign of budding self-possession a woman displays—assertiveness, say, or ambition—her 'femininity' dwindles accordingly."

Isn't it interesting that a man can date and even move in with another person and not have his qualifications as a father called into question, whereas a woman can't? It can be tricky fighting enemies that have outposts in our own heads as we establish a new life, but we may end up battling more fiercely with the images of motherhood that others are invested in and are convinced that we should live up to.

Luckily, once we are on our own, we can devise our own version of motherhood, one that centers on our own needs and the needs of our children. Disposing of the ideal of the perfect mother and the perfect wife is always a good place to start. Because even those of us who consider ourselves independent and our own person are often surprised by how powerfully images of the perfect wife and mother can penetrate our psyche and take up residence in our minds. It may take a while for us to shed their influence as we reinvent our lives, especially when we've been in a destructive relationship that has, over time, eroded our self-confidence and self-expression. As author Dalma Heyn reminds us:

> *Certainly, the women I spoke with never actually considered them-selves Donna Reed raw material. They felt poorly qualified to fit such a mold of selflessness and sexlessness. Nevertheless, at marriage they each began a process of self-revision, altering or burying those parts of themselves that they perceived to exceed or violate it. Their feel-ings and knowledge and experience—that is, what they felt in their bodies and knew about themselves and understood about men and sex and relationships, slowly collapsed, yielding to imaginings of what they would feel and know and experience once they became wives. They spoke of this someone new with an irony that belied their acceptance and anticipation of her, noting often that their own real feelings fell appallingly short of what they thought a wife's feelings should be . . .*

Leaving a destructive relation-ship can be a powerful catalyst for redefining who we are and recap-turing what has always been best in us. Yet even for those of us who remain attached to the problem person—either because we have children or have decided to stay together for now—disentangling ourselves from the influences of

Luckily, once we are on our own, we can devise our own version of motherhood, one that centers our own needs and the needs of our children.

external forces can lead to a journey of self-discovery and active exca-vation of our authentic selves, eventually tipping the scales in our favor regardless of whether the negative behaviors of the toxic indi-vidual persist.

Yes, the female identity is always up for grabs, but only with our consent. We can dismantle early training. We can become more aware

Even for those of us who stay, disentangling from the influences of external forces can lead to a journey of self-discovery.

of cultural programming that alienates us from our conscious feminine, and we can learn to embrace what is unique in ourselves in order to be more whole. Moreover, we can learn to say yes to what we want and no to that which is destructive to our essential self, regardless of what is required of us. And when we have a solid sense of who we are and what we want—an experience of what it's like to be treated in a loving, supportive, and healthy way—we are much less apt to tolerate anything less, including a relationship that is simply no good for us.

| 10 |

Never Wrestle with a Pig

I learned long ago, never wrestle with a pig. You get dirty, and besides, the pig likes it.

—George Bernard Shaw

Divorce is messy. It's painful, and even when it's absolutely the right thing to do, there's a feeling of loss. Divorcing a destructive individual can feel like wrestling with a pig. We go to the mat for a good cause, end up getting gunk in our hair, dirt under our fingernails—and feel rather beat up—and he has a blast. It's a terminally unfair situation yet, in many cases, unavoidable. Briana summed it up when she said: "Divorce is such a hassle. I think I should have just fixed him instead—it would have been easier!" All of us laughed, reflecting on the irony of her statement. Sure, there may have been days when the idea of fixing our husband actually looked less complicated than contending with divorce papers, lawyers, and strained interactions. But in actuality, the more distance we get, the easier it is to see that "fixing him" was only a fanciful notion with no basis in reality—definitely an idea that belonged under the "cherished illusions" category—and divorce was the price we paid for our freedom.

I Need a Divorce from My Divorce

Sadly, because control is so central to toxic men, divorce frequently becomes a forum for concentrated conflict instead of a process toward a mutually beneficial resolution. Whether blatant or subtle, destructive individuals view our leaving as an unacceptable rejection, escalating tension in an adversarial approach not dissimilar from the strategies he employed in the marriage. It can be jarring to the senses to see how belligerent his actions are, realizing that he's been this way all along. His antics grow more obvious—or maybe they just seem more blatant now that we've committed ourselves to a different course and cut emotional ties.

The problem is, these abusive tactics create unnecessary drama and hardship for those around him. Spiteful offensives and counteroffensives, clever ploys designed to weaken and upset us are put into action to get back at us for leaving. He may hide bank accounts, cancel our health insurance without notification, inform the principal that our children will no longer be attending private school, and successfully pull off other assorted tricks to create conflict and disrupt our lives. It can be hellish. Determined to get their way, even when they're "nice" about it, toxic individuals are notorious for purposefully undermining attempts to cooperate, whether children are involved or not. Certainly a destructive individual might go along with court orders or recommendations from his attorney for a time, but because he ultimately views cooperation as capitulation—some men go so far as to consider getting along a form of emasculation— the payback will surface in some form, derailing prior agreements to prove he's still in charge.

"My ex-husband always made sure he was late for exchanges," one woman told me. "He felt powerful making me wait for him with the two boys sitting in the car twiddling their thumbs. If I left after the time allotted by the custody decree, he would lie in court, claiming I was withholding the children from visits—a very serious charge. It got to the point where I had to buy a pack of gum at the store when we arrived and buy another one when we left so I had proof that I waited in compliance with the order. Games like these can really suck the life out of you."

Equally frustrating is when we acquiesce, handing them what they claim they want on a silver platter just to come to some form of resolution, only to discover that many of these men will refuse to accept terms they themselves dictated, simply to keep the fight alive. One woman who shared custody of her two-year-old son told me: "He hated the thought of letting me go, and it made him crazy to think I would flourish without him. So he did everything in his power to keep me engaged—and the courts allowed it . . . After a while it became so ludicrous

> "It took him fifteen years to lose interest in harassing me through the legal system."

that I'd tell people my ex-husband liked to date me in court! It took him fifteen years to lose interest in harassing me through the legal system." Despite their ugly accusations against us, they often don't want us to leave. Not because we're the love of their life, but because they don't want to lose an arrangement that's been working so well for them. That it was harmful to us is irrelevant.

Why does he keep the fight alive? There are many reasons, depending on the makeup of the individual, yet here are some of the most common ones:

- He wants to control you.
- He won't accept your leaving as anything but a personal betrayal.
- He thrives on the drama and conflict.
- He enjoys being a destructive force in your life.
- He's obsessed with what you do, who you're with, how you spend your time.
- He's terrified to let go and may be addicted to you.
- He likes to dominate you emotionally and psychologically.
- He hopes to weaken you so you'll agree to less than your share

of the assets; be susceptible to tactics of guilt, especially when it comes to the children; and fail to regain your personal power.

- He sees the conflict as a game and, if he's incapable of genuine empathy, the game must be won at all costs despite the pain it causes others, including his own children.
- He's desperate for your attention and needs others to see him as a victim.
- He is cruel and devoid of remorse.
- He views conflict and relating as pretty much the same thing.
- Conflict makes him feel alive and gives meaning (real or imagined) to his life.

Like it or not, the legal system, at least in the United States, rarely curbs frivolous lawsuits and belligerent entanglements via divorce court. In fact, in the estimation of many, family law has become an industry that is easily fueled by the antics of destructive individuals; the only ones who stand to gain are the attorneys, court-appointed psychologists, "specialists," and those who delight in conflict. For this reason, it's not easy to resolve contested issues. Even if we give in to their demands in the hope of moving on, they can still argue over the children, since custody issues can be reviewed for modification until the children are emancipated. In the end, we have little control over the lawsuits that come our way. We are required, by law, to respond to them despite our best efforts to terminate our involvement with a destructive individual.

How to Disengage

The good news is that despite ongoing litigation and continued turmoil, there are ways to disengage and avoid getting hooked by his disruptive tactics.

Number One: Figure out the composition of his psychological games and emotional terrorism.

Name them for what they are and get a sense of his strategies so you can see them coming. No, you don't have to get a Ph.D. in psychology, but it's helpful to assemble a general profile of his specific brand of his troublesome behavior. Although he may shock you with new methods to his madness on occasion, you'll be surprised how predictable his actions and responses can be. Patterns will emerge, so keep your eyes open.

Number Two: Stop expecting him to act like a reasonable human being.

He won't. He doesn't have to and he's not interested. The more you can stay in the present moment and learn how to respond with flexibility and a treasure chest full of appropriate responses to help navigate each particular situation rather than strict rules of engagement (except, of course, where those are merited), the better off you'll be. "I was such a respondaholic that whenever he'd act like a decent human being, I'd get sucked right in, responding as though we were going to work everything out in a sensible way. I did this because I was so attached to the way I wanted things to be instead of paying attention to how they really were. I even tried to overcompensate for his bad behavior by acting extra reasonable, which as I learned was actually a way of trying to control the situation—and him—in my own way. After a number of years, I'm now adept at relational martial arts and can hold my own despite what others do. I'm glad I took the time to learn more constructive ways of handling myself with men like these."

Number Three: Set appropriate boundaries and enforce them as consistently as possible.

For example, if he continues to drive to your house to pick up the kids when your court order clearly states that all exchanges are to take place in a public place, call the authorities every time he arrives. Make sure that the police file a written report, and remember to pick up a copy later on, in case you need it to apply for a restraining order. It may sound drastic, yet I can assure you: If he can get away with something of this level of importance, then chances are he won't take you seriously with any limits you set. *Note:* In some states and jurisdictions, the police will arrest both parties, and a judge could order "mutual restraining orders." Discuss the best strategy with your attorney. Holding him in contempt of court for violation of the order may be a better strategy in cases such as these.

Number Four: Don't take his behavior personally.

How he acts and reacts has nothing to do with you. After all, most of these men have narcissistic tendencies and consequently view the things you do to take care of yourself—including respecting and enforcing your own boundaries—as a personal affront. They are constantly on the lookout for any perceived betrayal—yes, even after you've left the relationship—and then feel justified in overreacting in a destructive and even abusive way. Noelle Nelson, Ph.D., author of *Dangerous Relationships: How to Identify and Respond to the Seven Warning Signs of a Troubled Relationship*, describes it this way: "Is this event or situation proof of my loved one's 100 percent total and complete attention and devotion to me 24 hours a day, or does it in some way demonstrate that my love's attention and devotion is less than 100 percent?" Again, even when you're no longer in the relationship, he probably still sees you as belonging to him. Thus he continues to measure your actions by the same yardstick he used when you were together.

> Even when you're no longer in the relationship, he probably still sees you as belonging to him.

Number Five: Don't react.

Act. When he tries to elicit an emotional reaction from you by saying outrageous things, swearing at you, belittling you in front of the children, or deliberately lying, use mental strategies to focus on your priorities. Focus on what you are trying to accomplish within the situation. Try not to blow up—even if he is egging you on. Think of it this way: If you argue with a two-year-old, in no time at all you'll begin to sound like one. The same rule applies here regardless of the fact that you're interacting with a seemingly grown man. Feel free to say, "I'll have to think about it," "I'm not sure if Michael has school that day, so I'll get back to you," "I'll talk to you at another time when you're feeling better." You have every right to create verbal distance from him and opt not to engage until you feel ready to take the issue on or let it die its own death.

Number Six: Be proactive.

If you suspect that he will lie to you when the children are in his care, think ahead. If they're over five years of age, they're old enough to use a cell phone. As one tech-savvy mom pointed out to me: "I didn't trust him to make good judgments as a parent when we were together, so why depend on him now that we're separated? Instead of worrying if their cold has turned into an ear infection over the weekend, I can phone the girls privately to see how they're feeling. The tone of their voice and other verbal cues provide me with so much information that I can determine whether I need to intervene or not." If you can't trust him to make sure the children have their costumes for the school parade, then purchase some spares just in case and leave them with their teachers. They don't have to be adversely affected by his inability to incorporate others' needs. Remember, you don't have to wish he'd do things differently, though you can be overjoyed when he does come through, as long as you cover your own bases.

Number Seven: Vent when you need to in order to avoid emotional constipation.

Scream in your car. Call a friend. Seek out advice and guidance from other women who married similar men and have been there. Cry a thousand tears if that helps you let go of the grief and heartache.

Number Eight: Take good care of yourself during this time.

It is unrealistic to expect yourself to contend with conflict, litigation, negotiations, dividing property, helping the children adjust to the separation, and everything else involved in a divorce as though these were just one more item on your to-do list. This can be a highly emotional time, and even if you're feeling much better now that you're out of the house, there are many changes taking place; if you have children, they will need your support, patience, and understanding. Be sure to rest. Sleep. Take hot baths. Get a massage. Have your nails done. Eat a good diet. Surround yourself with loving friends. Go for walks. Swim. Notice rainbows and rose petals laced with dew. Anything that helps you to see that your world has not been completely consumed by the divorce.

Number Nine: Humor cleanses the soul and can help you to keep a clear perspective.

It also releases pain and acts to counterbalance stress. Comical movies, Broadway plays, grabbing a hamburger at the local Irish family bar to hear the locals tell jokes . . . don't be afraid to laugh, despite the seriousness of what is going on between you and your troublemaking guy as you bring the relationship to a close. Carol Burnett, Groucho Marx, Jonathan Winters, Robin Williams, Lucille Ball, Billy Crystal, Gilda Radner, and *The Daily Show*'s Jon Stewart have all worked hard to stir up your laughter, so find out what tickles your funny bone and revel in it.

Number Ten: Stop depending on your ex.

Failure to appropriately cut emotional and logistical ties, especially while going through the divorce process, can be detrimental to your health. Separating from someone you once loved enough to marry and have children with is one of the most painful experiences one can have. To mitigate the pain, some women stay in touch with their ex, not merely for the sake of the children but to postpone the inevitable end. Then they end up with what I call a "separation that isn't a separation": They experience none of the benefits of separation—moving on, feeling free, establishing independence, healing emotional wounds—but all of the deficits, such as seeing him take up with a new woman, giving up time with the children, and struggling to survive financially. My advice is, when you break up, make it a real breakup. At first, like the surgical amputation of a limb, it will hurt like hell. In the long run, you will heal more quickly, more cleanly, and more completely.

As Barb Scala, attorney, divorce coach, and co-author of *Sanity Savers: Tips for Women to Live a Balanced Life*, pointed out during a phone conversation: "Because their sense of self has been weakened, many women in destructive relationships lack the confidence to make good decisions on their own behalf and instead continue to engage with their future ex-spouse during the divorce process, relying on him to tell them what to do. I say, 'Don't!' One of my 5 Ways to Bloom is to be with positive people. I encourage women to surround themselves with a nurturing support system and to move away from people such as a controlling spouse who zaps your energy and strips away your self-esteem. It's important at the get-go to make boundaries and shed the comfort zone of control by taking brave steps to trust in your own abilities and risk making a wrong decision. Only then can a toxic marriage be truly over

> Divorce, if it doesn't kill us, will definitely make us stronger.

so a woman can go on to live her own life." To depend on him to offer sound advice, especially on your behalf, is like asking the fox to guard the chicken coop. It's just not a good idea. Luckily, as you strike out on your own, your strength will return, as will your confidence.

Yes, it's true: Divorce, if it doesn't kill us, will definitely make us stronger. It's not a trial by fire any of us would have opted for, if we had the choice—it's hard on us, and hard on our children. Yet sometimes the hard choice is the best choice, and the better able we are to detach with love, uphold our boundaries, and act on our own behalf with guidance from those we trust, the more easily we'll turn an ending into a new beginning.

| 11 |

Learning to Discriminate

The word *discrimination* often connotes prejudice and exclusion. However, there is a huge difference between discriminating *against* others on the basis of ignorance or emotional reactivity and fine-tuning your senses to take care of and, sometimes, to protect yourself. Developing interpersonal sensitivity and a discerning intuition is essential to well-being. After all, even if you're open-minded, that doesn't mean that anything goes. Learning what works for you and what doesn't, what you're comfortable with and what you're not, is an essential part of self-care and self-preservation. By determining the perimeters of your comfort zone, you create boundaries, not to shut others out, but to invite their involvement within limits comfortable to you and appropriate for the situation. Think of it as a form of maturity based on self-respect and self-knowledge.

Learning what works for you and what doesn't, what you're comfortable with and what you're not, is an essential part of self-care and self-preservation.

At one of my favorite Starbucks coffee shops in St. Louis, there are two lively men who work behind the counter. One young man takes my order, and the other, the barista, prepares my coffee. Without fail, whenever I order, they are sure to make a big show of it: "A grande mocha with only one shot of espresso, decaf, regular milk, one *half* pump of chocolate, no whip . . . a glorified milk for the lady!" They then give each other a high five and shout out in unison, "High maintenance!" and we all laugh. It's become a routine joke, a welcomed brand of levity. But one day a handsome, finely dressed man was in line behind me, watching the entire routine. When they shouted out "High maintenance" he chimed in: "No, I'd say she's a woman who knows what she wants!"

And there you have it. It had taken me months to perfect my coffee to taste, to get it just the way I wanted it, and to this man I clearly knew my own mind. Now don't get me wrong. If I structured all my choices in the same way I order my coffee, I'd drive myself and everyone around me crazy. But the truth is, knowing when things need to be exactly a certain way and knowing when to be flexible, knowing which battles to choose and which ones to let go of—all of these are aspects of discrimination. We shape these choices around what is best for us. As we learn to define and refine what works for us, what is healthy for us and what is not, we build a more solid foundation of self-knowledge, making it more difficult for destructive people to find entry points into our world. Truly, a woman who knows what she wants—and what she doesn't want, especially when it comes to relationships—keeps her priorities straight so that she doesn't become entangled in problems that aren't hers to solve.

> Knowing when things need to be exactly a certain way and knowing when to be flexible, knowing which battles to choose and which ones to let go of—all of these are aspects of discrimination.

Essence Versus Personality Versus Character: Are They Aligned?

Being strongly intuitive and highly relational, I have a tendency to see the best in others because their essence is so obvious to me—and from an essence perspective almost everyone appears as a child of God. Essence is the divine spark that resides inside of each of us regardless of personal issues, addictions, and psychological disturbances. It's an energetic core, if you will, that illuminates and animates our very being; it's the light you see in another's eyes.

Despite the beauty of essence, it doesn't necessarily inform the personality, especially if there are psychological or physiological imbalances, addictions, or dissociative disorders. Dissociation from one's essential spiritual nature—one's essence—can and does occur as a result of invalidating, abusive, and unloving experiences. Even socialization that overrides one's authentic voice can sever the connection, as in the case of highly developed intellects that have little emotional intelligence. As a result, when I approach others' essence and forget to open my eyes to the other components of who they are, I can get blindsided when aspects of their personality start to emerge—particularly undesirable words and behaviors, since they contradict the beauty of the connection I'm experiencing. Make sense?

Think about the time you met a man and felt connected. You could see he was a good person even though he also seemed to have some problems. Chances are, if you focused too intently on the ephemeral connection instead of holding it up for scrutiny alongside his personality, you probably missed some important clues. Like most of us, if you're not careful, you might negate or minimize the unpleasant paradox staring you in the face instead of paying attention to the discrepancy between the goodness inside and the problems that are surfacing through the personality—and that can lead to trouble.

Now, in the case of sociopaths, psychopaths, and individuals with borderline personality disorder, it can be dangerous territory. After all, they appear to connect, powerfully, both psychologically and emotionally, yet they are also experts at hiding their true motivations and intentions, and in most cases are severely cut off from true empathy, love, and spiritual essence. There's a disconnect that is actually evident in the structure of their brain.

In my experience these types of men have turned away from their own essence and instead are operating from a more mental and material orientation, deriving satisfaction from manipulating others to get what they want. They are uninterested in real relationships with others and instead use manipulation, control, and mind games to steal money, to improve a bad credit report, or put a roof over their head. Though these types amass what they can, rarely do they experience a genuine sense of fulfillment. Insatiable, they continually seek out new conquests. They are cut off from their own source of spiritual energy—essence—and so they attempt to get filled up from others.

"He's Very Empty"

While these types of individuals are on the extreme end of the spectrum, the same pattern can be common among a number of the destructive individuals described in the profiles listed in chapter 2. That is why recovery programs and many psychotherapists, especially those with a transpersonal bent, work to cultivate a spiritual connection to the self—and new therapies are evolving to "repattern" areas of the brain for better integration among conscience, intellect, and the feeling centers. Otherwise, distortions in the personality can overwhelm healthier aspects of the individual and start running the show. Cut off from essence, these distortions often become cons resulting from psychological fragmentation or, in some cases, simply from a lack of moral character and the development of a conscience. In the extreme, a person like this appears soulless. As Anne Bird, Scott Peterson's half sister who desperately wanted to believe he wasn't guilty of the murder of his wife, Laci, told reporters: "He is the most empty person. Everything he does seems to have been copied from someone else . . . I think he's very bright, but he's kind of soulless. He's very empty. Somehow he's been lost."

It's sadly ironic that many people who aspire to be spiritual, to see the good in others, and to love and accept others unconditionally are as a result highly susceptible to exploitation by those who operate from an entirely different set of rules. Unfortunately, I see cases of this all the time: A destructive man, including a more extreme type such as a sociopath, attracts a woman with a pure heart and good intentions. Then, once she has fallen in love with him (or more accurately with his counterfeit image), he proceeds to inflict deliberate harm on her, knowing that she, unlike him, is too highly principled to retaliate against him or to treat him likewise. Destructive men exploit women with good character and noble intentions. If these men were to pair off with women just like them, they'd never be able to pull off their dirty deeds! So as the time-worn phrase puts it: "Buyer beware." The Christian scriptures also capture this in the passage: "Be as wily as a fox but as innocent as a dove."

When a destructive person comes to rely on less-than-noble motivations, consciously or not, his character is compromised. As time goes on he may grow less and less capable of expressing virtuous qualities and what is best within him. Disconnected from essence, his internal compass can be defective, and so the quality of his character is diminished. He simply doesn't have the capacity to operate from a place of integrity, and his actions reflect it. As a result the goodness you catch glimpses of is rarely or inconsistently expressed—and with certain men may seem to be nonexistent.

An older woman, Julianna, herself an artist, put it eloquently when she said: "I experienced moments when something profound shined outward from him, if even for an instant, and I tightly grasped on to it, hopeful that this delicate, tiny pearl was a real reflection of him. But then I strung the pearls together in my mind, as though on a necklace, pretending that this grouping of pearls represented who he really was or who I wanted him to be. I simply dismissed the long pieces of string linking the pearls together

Pay attention to the balance of the equation. How often is he authentic? Are the enjoyable aspects of his personality out of balance with the nasty side?

because it was too painful to accept that the appearance of the pearls was so rare and that the in-between moments were so miserable."

The occasional appearance of the goodness in the individual and the positive aspects of his personality that, when genuine, reflect his true essence can be seductive and keep us hooked since we're justified in saying, with some certainty, that "he's not all bad." But what you really need to pay attention to is the balance of the equation. How often is he authentic? Are the enjoyable aspects of his personality out of balance with the nasty side? Is his charming, humorous softer side merely a cover-up for the less desirable characteristics of his personality? Are his good traits actually tools of manipulation instead of genuine expressions of who he is?

Like it or not, when it comes to problem people, the personality may be pieced together like a patchwork quilt. The positive aspects of the individual's essence rarely emerge since their expression requires some level of genuineness and good intentions—and this is difficult to do when there is so much internal fragmentation. When such a disconnect occurs, the alignment among these various aspects of the individual is off-kilter in much the same way that the vertebrae in the spine can be thrown out of line, resulting in disruption of the nerves' proper functioning.

Authors and psychologists Neil Jacobson, Ph.D., and John Gottman, Ph.D., describe a scenario in their book *When Men Batter Women: New Insights into Ending Abusive Relationships* that clearly demonstrates the disconnect between the deeper aspects of the destructive individual and his personal actions. While the case they cite is that of a physical batterer, the dynamics can be similar or identical in the far more common instances of emotional abuse and psychological domination. "When Don saw the blood on Martha's face, he knew he had lost it, but he told himself that she deserved it. Only a small part of him, dimly—like a faint whisper in the corner of his brain—wanted to cry like a baby and beg forgiveness . . . By the next day, he regained his old charm and had managed to squelch that dim light of remorse."

Why is this so important to look squarely in the face? Because so many of us, like Julianna, want to hold on to any thread of goodness we sense, observe, or experience in the man we love. Love can be blind. We want him to be the sum of only his good parts—or we actively minimize the bad—even though his prevailing patterns are unavoidable. We want the good without the bad. It's this tendency that can prevent you, or any of us, from seeing people for who they really are, how they choose to behave, and what portion of their healthy self, their essence, they are actually expressing on a consistent basis.

> Why do we often minimize the bad parts of the destructive individual? Because we want him to be the sum of only his good parts.

Remember, it takes a while to see past the initial attraction or the dynamic or heartfelt connection. Sometimes you are being charmed, manipulated, and conned, at other times the destructive individual simply has too many unresolved problems that outweigh what is good about him. It's up to you to be mindful of what his words and actions are really conveying. Read between the lines. Trust your gut. If you find yourself furrowing your brow each time he attempts to talk you into something, especially if you're uncomfortable with it, pay attention. Does he tell you he occasionally drinks too much? Does he admit he had problems with anger *in the past*—but insist he's over it now? If so, listen up! Everyone gives off verbal and nonverbal clues. Even those who are skillfully adept at impression management can send off warning signals as they attempt to captivate and draw you in.

While you may not be able to fully assess every person you

> Do the math. How much of his personality seems to be a genuine reflection of something deeper, and how much of his goodness is clouded over with darker aspects?

encounter on the spot, you can certainly exercise critical thinking and some common sense. Do the math. How much of his personality seems to be a genuine reflection of something deeper, something of substance, and how much of his goodness is clouded over with darker aspects of the personality that, in the end, could mean trouble for you?

Seeing People for Who They Really Are: Actions Speak Louder Than Words (But Words Say A Lot)

When it comes to destructive individuals, interpreting words and actions can be tricky. All of us can make well-meaning promises in the hope that we can fulfill them. We want to help. We overextend and so some commitments fall by the wayside, much to our chagrin. We do our best to be women of our word, fully knowing there will be times when we come up short. At other times we make excuses that allow us to brush a request aside. However, for destructive individuals, the integrity of words and fulfillment of promises are of little or no importance. Instead, words are callow tools to make certain they get what they want, regardless of the consequences for you.

New Age men, for example, find ways to manipulate by appealing to the cause and effect of potential karma, or they might blame their behavior on a "past life." Passive-aggressive types try to sell you on the idea that their words do not contradict their actions, even when it's clear that the two are hardly in alignment. Other destructive individuals use words to convince you that their opinions and ideas are more relevant than yours, certainly more accurate than yours, and they think nothing of discounting your own opinions about what's best for you. They'll talk you out of taking care of your own needs and desires whenever it clashes with what they want.

Face it, it can be painful to see people for who they are, yet it's critical to do so, especially when you are dealing with a man who claims he has your best interests at heart . . . but really doesn't. Ask yourself: *Is he true to his word? Do I often spend time figuring out what he really means? After a conversation or argument do I tend to feel off? Does he have a tendency to twist my words so that I have to explain myself over and over again?* And last, *When I confront him on his behaviors or tell him I don't like something he said or did, does he find ways to make me wrong?* Think about it. It usually doesn't take long for the patterns to emerge, but it can take a while for you to accept the inconsistencies of his words and actions as a problem that you don't have to solve. Not this time.

Here's a quick checklist as you move forward:

☐ Does he use words to discount or invalidate your feelings?
☐ Does he find ways to talk you out of what you know is true for you?
☐ When you tell him what you need, does he promise to give you what you want then go back to the same old behaviors?
☐ Is he a different person when the two of you are out with others?
☐ Are words used as a weapon to make you feel inferior, stupid, and worthless?
☐ Are veiled threats used to keep you in line?
☐ Does he lie to you and then deny his actions or turn the discussion into a heated argument so that you'll back down and drop it?
☐ When he asks you what you want, does he actually respond to your requests or brush them aside for "a better idea"?
☐ Is he skilled at finding ways to avoid taking responsibility for his actions by twisting words, making jokes, or insisting that you misinterpreted him?

Words can elevate the spirit or crush it.

Whoever said, "Stick and stones can break my bones but words will never hurt me" was very wrong. Words can elevate the spirit or crush it. In fact, words can turn lies into truth—quite literally. A destructive individual can, with both words and actions, shape your self-perception. In other words, he will have you believing things about yourself that simply have no bearing in reality, but once they take up residence in your psyche you'll believe them to be true. They've become part of your own belief system despite the fact that they are nothing more than control tactics designed to derail your self-esteem, self-worth, and accurate self-perception. Once this happens, the misconceptions planted in your brain can be difficult to exorcise from your thoughts, especially if they have been incorporated into what you perceive to be your identity. Gary Robertson, a clinical psychologist who is also certified in energy psychology, has this to say: "Words, and actions, speak volumes. They offer life-affirming truth; they can also distort the truth. Listen to what you're being told. Watch his actions. Take time to sort out whether his actions—or his words—are as honest and sincere as he'd like you to believe."

What Level of Consciousness Is He Operating On?

Men who genuinely like women have a different consciousness from those who don't. They don't see women as inferior and in need of control. They don't automatically assume traditional roles and believe that men should have the power in a relationship. They have some capacity for taking women's needs and concerns into account. Certainly that's not to say more evolved men don't have issues with sharing power, don't struggle to figure out the division of labor in the home, and don't find themselves feeling perplexed by some of the biological and cultural differences women bring to the table in a relationship. On the contrary, many of them do.

The difference is that these men are willing to "do the work," as they say in therapeutic circles. They are open to new ways of thinking and being in the world, and they are willing to make changes, to improve upon dysfunctional patterns, in order to come together in a relationship. Researcher and prominent psychologist John Gottman refers to this important distinction as being "open to influence," and as his work confirms it's an essential ingredient not only in successful relationships, but also in personal growth and genuine recovery.

In my work I often discuss the idea of "willingness" because it's such a powerful spiritual concept. Without it, genuine change is difficult. On my radio show, *Quantum Leaps*, I talk about the transformative power of accelerated change and how it can benefit our lives. I remind the audience that in order to take this leap in personal growth, individuals don't have to be ready, but they *do* have to be willing; otherwise my work is not as effective. To me, willingness is the gateway to change; it is the essential prep work that allows authentic change to happen, regardless of whether we're frightened or even apprehensive.

The research of David R. Hawkins, M.D., Ph.D., confirms my findings. In his book *Power vs. Force: The Hidden Determinants of Human Behavior,* he uses a scientific method to calibrate human consciousness in order to delineate spiritual development. He writes:

> *Willingness implies that one has overcome inner resistance to life and is committed to participation. Below the 200 calibration, people tend to be closed-minded, but by level 310 [willingness], a great opening occurs. Growth is rapid . . . At this level, people become genuinely friendly, and social and economic success seem to follow automatically . . . They're also willing to face inner issues and don't have major learning blocks.*

Dr. Marcia Linehan, who developed Dialectical Behavior Therapy (DBT), emphasizes the importance of willingness in achieving change, but she goes farther to contrast it with willfulness. Willingness promotes recovery and growth, since it consists of openness to different ways of thinking, feeling, and behaving. Willfulness, on the other hand, inhibits recovery and growth, since it is based on closed-mindedness, on a "my way or the highway" mentality.

What Is Dialectical Behavior Therapy?

DBT is a systematic and eclectic combination of cognitive and behavioral therapies. It was designed by Marcia Linehan, Ph.D., who based the program on her own research findings and studies of the attitudes, skills, and practices that help people live effectively, regardless of the circumstances of their lives.

Among other components, the program teaches mindfulness, emotional regulation, self-awareness, and self-soothing. It also provides strategies to help people avoid destructive behaviors toward themselves and others. Although originally applied primarily to those suffering from borderline personality disorder, it has been effectively used with other kinds of problems, such as depression and anxiety. DBT, in fact, contains the kinds of skills that anyone—with or without a mental disorder—would benefit from practicing.

Gustav Geiger once wrote: "The position of women in a society provides the exact measure of the development of that society." New Age manipulators, religious tyrants, self-proclaimed progressives—really any type of problem person who views women as less-than—is living proof that there are plenty of ways to act "spiritual" and "evolved" without having achieved a level of genuine growth that would translate into enlightened action, especially when it comes to the treatment of women. Think about it: How many social and political activists, religious reformers, and spiritual gurus have truly elevated women's position in society? While they were fighting against oppression, when it came to women were they oppressing?

I remember reading an article written by a woman who had joined the men of the New Left "to usher in a New Age." They vowed to work toward greater social equality, yet regardless of the fact that she had been top of her class at Yale, instead of inviting her to engage in discussions the men relegated her to serving coffee. These "enlightened" intellectuals unilaterally determined that she

There are men who have a well-developed character and an innate sense of women's worth—and act accordingly.

would do whatever was necessary to support their heroic endeavors: typing their papers, addressing envelopes, and cooking meals. Their treatment of her was no different from the injustice they were railing against, and over time it had the same effect on her as a destructive relationship. Because of their denigrating treatment, she began to question her intelligence *and* her worth!

On the other hand, there *are* men who do not profess to be spiritually superior, and yet they have a well-developed character and an innate sense of women's worth—and they act accordingly. These men don't exhibit unreasonable resistance when it comes to sharing power in a relationship. They are comfortable with a woman claiming her own personal power since they know it will not rob them of theirs. It's an important contrast. Though these men, just like women, are not perfect, they are willing to change. Muhammed Yunus, who won a Nobel Peace Prize for his work, afforded women the opportunity to transform not only their own lives but also their families, communities, and country by offering microloans. No one had to convince him of women's worth and their ability to bring about possible change for all.

So as you move forward, consider carefully the consciousness of the men who cross your path, especially those who want to be invited into your world. Just because a man is intelligent and well read, has practiced a host of spiritual disciplines, and has attended personal empowerment workshops doesn't mean he's a genuinely good guy. He may be donning the robes of the modern prophet—a well-put-together business suit with the latest self-help book in hand—while, in reality he's still eager to ensnare you and whittle your self-worth away.

Paying Attention to Red Flags

Once you've left the relationship or at least gotten some distance from it, you'll be amazed at how much easier it is to see red flags. Reflect on the behaviors you contended with—and if you are co-parenting, pay attention to the mind games he continues to use to hook you. He may say things to get you to react emotionally so that he can be in control: "I don't think you're feeding the children properly," or "They look like orphans, when was the last time you bought them clothes?" He may become inappropriately personal as a way to test your boundaries and to see if he can coerce you into explaining or defending yourself: "Have you put on weight?" "The kids tell me you're seeing someone . . ." "Did you go out of town when the girls were at my house?" If he can get you to divulge personal information, he can feel like he's the one calling the shots.

If you've recently met someone who seems interested, pay attention to the signals he's sending. Is he overeager to get to know you? Do you find yourself spilling personal information about your financial status, employment, or lifestyle when you haven't known him long? Does he stare at you intently while you're talk-

Most importantly, listen to your gut.

ing, perhaps to the point that it makes you uncomfortable? Or does he use charm to make you feel at ease and relaxed? Do you find yourself falling in love fast instead of enjoying a relationship that slowly develops over time?

Perhaps most importantly, listen to your gut. Do you feel pressured to become intimate before you're ready? Does he engage in activities you're not comfortable with, such as drinking and driving? Is he already talking about marriage and painting a picture of a happy life together after only a few dates? Even if it feels flattering and taps into the part of you that really wants a lasting relationship, beware!

If he's truly interested in developing a commitment, he won't feel an urgent need to seal the deal.

However, it's also important to note that predators may operate a little differently. Though they often steer the relationship in the direction they want it to go, they can exude apparently endless patience so as not to frighten you off. Be mindful of the "now the gas is on, now it's off" pacing they are notorious for, as it is thoughtfully calculated to move you forward as though in a chess game—*his* chess game. If you appear nervous or suspicious, he will back off for a time, hoping you'll come to him, and when you do the forward motion resumes.

Lisa described her experience this way: "He rarely talked about himself and wasn't eager to divulge personal information. He kept the focus on me, sometimes showering me with gifts and compliments. Yet when I would tell him I couldn't spend so much time together on account of my children, he would automatically invite himself over to my house as though a commitment was already established. If I hesitated, he'd tell me that he understood and then back off, but I'd feel guilty and invite him to come over and watch a movie with us. I became more and more uncomfortable and finally listened to my gut and broke things off. Sure enough, he became verbally abusive the minute I told him I didn't think the relationship was a fit for me."

If you're unsure of what, exactly, the red flags are that you're seeing, talk to other women who've been there. Have friends "drop by" the restaurant when you're out on a date so they can meet him and see how he responds to sudden interruptions. Is he a bit put off since he really was hoping for some private time with you? Or does he seem so upset that you find yourself placating him and apologizing? Don't expect your friends to be able to completely figure him out. But if you're concerned—even if you think he might be the one—check him out. After all, there's a reason why men used to court women and meet their families. Set the pace and don't be afraid to put another pair of eyes on him. The patterns and behaviors you tend to be blinded to may be obvious to someone else—and it could end up saving you a lot of heartache.

Innocence and Naïveté Re-examined: Seeing Who People Really Are and Trusting Life Anyway

No matter how intelligent you are, remember that all of us have blind spots. Destructive behaviors can seem normal if you come from an abusive or dysfunctional family, and until you come to experience and understand healthy behaviors, you may not be able to detect a seemingly obvious problem person coming your way. Don't despair. It takes time to learn how to decipher these toxic behaviors and untangle any emotional or psychological knots you may have developed over the years. If you're getting out of a long-term relationship or a short-term one that really did a number on your head, you probably need time to heal and regain a more balanced perspective. Being involved with a destructive person can infect your thinking, normalizing the abnormal, and you may have to allow yourself a period of relationship detox in order to regain your equilibrium and come home to yourself. Quite literally, you will have to retool your brain and update your perceptions of people.

Despite the obvious contradictions involved in a destructive relationship, it's tempting to cling to the notion that everyone is good, deep down. But now that you've experienced another reality first-hand, it's difficult not to "have the scales fall from your eyes" (as my friend Trisha says). Not everyone is good, not everyone chooses to fulfill his or her potential, not everyone is interested in doing what is required to participate in a healthy relationship, and if you stubbornly disregard these facts of life you may find yourself right back in a bad situation.

The uncomfortable truth is that people run on a spectrum. Just as there are genuinely good people, there are also those with bad intentions; in some cases the worst of intentions. All you have to do is watch the evening news. Predatory individuals lack the ability to feel remorse and empathy, and do not exhibit any kind of conscience. This has been proven by scientific brain research that has found psychopaths to have abnormally low levels of right insula activity, the emotional and empathetic function in the brain. Like it or not, none of us is immune. In fact, according to the authors of LoveFraud.com, the person most in danger of being fooled by a psychopath or sociopath is someone who is generous, gives people the benefit of the doubt, and is financially stable. It's worth looking at the quiz offered on this Web site since it clearly demonstrates that you need not be the product of an abusive family, an alcoholic home, or a troubled childhood to fit the profile of an attractive mark. Basically, you just have to be a decent person.

> The person most in danger of being fooled by a psychopath or sociopath is someone who is generous, gives people the benefit of the doubt, and is financially stable.

Certainly it is worthwhile to explore the dynamics of our families of origin, since it's worth understanding which dysfunctional patterns may play a role in involvement with a destructive individual. Unearthing any prior abuse can help to unravel psychological issues that are keeping a woman stuck. Additionally, self-defeating behaviors can be replaced with more effective ways to be in the world—and in a relationship. Past history does matter. Yet when it comes to predators and other less-than-savory characters, you might just be their ideal woman not because there is anything wrong with you or anything dysfunctional about your family of origin, but simply because you're a nice person.

Don't be afraid to see people for who they really are. Don't automatically assume that others are good and that they're acting out of good intentions; that can be a form of denial and a way to perpetuate your naïveté and powerlessness when it comes to discriminating among different types of people. After all, intelligence is not the same as wisdom. Learning to trust your own perceptions despite the pressures and opinions of others may take some time. You can still believe that people are good at heart, yet it's also essential to learn to live with human contradictions. Not everyone has your best interests in mind.

In her book *Women's Reality: An Emerging Female System in a White Male Society*, Anne Wilson Schaef, Ph.D., sheds light on this internal conflict so common in women:

> *Women may shy away from developing mature and independent identities because they fear the loss of innocence . . . But there is a difference between innocence per se and childlike innocence, or naïveté. In order to maintain a childlike innocence, one must never grow up or be aware of one's surroundings. In other words, one can never have one's "consciousness raised." We fear that if we become "aware" we will no longer be able to hope. We will never be able to "fall in love" again. This is an embodiment of the "either–or" syndrome. Either we must hold on to our childlike innocence, or we will become cynical and hard. Either we must forego growing and changing, or we must accept the fact that we will be alone and joyless forever. What we forget is that we can have our feet on the ground and our head in the stars at the same time. We can be whole people while enjoying the other wholeness of being in love.*

Can letting go of these naive beliefs be painful? Yes. Will you feel grief, anger, and occasional cynicism as you release innocent notions? Probably. But will you also be more complete in who you are and better able to embody the genuine wisdom that can only come from experience? I believe so. A destructive relationship can shake us up; it can awaken us, so that we have the opportunity to move beyond naïveté—a dangerous place of ignorance—that can leave us vulnerable and dismissive of our own well-being. Some of us come to this new place of knowing with grace; others kick and scream, furious at having to relinquish an illusion that may have, at least partially, defined us. As Dr. Schaef writes:

As we mature into full adulthood . . . many of us find that the position of childlike innocence is impossible to maintain . . . We find we must begin standing up for the rights of others as well as those of our children and ourselves. We are plunged into awareness. And we are terrified! What happens is that we're faced with having to make a profound decision. We feel we have reached a "turning point" of Faustian proportions. Do we ignore oppression—and in essence perpetuate it? Or do we grow—and risk losing our childlike innocence forever? For many women, this choice involves a move into a state of anger, cynicism, and bitterness. It is important to remember that this is a temporary state and one of growth. Most women are afraid of being angry, cynical, and bitter for the rest of their lives once they take the first step in that direction. However, as we learn to embrace our anger, cynicism, and bitterness and work through it, we move into another developmental stage, one of "innocence with wisdom" . . . We can trust our perceptions while remaining open, vulnerable, and loving.

As Sophia put it: "I had to wake up and replace my childish notions with a more substantial wisdom. Now my eyes are open to both truths. I get to decide which part of the spectrum works for me, realizing that people fill the entire gamut."

With wisdom comes freedom—and responsibility. You have to learn to say no even if it hurts others' feelings; to set boundaries—which can be unpopular, especially if you've been a people pleaser; and to reject those who wish to harm you emotionally, psychologically, physically, or even spiritually. If you trust yourself, you'll trust life regardless of its unpleasant and occasionally disturbing dichotomies. You'll come to see people for who they really are and decide to trust life anyway!

Trusting Your Intuition: You Know More Than You Think You Do

Think back to the instances when you allowed the toxic man in your life to override your innate sensibilities. Study the scenarios.

Remember the feelings. Think about the pangs in your gut. Chances are there were many times you received warning signals viscerally in your solar plexus—or perhaps your thoughts raced and your pulse quickened—yet you found ways to silence them or put them aside with rationalizations. "He's always quick to anger after visits with his mother. He didn't mean to take it out on me—again." Well, now is the time to rekindle those vital instincts that can serve you so well. You needn't begin with a sophisticated system of warning bells. Simply excusing yourself to make a phone call when a situation doesn't feel right can be a wise course of action. Knowing when to consult with a trusted friend who knows the ropes when you have questions about someone you've recently met is always smart. Learn to listen to what your instincts are telling you.

Intuition is a powerful tool of detection, but until you can read its messages with accuracy, it is best to pay close attention to your level of bodily discomfort. Here are some strategies for dealing with warning signs . . . even if you're not quite sure where they're pointing:

- Ask questions. Ask more questions.
- Bring up discrepancies in his story as though you're "just curious" and may have misunderstood. Contradictory information can be ferreted out this way if you suspect he's lying.
- If you're uncomfortable with an offer to go to his place or dine at a secluded restaurant, insist that you only have a limited amount of time and will take a rain check.
- Feel free to say: "I'll think about it," "I'm not sure if I have an opening in my calendar," or "Let me get back to you" in order to give yourself time to sort through your feelings and consult others for advice if you feel uncertain. It's okay to stall until you feel sure about him.
- If your gut is uneasy, keep your eyes and ears open to clues that might tell you why.

What's the Real Story?

Brenda met Douglas on a flight to Denver. He seemed like an especially nice guy. When she returned from her trip, she found a message from him on voice mail, asking her out on a date. She made sure to meet him in a public place where they could sit and have a cup of coffee. The first date went well so she agreed to see him again, even though she felt a bit ambivalent.

During the second date she found him pressing her for information about her profession, telling her he was really enthusiastic about learning more about her methods. Yet Brenda felt he was trying to acquire free knowledge and advice. She became so uncomfortable that she decided it best to set a boundary. "Doug, I'd be happy to give you advice on a professional basis if your company would like to hire me as a consultant, but I prefer not to discuss my professional secrets in a personal setting. After all, it is my bread and butter." He told her that he understood.

Yet Doug continued to find ways to bring up topics that required Brenda to divulge information about her work. After insisting for the third time that he respect her boundaries, she got the same old song and dance. "I completely understand. I won't do it again." He did, and like most passive-aggressive men he simply dismissed her wishes and persisted after what he wanted.

Brenda broke things off with him after their fifth date. Doug, being such a "nice" guy, pleaded his case, insisting that he had done what she asked and that there was no reason for her to be angry. Luckily, Brenda had paid attention to her gut reactions from the beginning instead of dismissing them or minimizing Doug's actions—and this made all the difference. She got to see that she was right about her hunches. However, it's important to consider that in Brenda's case, Doug was a relatively safe guy to test her theory on. Others are not, and it's essential to determine whether you are safe to find out what, exactly, your intuition is trying to say.

- If everything looks good on the surface but you still feel uncomfortable . . . pay attention.
- If you're certain you're not interested, let him know that you don't think you're a match and "thanks but no thanks." Remember, the more you go against your own boundaries and drag things out, the easier it will be for him to control you as time goes on.
- If you feel totally in love, take a step back to see if you're blinded by the thrill of attraction and the attentions of someone interesting. Intoxication with alcohol or a flood of chemicals in the brain can also impair your judgment and the ability of your intuition to function on your behalf.
- Try giving *yourself* the benefit of the doubt for a change and see what it feels like.

Many people overestimate their ability to detect lying and dishonesty in others. Even professional practitioners, such as psychologists, psychiatrists, forensic examiners, and others with advanced education in human behavior, can have as much trouble detecting lying as the average layperson. So these experts can't detect dishonesty very well, how much harder must it be for the average woman who is eager to find a life partner and therefore all too ready to see only the best in her potential Mr. Right?

Understanding the Currency of Life Force Energy and the VNP: Valued National Product

Economically speaking, it's no secret that women's currency is undervalued. The good news is that while you may not be able to immediately change public policy, when it comes to relationships—that is, mature relationships—negotiating the terms is commonplace. "If I quit my job to raise our children, then you will be the one who brings home the paycheck." Or, "We both work outside of the home and so we'll need to share the chores in order to be a solid team." In situations such as these, both people's currency is brought to the table so a fitting balance can be put into place to ensure that the relationship thrives.

Now take a moment to think about your currency. What are the talents you offer? What qualities do you bring to a relationship? What are your strengths and what are your weaknesses? It's helpful at this stage to carefully consider your worth. Chances are that you've forgotten some valuable traits, especially if you received criticism and invalidating remarks that whittled away your self-esteem. Dig deep. Ask your friends what they think is special and unique about you? What do they think you do better than anyone else—plan parties? Parent? Solve computer problems? Reflect on what you have to offer. Feel who you are. Know what you have to give; not what you have to give away but what you have to give to others. This is your currency.

Destructive individuals don't value your currency except as it serves them. In most instances they are takers who, to remain in control, will not make equal exchanges; ultimately, the score must remain in their favor. As you begin to learn to discriminate, you will find that men who truly appreciate you, and your currency, will relate differently to you. They will take your opinion seriously. They won't feel threatened by your talents, and they will not attempt to misuse your "goods" for their benefit.

You must value your own currency by valuing yourself. If you don't, a problem person can sense it a mile off.

But here's the tricky part. You must value your own currency by valuing yourself. If you don't, a problem person can sense it a mile off. Certainly, you don't have to be an Amazon or shout out your personal tough-girl résumé from the rafters. Simply begin to grow your confidence in the qualities you possess, especially if the tactics of the toxic individual have taken their toll on your self-worth. Take them back and reclaim them one by one. Behaviors that illustrate ambivalence, too much people-pleasing, "Sure, whatever you'd like to do," and lack of personal power can send the wrong signals.

My friend Sandra has a comical summation of the way she felt after her toxic marriage ended as she picked up the pieces of herself. It goes like this: "I gave my battle cry for all women who had wrongfully been stepped on: 'Doormats to unite!' That is, if it's okay with everyone . . ." It took her a while to feel whole, yet as she observed others' treatment of her, she began to quickly catch on about which men showed respect for her and which simply wanted what she had to offer without concern for her needs.

Interacting Is Not the Same as Relating

Destructive relationships do not foster intimacy or consistent exchanges of love. On the contrary, they are based on power and control. Whether it's an alcoholic putting his booze first and tacitly expecting you to go along with the behaviors that accompany it; a passive-aggressive who strings you along so he can call the shots; or a wealthy, accomplished individual who uses money as an enticement as well as a weapon—all the men described in this book are more likely to establish patterns of interacting than of relating. Why? Because relating requires emotional connection, vulnerability, and mutual respect, and these qualities are always in low supply when it comes to dealing with toxic men.

Scientific studies have shown that regular doses of connection-type activities are essential to oxytocin production—the chemical that enhances bonding and attachment. Anthropologist Helen Fisher says: "Massage. Make love. These things trigger oxytocin and thus make you feel much closer to your partner." In other words, regular and sustained touch, talk, and attention, imbued with love, need to take place to create the kind of authentic intimacy that sustains a relationship. Simply interacting and participating in a push–pull dance that is unsatisfying leads to emotional deficits and, eventually, loneliness. Anne says it best: "We went everywhere together, yet never had I felt so alone." If a man is toxic, narcissistic, addicted to substances, work, or porn—or just plain emotionally unavailable—there will be little time for relating because he'll be too busy running his own game. Learn to tell the difference, since many destructive individuals genuinely believe their own lies or may have an inaccurate self-concept, believing that they are giving you an emotionally satisfying experience when, in reality, they are interacting with you as their needs—and sometimes their whims—dictate.

Don't Settle for Less: "I Want a Real Relationship (with Myself and Others)"

If you really, truly want a real relationship, you've got to get real. Now is a good time in the discrimination process to take an honest inventory about who you are and how you are in a relationship. If you have a tendency to pour on the charm to attract a mate, then wonder why he feels betrayed once he discovers that the woman he fell in love with is someone else, it might be time to rethink your strategies. Emotionally pulling someone's strings to make him desire you is not the same as getting to know someone. It is, instead, a recipe for disaster. If you are wedded to the idea that there are separate rules for men and women, I can guarantee that you're setting yourself up for antiquated gender dynamics whereby the man is in control—even if his methods are dressed up in the latest garb! Charlotte Kasl, Ph.D., author of *If the Buddha Dated: A Handbook for Finding Love on a Spiritual Path*, talks about John Gray's Mars and Venus perspective:

> *His book is based on stories the culture has created about all men and all women, stories that reinforce the false core. For example, in talking about the problems strong, independent women have in attracting*

men and how women need to need men, he writes: In the old days, a woman was in many ways helpless to provide for herself. She clearly needed a man. This helplessness actually made her very attractive to men and gave a man confidence to pursue her and the sense of purpose and responsibility to provide for her and be supportive.

The image of a man protecting a helpless woman sounds like a parent–child relationship, not one of two equal mates. It is clearly a cultural stereotype that deprives both people of their human potential and wholeness. Inequality of this sort is a prescription for a deadly relationship. In fact, it's not a relationship at all, it's two masks living together.

Dr. Kasl continues: "If someone falls in love with our mask, we have two choices: either we wear the mask and risk losing ourselves, or remove the mask and risk losing the relationship."

So, at this juncture, take a moment, take a month, take a year to determine how willing you are not only to *have* what you want in a relationship, but to *be* what you want in a relationship. It may be time to heal the past. Go into therapy for awhile to sort things out. Find a somatic psychologist or an Eye Movement Desensitization and Reprocessing (EMDR) or DBT practitioner to help rid you of post-traumatic stress symptoms, or of the accumulation of hurt, pain, and disappointment you've endured. Take a vacation. Start exercising, eat healthy foods, and rediscover your passions. Get some distance from harmful situations and people that pull you down. Join a 12-step group such as Al-Anon. Develop a new relationship with yourself and discover how you can be authentic, insightful and operate with integrity. After all, you will eventually need these skills—and a core self—to have a meaningful relationship with someone who truly loves and respects you.

> Take a moment, take a month, take a year to determine how willing you are not only to have what you want in a relationship, but to be what you want in a relationship.

What's EMDR Therapy?
Eye Movement Desensitization and Reprocessing (EMDR) is an advanced technology for releasing traumatic memories, changing negative core beliefs and unproductive behavioral patterns. It is also used for overcoming addictions, OCD (obsessive-compulsive disorder), and accompanying compulsive behaviors. It is especially effective with post traumatic stress and emotional distress. For more information go to emdr.com or webemdr.com

■ ■ ■ ■ ■

Learning to discriminate; to make distinctions; to tell the difference in others' motives and intentions; to better decipher intuitive messages and visceral red flags; and to more accurately size up and determine where a man is in his development and whether he's a good fit—all of these are important aspects of growing up and growing beyond the trappings of destructive relationships. They are tools of applied wisdom that are essential for women today. Additionally, they are the doors we ourselves walk through in order to come more fully into being and claim our own personal power, making more fitting choices for our sustained self-possession and well-being. As bestselling author and inspirational speaker Maya Angelou once said: "When you know better, you do better."

| 12 |

Sanity Comes First

"Sanity first" means taking care of yourself—vigilant self-care—and getting clear about your priorities, making certain you are not only part of the equation but *central* to it. It is nothing short of a radical act of self-love and applied wisdom. In *The Woman's Comfort Book: A Self-Nurturing Guide to Restoring Balance in Your Life*, Jennifer Louden puts it this way: "When we practice self-care, we start refusing to stay in relationships, jobs, and attitudes that depend upon our hating ourselves. We begin to see possibilities where before there were only habits."

What Would a Healthy Person Do?

Now that you've moved away from the insanity of a destructive relationship, it's time to create more sanity in your life. Figure out what that means for you. Have the residual effects of a toxic relationship left you feeling insecure? If you were involved with a compulsive liar, are you feeling overly paranoid? Having left an alcoholic or other type of addict, do you now find yourself trying to control others in the same way you tried to control the substance abuse? Dysfunctional patterns you carried into the relationship may have been exacerbated to the point that you don't feel quite like yourself. Or if your relationship barraged you with bizarre behaviors and disorienting maneuvers that you were forced to counter flying by the seat of your pants, you may still feel a bit crazy. Take time to find out what recipe, what loving magic, is needed to remedy the situation and restore you to sanity. You are worth it!

> Take time to find out what recipe, what loving magic, is needed to remedy the situation and restore you to sanity.

If sex addiction or substance abuse was part of the problem, you might want to check out a 12-step program. After all, addiction is a disease that spreads, and it could have insidiously altered your thinking, your behaviors, and your approach to life. If your self-esteem is at an all-time low, be kind to yourself, pamper yourself so that the real you who feels thrown about like confetti can be pieced back together. Take hot baths. Heal. Get healthy. If your confidence has been shaken, before you make big decisions, run them by people you trust. If you find that you're reacting to those around you, meditate, swim in the ocean, take refuge in cathedrals or art museums, get quiet with your cat, watch a movie, do whatever you need to do to get some serenity.

It may not happen overnight, but if you allow yourself some part of every day to relax in body, mind, and spirit, you'll regain your center. Perhaps a retreat is in order, or a workshop that can help you to get your head on straight. Maybe you need a vacation. Take one. It's essential that you make time and take the space to reconnect with yourself—no one can do this piece for you. No one. Not a new boyfriend; a former lover; a best girlfriend; a new dog. Sure, these connections are valuable and offer essential personal nourishment, but they cannot replace or be a substitute for your relationship with yourself.

Be on the lookout for the dark side of nurturing. If you are treating yourself a little too much—and it doesn't matter whether it's to facials, massages, new clothes purchases, what have you—make sure you aren't swapping one stressor for another. On the other hand, if you feel soothed by ice cream or chocolate and are consuming large quantities in the name of self-care, you might want to expand your repertoire before you have another problem on your hands.

In Jennifer Louden's *The Woman's Comfort Book*, she discusses nurturing gone awry: "Why do we sometimes allow comfort to limit our potential? Why do we sometimes comfort our-selves in not-so-great ways? To avoid responsibility, to hide in self-delusion, to remain self-righteous and safe from failure, and to avoid fear or anxiety are

> We've all ventured into self-care as an avoidance technique. We've all gone to the dark side.

possibilities." I would add . . . to numb ourselves from pain, to avoid moving out of naïveté, and to keep ourselves stuck by blaming other people or past circumstances. Not that Dr. Hannah and I have ever done these things ourselves, but we've read about it!

Seriously, we've all been there. We've all ventured into self-care as an avoidance technique. We've all gone to the dark side. Jennifer Louden says: "Entrenched patterns, pressure from friends or colleagues, and a deeply held belief that we don't deserve this good fortune, coupled with a lack of awareness, often lead us to comfort ourselves in an empty or self-abnegating style." As one of my clients confessed after her breakup, "I discovered that everything I'd been doing to 'nurture' myself ended up being bad for me. I had to find nourishment for my body, mind, and soul that didn't involve eating, shopping, or spending money with abandon. Once I turned things around, I could better experience what I would call true happiness. What a difference!"

In *Women Who Run with the Wolves*, Clarissa Pinkola Estes, Ph.D., talks about the dark side of nurturing in terms of a woman's "soul famine," which can result from abuse or oppression at the hand of another, or by the culture in which she lives, denial of her authentic self—and the expression of it—or rejecting the authentic self in order to fit in. What is important to note is that soul famine can make any of us susceptible to self-destructive behaviors whereby we turn nurturing activities into compulsions that, if we're not careful, can become addictions:

Overkill through the excesses, or excessive behaviors, is acted out by women who are famished for a life that has meaning and makes sense for them. When a woman has gone without her cycles or creative needs for long periods of time, she begins a rampage of—you name it— alcohol, drugs, anger, spirituality, oppression of others, promiscuity, pregnancy, study, creation, control, education, orderliness, body fitness, junk food, to name a few areas of common excess. When women do this they are compensating for the loss of regular cycles of self-expression, soul-expression, soul-satiation.

Put Yourself in the Equation

As you've probably figured out, and indeed, learned from experience, destructive relationships starve women; they shrink us to fit someone else's requirements and, if we're not careful, they can turn us into imposters as we distort our true selves in an attempt to survive and keep our deeper vitality intact. To again quote Dr. Estes: "The vision a woman has for her own life can also be decimated in the flames of someone else's jealousy or someone's plain-out destructiveness toward her . . . No woman can afford to let her creative life hang by a thread while she serves an antagonistic love relationship . . .

In all likelihood your toxic relationship left you hungry if not soul-starved. Perhaps previous deficits were partly responsible for your involvement in such a relationship; the promise of a nourishing and loving connection seduced your heart. Yet even if you entered into the relationship with some holes in your soul or a hungry heart, chances are the problem was compounded by the tactics of the destructive individual. By their very nature, these tools of control are designed to sever a woman's relationship with her true self. Think about it. What does a colonizing power first do to the original inhabitants if it wants to overpower them and leave them emotionally, psychologically, and spiritually decimated? It removes all the rituals, spiritual practices, creative endeavors, and methods of personal expression that are the heart and soul of the culture. Devastated people are much easier to control. Sufficient wounding of the psyche can make any of us, no matter how bright, no matter how strong, lose our soulful moorings, if only temporarily.

> **Devastated people are much easier to control.**

The good news is that there is a remedy. It's an elixir of your own design; a personalized program of self-care to revitalize your mental health, renew your physical well-being, and beef up your spiritual core. Engage yourself in satisfying activities and experiences, take time to come home to yourself, feel what is in your heart, act on it, and be sure to avoid those who wish to keep you down.

My good friend Sue, who came from a highly dysfunctional family and as a result married a man who operated in much the same way, tells me that she often asks herself, *What would a healthy person do?* Upon exiting her marriage, she realized that she hadn't acquired healthy patterns for self-care. She wasn't even certain she knew what it meant for her, so she made an effort to find out. "I read every self-help book I could get ahold of, I wrote in a journal, I tried therapy and put what I learned into practice. I now know when a mindless activity is just what the doctor ordered or when I need something nourishing like a creative project, a bath, or a nap. I can better tell when I'm off-balance and,

> **Vigilant self-care is a lifestyle choice.**

more importantly, I now know what to do about it because I am in touch with my own needs. It's simply part of my lifestyle at this point. I couldn't conceive of living any other way!"

Take the opportunity to take better care of yourself and really learn what sanity and self-care means *for you*. Remember, what fits for a friend may not be your spiritual succor and may not be emotionally fulfilling or your brand of real soul food. You have been through an ordeal. Your self-esteem is capsized, and it's time to right your ship. In *Emotional Sobriety: From Relationship Trauma to Resilience and Balance*, Tian Dayton, Ph.D., describes it this way:

The ability to self-regulate, to bring ourselves into balance, is key to emotional sobriety. But when our limbic system has become deregulated through chronic stress or crisis, our emotional rheostat loses some of its capacity to regulate itself. When we have a hard time regulating ourselves, our moods, relationships, life, and emotional balance are affected . . . Science can now illuminate why approaches like psychodrama, 12-step programs, group therapy, journaling, bodywork, yoga, exercise, and massage work . . . why changing the way we live and the nature of our relationships can change the way we think and feel, and vice versa; and why fixes don't work but why a new design for living does.

In fact, during the last few decades science has been taking a careful look at the neuropsychological mechanisms that bring about the positive, stress-reducing effects of talk therapy, meditation, support groups, and even just having a good cry on a friend's shoulder. Although far too complicated to summarize here, the findings suggest that not only does the brain drive our emotions and behavior, but our behavior and emotions literally cause change in our brain! This is why studies have found that, for some cases of depression, psychotherapy alone can be as effective as drug therapy alone. That's because psychotherapy can modify how we think, which in turn can alter how our brain functions.

Make Promises You Can Keep: Five Ways to Keep Your Soul Intact

For now, despite what is swirling around you—divorce court, face-to-face exchanges, division of property, he won't stop calling or you can't seem to get him out of your head—keep the focus on yourself. Don't get me wrong. If you need to purge clothes that he picked out for you or burn some photos and old love letters, by all means do so. It can be cathartic. If you need to move halfway across the country or to a different continent, go ahead. You can even complain endlessly about him to friends, but only if you don't do it at the expense of taking care of yourself. Believe it or not, anything and anybody can be used as a distraction. If you find that you're avoiding revitalizing activities and only have time to lament the past, you'd better find out why—because it's insane.

Taking the focus off the pain is important. So is making a commitment to yourself and being responsible for your own well-being. Here are five promises that, though simple, have far-reaching results. They'll even produce some miracles if you integrate them over time so that they become part of your lifestyle instead of a temporary fix. You won't do them perfectly, so don't even try. The point is to love yourself enough to do them as you can, when you can.

Number One: Ask yourself what you need, every day.

At first you may not be sure. Doesn't matter. Keep asking. Are you tired? Do you need time with your children? Are you missing visits to the museum to view your favorite works of art? Even though you might not be able to do what is needed *right now*, planning to give it to yourself and figuring out when it's possible to schedule into your calendar can be psychologically rewarding. Letting yourself know that you care enough to consider what your soul is calling out for, what your body and mind need, sends a powerful signal to the psyche. It's the equivalent of a love letter—*to yourself*. And isn't it empowering to know that your self-care is not contingent upon the actions of others? Any others give you is a wonderful, heart-warming bonus!

Number Two: Nourish your soul.

Whatever keeps your faith strong, do it. If it's involving yourself in music; practicing a spiritual disciple; spending time at your place of worship; communing with nature; having close, connected time with loved ones; dancing in front of the mirror naked; whatever it is, make sure it is part of your life. Don't deprive yourself of soul food.

Number Three: Give up perfectionism.

Not all of us are bona fide perfectionists, but even small doses of perfectionism and its related behaviors can be self-defeating. What's involved in giving them up? First of all, it's important to be gentle with yourself when you make mistakes; genuine mistakes, not excuses for irresponsible behavior. Be mindful. Some things cannot be figured out until we're actually in them. Saying "I should have known better" and beating yourself up is a waste of time. If, on the other hand, you neglected warning signals, take notice so you can have the opportunity to do better next time. Second, love who you are. Be honest about your problem areas and make a commitment to learn healthier behaviors, yet do it with love. I can promise you, you'll achieve better results—and have so much more energy to create the changes you want.

> Employing joy, self-love, and inspiration are far more effective tools for doing things differently whether it is weight loss, strategies for success, or reworking the structure of your life.

In fact, Debbie Johnson, author of *Think Yourself Thin* and *Think Yourself Young*, uses scientifically based applications of focused imagination as a way to activate change. As her books illustrate, employing joy, self-love, and inspiration are far more effective tools for doing things differently whether it is weight loss, strategies for success, or reworking the structure of your life.

Number Four: First things first.

Most women reflexively place others before them and, as a result, get caught up in others' dramas and agendas while losing sight of what is truly important. We mix up emotional priorities and then have trouble putting first things first, especially if putting ourselves first is what is required. We accommodate beyond what is reasonable. Author and lecturer Anne Wilson Schaef, Ph.D., is right on the money when she says: "When I'm all hassled about something, I always stop and myself what difference it will make in the evolution of the huma species in the next ten million years, and that question always helps me to get back my perspective."

Learn what your real priorities are, and then learn to place them in their proper order. They might be out of whack or need some fine-tuning. In fact, it is highly likely that they will need some updating if you've been involved with a toxic individual. Take some time to figure out what matters to you most and act accordingly. There is power in priorities. Besides, it can make your life much easier by helping to moderate your time and energy expenditures. Think about it—if it's not of genuine importance, why bother?

Number Five: Don't go to the hardware store for milk.

Yes, it sounds funny, but it's quite profound. If there are people you can't depend on, don't keep asking them for favors. If your parents are emotionally unavailable and don't get you, don't keep expecting them to understand your deepest thoughts and desires. You get the idea. It's really important to understand who people really are and what they can offer. Not what you want them to give you, but what they are actually capable of giving you. Basing your expectations on what is instead of how you want things to be saves you a lot of heartache, disappointment, and potential conflict.

Believe it or not, this is a powerful way to take care of yourself. You stop placing your destiny in incapable hands; you no longer cast pearls before swine and expect certain people to share your views or even understand what you're saying; and you don't waste time and energy trying to control others so they act, think, feel, and behave as you would like. Instead you select those you can trust. You decide who is on your wavelength, and you apply wisdom when it comes to loving others and holding them in confidence. Like accepting life on life's terms, you accept others on their terms. You can't force them to change, so isn't it wiser to choose accordingly? Accepting others as they are even if you don't like the truth of it is a sign of emotional

spiritual development and increases the odds
...stence.

...ing from a person who is incapable of giv-
...d saying goes—like barking up the wrong tree. I've
...n a number of clients who hoped that a parent who was
...ant and unemotional toward them throughout their childhood
would suddenly become loving and affectionate toward them now,
when they were adults. In my estimation, this is an exercise in futility, a waste of time and precious life energy. Generally, people don't
change that much. The only change we can or should expect is the
change we can make in our responses toward others.

Finding Support and a Support Network

Support networks come in many forms. For some of us, our family
provides love and support. For others, it's our handpicked family of
choice. Still others seek out support groups, book clubs, and sports
teams. They take a photography class to be with others of similar
interests. Or maybe flying lessons . . . Perhaps one group doesn't fulfill all our needs, and so we divide our time among several.

No matter what route we go, one thing is central: We all need
support. Not to belabor the point, but if addiction was part of the
relationship dynamic, it makes sense to find a knowledgeable group
so you can educate yourself about the disease and its manifestations.
In cases where children are involved, it can be a lifesaver, helping
you to react less, helping them to understand Daddy's behavior more
so they don't personalize adult problems that don't belong to them.
Even if you hang out at the local cafe to chat it up with the locals,
great! Isolation can be an impediment to healing as well as an impediment to happiness. It's not emotionally or psychologically sane. So
piece together the combination that works best for you and ask for
the support you need.

In the Sisterhood

Helping one another is part of the religion of our sisterhood.

—LOUISA MAY ALCOTT, WRITER, ABOLITIONIST, AND EDUCATOR

Women *love* to gather—and it's actually *good* for us! Having a close group of girlfriends is invaluable. It keeps us mentally and emotionally healthy. In fact, when women get together the level of the hormone oxytocin elevates so we feel more relaxed. And being innate bonders, it's natural for us to join together with other women. As Shelley E. Taylor's research shows us, women under stress seek out the company of other women to help keep us in balance.

Tend and Befriend

Research by Shelley E. Taylor at UCLA re-examined the differences between men and women when facing danger. Previous studies on stress were conducted with male subjects, so this new study focused on women's biochemical reactions. It was discovered that women have a tend-and-befriend type of response rather than a "fight-or-flight." Women's instinctive tendency to stress is to nurture their young, cook or clean, and seek social contact and support from others, especially females.

My friend Kari Henley, founder of GatherCentral.com, has devised an array of gathering groups for women so they can stay connected during good times and bad. Kari loves to point out that unbeknownst to many, heart disease is the number one cause of death among women; moreover, a study by the UCLA Department of

Psychiatry found that the number one contributor to heart disease is not obesity or stress, but loneliness. With women being so relational, the social isolation of the present day can actually kill us if we don't make efforts to surround ourselves with meaningful friendships—preferably more than four friends each. (Studies found that those with fewer than four friends were more than twice as likely to die of heart disease!)

Look beyond fast-food friendships to a circle of quality friends.

But quality matters. Not only are fast-food friendships unsatisfying, but it's essential to be aware of the type of women you let into your circle of friends. The Quantum Leaps Aficionados Pod (as they call themselves) is a network of women's groups who jump-started their life with a Transformational Life Coaching session with me and then went on to formalize ongoing support for accelerated personal growth and creative life change. The Aficionados stress the importance of being with authentic women of high integrity. After all, trust is deeply important when it comes to feeling safe within a group setting. These women make sure the code of the group is upheld; otherwise, as we all know, gossip and criticism can threaten solidarity—not to mention the ability to open up, laugh, and reveal our unique selves. As Marianna often quips, "I love to hang out in the sisterhood!" Take some time to find one, or create one, for yourself . . . and surround yourself with the power of being among true sisters, all of whom have an incredible story to share!

Sanity, serenity, and sisterhood!

| 13 |

Why Keep Fighting Your Essential Self?

The writer Anaïs Nin once said: "We do not grow absolutely, chronologically. We grow sometimes in one dimension, and not in another, unevenly. We grow partially. We are relative. We are mature in one realm, childish in another." In truth, we never completely arrive because we, unlike the Powers That Be, are not all-knowing. We cannot always see ahead. We get hooked and entangled in scenarios that squeeze us into greater knowing even when we're certain we didn't sign up for *this* particular ride!

I remember one lovely client, Rachel, telling me, "I can't be married to an alcoholic—I'm Jewish! Jews don't do alcoholism!" I responded, "Oh, you're right, I forgot. You're the Chosen People, but not chosen for *that*!" We both had a good laugh and then went about the business of transforming her life—her life with an alcoholic. When in the middle of our session she lamented, "I should have seen it. I'm so smart. I should have figured it out!" I reminded her that every one of us will at some point be confronted with unfamiliar scenarios and alien behaviors that will require us to develop new life strategies. Some things we have to find out through trials and tribulations. Life is our teacher. At other times, when we're ready, the professor appears; the leaflet drops into our lap; we hear a story on TV that opens us to a new level of awareness. But it is up to us to develop it or not. Honestly, it takes a level of humility to admit that we may have made bad choices; we may have stayed too long. Remaining stuck in self-pity, self-hatred, and self-blame serves no one, least of all us.

Self-Blame: Taking Responsibility for People, Events, and Situations You Cannot Control

To take responsibility for people, events, and situations you cannot control is, quite frankly, a self-centered position. It's a tad arrogant to think you have that much power over others as well as power over the cosmic swirling of events that transpire every day, whether under your own roof or in some distant land. Don't get me wrong. We *are* powerful. We *do* make a difference. The actions we choose do have an impact; they reverberate outward, affecting the lives of others. Yet taking responsibility as if you could determine the outcomes, as if you could calculate the free-will-to-divine-intervention ratio and actually exert enough control over the destiny of others . . . well, I get exhausted just thinking about it!

No matter how intelligent you are, no matter how aware, you will always come up against situations that you do not understand and, once again, will find yourself on a learning curve. My friend and colleague Deborah Genovesi likes to say: "Life is one big learning curve. Once you get off that learning curve, you're dead." I couldn't agree with her more. As the Al-Anon slogan goes: "You didn't cause it, you can't cure it, and you can't control it." It's a potent reminder that only so many things are within our control. The point is to become comfortable with that "limitation" because, in the end, it frees you up to be responsible for what is truly important for the only person you ultimately do have control over: you.

Lately I've observed an interesting phenomenon that can exacerbate over-responsibility for others' behavior and set you up for a dangerous cycle of self-blame. It's a New Age version of "you brought it on yourself." While it's important to explore unhealthy patterns and behaviors that can keep you locked in a dysfunctional cycle in which bad-news individuals are continually drawn to you, to act as if you are at fault for their destructive behaviors or you are "bringing this on yourself" without consideration of the interplay between individuals is ridiculous. And in cases where the main reasons a predator is attracted to you are that you're kind, generous, give people the benefit of the doubt, and are financially stable, blaming the victim is abusive and inappropriate.

Sure, we must take responsibility for our actions. Fair enough. But using this tack to chastise yourself for becoming enmeshed in a bad situation is counterproductive and, quite frankly, will only serve as a way to make you feel worse. Perpetually trying to figure out what you've done "wrong," believing that it must have been something you did to bring this upon yourself, is insane. Shit happens—and sometimes it happens to *you*. That doesn't mean it was within your control. Instead of saying, *I should have, I could have . . .* , think in terms of: *What can I do now that I have more information about myself and others— and a better sense of the extent of my reach when it comes to changing other people and shaping events?*

A psychologist I was privileged to meet during my sixteen years in family court proceedings often quoted me the Serenity Prayer. It goes like this:

God grant me the Serenity to accept the things I cannot change; the Courage to change the things I can; and the Wisdom to know the difference.

It's an important measuring stick because it calls upon you, upon each of us, to assess every situation with prudence and wisdom and then act with discrimination and commitment.

Beating Ourselves Up for Our Mistakes: "How Could I Have Fallen in Love with an Abuser?"

"I should have known better. All the signs were there," we hear ourselves say. It's a familiar lament. Yet remember, we are relational. Each one of us falls in love with someone who is flawed. Can we know ahead of time how badly wounded a person is? How addicted? How toxic? Often we can't. Relationships, like life, are like peeling an onion, and it can take some time for the rotten pieces to emerge. Even when they do, we may minimize, deny, or simply be uncertain how to interpret what we're experiencing. Besides, we may fall in love with someone's essence or potential, and the powerful feelings in our heart overshadow the ugly truth that we're in a destructive relationship.

Now, if you have a tendency to fall for bad-news individuals, learning more about healthy relationships—how they work, what they look like, and what's involved in being in one—may well be worth your time. Destructive men come in many forms, no doubt. Yet as John Gottman, Ph.D., and Nan Silver point out in *The Seven Principles for Making Marriage Work:* "The determining factor in whether wives feel satisfied with the sex, romance, and passion in their marriage is, by 70 percent, the quality of the couple's friendship. For men, the determining factor is, by 70 percent, the quality of the friendship. So men and women come from the same planet after all." True, we can't always control who we fall in love with. However, we *can* choose who we want to be involved with and to whom we commit. It's an important distinction that affords us the opportunity to make different choices in the future. Just because you love someone doesn't mean you must sacrifice your well-being to be in a relationship with him. On the contrary, you owe it to yourself to choose a scenario that's a better fit. Be grateful you have the capacity to love. Now it's up to you to decide how to wield such an exquisite force and with whom. Beating yourself up only serves to make you miserable. It makes you wrong for having loved.

In fact, common wisdom among Imago Relationship therapists, who view intimate partnership as a path toward healing and growth, is that with every relationship—as long as we are growing in consciousness and becoming more aware of how our childhood wounds are getting reactivated—it grows more likely that our *next* relationship will be more conscious and fulfilling for us.

> We can't always control who we fall in love with. However, we can choose who we want to be involved with and to whom we commit.

Avoid the Guilt Traps: Dealing Constructively with Anger, Frustration, and Fear

It's not unusual to feel guilty for having left the relationship. Regardless of the fact that we know it was the right thing to do, our minds can play tricks on us. Don't forget, not only are women relational, but we are also encouraged to believe that the responsibility for the success or failure of a relationship rests on our shoulders. As a result, we can come up with all kinds of scenarios whereby we could have done something differently, we could have been more agreeable or more understanding and then it would have worked. We wouldn't have had to leave. While reflection is important and pinpointing mistakes can be helpful, guilt only perpetuates self-blame and the illusion that we could have made things different *somehow*.

If you continue to deal with the problem man in efforts to share custody and time with your children, he may work hard to play on your sympathies and make you feel bad. He's more than happy to have you take all the blame since he has no intention of admitting any wrongdoing. Or if he does, it can be a manipulation to draw you back in emotionally, making you think, one more time, that maybe he's changed. Be careful. If you're feeling guilty, you're susceptible to others holding you accountable for things that you are only partially responsible for. Don't buy into it. If you need to, write out a list to remind yourself of all the things you did in an attempt to improve the situation, all the things he did to sabotage stability and emotional connection, and why you finally decided to move on. Get a more realistic perspective. Nothing is wrong with you because you wanted something better, you desired a more loving relationship, and you didn't thrive on conflict. In fact, everything is right with you for these very reasons. Don't give the power to validate your actions to him or anyone else for that matter. Guilt only severs you from the confidence of knowing you made the best choice, even if it wasn't the easiest one.

When it comes to anger, frustration, and fear, first and foremost, remember that these emotions are normal. You have been through an ordeal. Once you get beyond some of the pain, anger usually bubbles to the surface. Feel it and use it as a constructive force in your life, not a destructive one. If you're feeling unhinged, scream in your car. Call a friend who is comfortable with a tirade of release and move through the anger. Chances are, you stuffed your anger down for a long time and allowed it to

Anger and love are powerful forces for change. Don't use one without the other.

fester into resentments. That they are coming out is a sign that you are ready to heal and reclaim your identity. You may even be angry at yourself for giving yourself away to someone who treated you so badly. Have compassion for yourself. Gnaw on a pretzel. Laugh until you cry. Especially if you're feeling frustrated and fearful about handling your own life, use anger to break through the inertia. As a therapist friend once told me: "Anger and love are powerful forces for change. Don't use one without the other."

The process of ending and healing from a bad relationship, with its roller coaster of conflicting emotions, is quite similar to the grieving process when we are faced with our own death or that of a loved one. As initially proposed by Elizabeth Kübler-Ross, the process takes place in five stages. These stages—shock, denial, anger, depression, and acceptance—are the human psyche's way of adjusting to a major loss. The stages may emerge even in those cases where a woman is the one to break off her relationship with a destructive man. It is, after all, still a loss; the loss of what could have been, the loss of a dream, the loss of the comforts of having a partner. It is, in fact, a kind of death.

Moving Past Self-Doubt: "Can I Trust Myself to Be in a Healthy Relationship?"

Destructive relationships can shake our confidence and make us wonder not only if we're worthy of a good relationship but if we're even capable of having one. Certainly, for all of us, there's room for improvement. And don't forget, the limbic system in the brain which regulates emotions and helps to keep us balanced has probably been affected by our experience; truth be told, we may not be at our best when it comes to discriminating between the good guys and the bad ones. Compound this with other emotional adjustments such as dealing with being alone and having to handle all of the household responsibilities—plus any children—with limited assistance, and you have a situation ripe for a destructive relationship. After all, desperation, a hungry heart, and loneliness can be beacons to a problem person, especially one who would love to "be nice" and rescue you.

Does that mean you should lock yourself in a closet until everything is at its best? Absolutely not. Just be aware of what's driving your need to be in another relationship. Be like my friend Sandra: "I always run a guy by a group of friends known as the Bozo Committee. They simply have a better radar system than I've ever had for whatever reason and I can depend on their input." Make it fun. And don't be afraid to ask yourself the question posed by Dr. Kasl in her book, *If the Buddha Dated:* "My question about any rules or prescriptions for love from a spiritual point of view are these: Do they help people relate from essence—that clear-seeing part of us that is love, kindness and true—or do they limit people and separate them from their authentic self?"

When it comes to a practical plan, I highly recommend Dr. Barbara De Angelis's book, *Are You the One for Me?* It's a thorough assessment of both sides of a relationship—yours and his—and she's not afraid to venture into the territory of destructive relationships. Another approach is to make a list that has three components. In one column make a list of what you need in a relationship. In another, write down all the things you will not tolerate: addictions, affairs, verbal, psychological, and emotional abuse, spending problems, issues with children, and so on. Be thorough. Knowing what you don't want is just as important as knowing what you do want. Last, write down things you may not be thrilled about but can accept in the name of "we're all just human."

Knowing what you don't want is just as important as knowing what you do want.

Carry your lists with you when you go on a date. Halfway through dinner, excuse yourself to the restroom and review them. If you find yourself giving him the benefit of the doubt when the answer is already evident, be mindful! "He's already had three drinks, but it doesn't necessarily means he's an alcoholic," you say. True, he may not be an alcoholic, but it is a red flag. Break an old pattern and pay attention. Even if you decide to go out on another date, you can make certain that you continue to keep an eye on any concerns you have instead of relying on old habits—habits that probably helped to get you into a pickle in the past. Take yourself seriously—and don't get serious before you're certain he is worth the investment and that, with him, you're authentic self can shine!

■ ■ ■ ■ ■

Self-blame, self-hatred, self-doubt . . . the panacea? Love, forgiveness, patience, acceptance, compassion, and gratitude toward yourself and the incredible life you have been blessed to live as well as the amazing one you are now creating. As the poet Hafiz once wrote: "I wish I could show you, when you are lonely or in darkness, the astonishing light of your own being." Remember this light—it is you.

| 14 |

Having a Better-Than-Normal Life

Regroup, renew, and reinvent. These are the three stages and phases that you will go in and out of for the rest of your journey. It is a journey forward, not back . . .

—LAURA CAMPBELL, LIFE TRANSITION COACH AND FOUNDER OF
DISCOVERTHEDSPOT.COM

Be grateful. You could have waffled. You could have allowed the status quo to prevail and been held captive to inertia. Did you? No. You made a choice, a powerful choice, to reclaim yourself and your life. Celebrate! Will it all be chocolate and roses? Probably not, yet as you shape your routines, waltz cheek-to-cheek with the challenges, and fully inhabit your own skin, you'll feel something deeper moving in you—and in your life. You've grown and become wiser. You know more about your weaknesses and behaviors that can hook you into old patterns and now you have more choices about how to respond, when to say no, when to let go—and when to run! You get to walk with your own imperfections, knowing that your humanity is your strength as well as a doorway to greater knowing that will continue to inform your life, daily. Flow happens. The ineffable currents that pulse through you bring rewarding surprises and lessons from deep within. As your awareness grows, you experience divine timing and manifest your dreams by merely whispering them in your own ear.

Magic can happen despite what is taking place around you. Trust yourself and you can trust your life.

Flourishing Despite the Ups and Downs

No matter what details remain, no matter which issues are unresolved, you are off the runway, have taken flight, and are moving toward a new destination. Enjoy what is good. Relish the novelty. Although there will be setbacks and less-than-jubilant days, as you come back to center and expand into your new situation, no matter how humble, no matter how grand, the opportunity to reinvent yourself is wide open. Dive in. And when you feel low, think about how far you've come and what you left behind. You had a vision of something better. Continue to imagine it and mobilize your energy toward creating it, one day at a time. Any setbacks are temporary, and may actually point you in a different, more interesting, direction. Be resilient. Have chutzpah. Remember that you are a testimony to success.

> "I have more of myself to share with my children. We play more, laugh more, and cry less."

Mary Elizabeth put it like this: "Now that I deal with the destructive man in my life only minimally, I have more of myself to share with my children. We play more, laugh more, and cry less. I've gone back to massage school to complete my degree and was surprised to find that the students, though younger, welcomed me with open arms. They like me. I feel like I'm the cheerful person I used to be but there's also more substance. I feel a bigger identity growing inside, and everyone, especially my family, benefits."

Joining forces with life is nothing short of a leap of faith. It's a leap worth taking. It forms a partnership. You are free to fall in love, to become re-enchanted, not in the sense that you return to a state of naïveté; rather, you develop a deep trust that prevails despite hardships and surface dramas. You have entered more fully into the stream of life and, as such, you will redefine yourself and your existence as needed. Having passed through the gauntlet of a destructive relationship, you are primed for full participation and it is up to you to open to higher guidance in order to go to the next level and invite in unimaginable authenticity.

Yes, you may be frightened to take such a quantum leap. No matter, It awaits and the timing is up to you. In Martia Nelson's book *Coming Home: The Return to True Self*, she reminds us of what is required to take the leap and what rewards are available:

> So often in our daily lives we block things we don't want to hear because of the conflict we'll feel. Yet in turning to higher guidance we ask for the truth. To the degree that we want to expand beyond our previous limitations, we long for it. But to the degree that we still want control over the details of our lives, we resist the truth and fear its touch. The pull toward truth is often equaled by our resistance to it; the ambivalence is our reluctance to choose between empowerment and control.

Having passed through the gauntlet of a destructive relationship, you are now primed for full participation in life.

It is precisely this ability to commit to an authentic life, one of truth, that enables you to create a more meaningful intercourse with existence so your center holds regardless of the actions and agendas of others. By incorporating vigilant self-care, wisdom, survival smarts, courage, and genuine self-possession whereby you listen to your intuitive inner voice, you will flourish even with the fluctuations that will inevitably come your way. Just remember, no matter how empowered you are, or how strong you become, you need not do it alone. On the contrary, invite in others who understand. Not to dwell on the past but to help you to develop a greater understanding of what transpired so it has significance instead of becoming a past regret. It has shaped you. It did not break you.

The Possibility of a New Relationship

"One day my heart just opened up and I knew I was ready to love again, to make love again, and to open to someone special. I didn't have to jump into the first thing that came along. I was guided by self-respect and though I felt honored to have the attention, I knew I wanted more genuine connection whether it lasted two weeks or twenty-five years. By changing myself, I changed my approach to relationships; I was guided more by confidence than neediness or the fear of being alone. To me, that's liberation!"

> Remember: The destructive relationship shaped you, it did not break you.

There will come a time when you feel ready to engage in a new relationship. Or at the very least contemplate one. Maybe a former lover has moved back into town; maybe there's a friend with whom you can have a flirtation, enjoying the rumbling of feelings, the attraction, and the scent of love. Though you may be hungry, don't let desperation drive you. The lessons of the past are there to inform you; they are not there to hold you back. Indulge in the aliveness of your womanhood. Think. Get clear about what you want and what you don't want. Enjoy the possibility and invite it in. See who shows up. You never know what surprises await you!

One client, Julia, had such a funny experience when she finally felt ready to date: "I felt a shift take place inside of me right before I headed back to New York. Wouldn't you know it? On the first leg of the flight I met a really nice guy, kind and handsome. Then, on the second leg out of Denver, I sat next to a long-legged model who was sexy beyond belief. Why not? It was the lusty month of May! As if that wasn't enough, my shuttle driver was a gorgeous and exotic man from Argentina. We struck up a delightful conversation and when he dropped me off, he

> The lessons of the past are there to inform you; they are not there to hold you back.

He's Just No Good for You

gave me a kiss on the cheek, told me I was the most beautiful woman inside and out, and teased, 'Next time you're in the city, I'll marry you!' If you ask me, the universe was giving me a nod, tossing out a smorgasbord of men for me to enjoy in a safe way so I would feel more comfortable getting back in the dating fray."

Don't rush. It takes courage to love after coming out of a destructive relationship and confidence to cut things off if you smell a rat. Be creative. Try original methods of discernment. Elaine describes her approach: "I dated videos for a while. By that I mean that I watched romantic comedies and action films and quite literally studied the qualities of the actors, deciding what I liked and what wasn't comfortable to me as though they were potential dates. It was very helpful. When my friends introduced me to Eric, I could see qualities in him I liked in a variety of actors. I felt at ease. We fit together in such an effortless way. I never knew marriage could be like this. It sounds funny to say but I studied those videos, which made me more thoughtful about what, exactly, I wanted."

Just a quick word of caution here . . . be mindful as you re-enter the world of relationships. Many of us become caught up in another destructive relationship and recycle aspects of the past. Some of us think that this particular brand of problem person isn't going to be so bad until we discover that we're back in an old, familiar position, struggling to keep our self-esteem intact. If this does happen, don't be hard on yourself. These men wear many guises; it's difficult to know them all. And if you have a few issues left to confront and heal, some rough edges that are in need of change, take the steps necessary to deepen your learning and grow. That's the good news. You have the power to change. You've already proven it once. Don't despair if you have to go back and take a higher-level course. Just trust that you can transform the experience into meaningful wisdom. Don't give up on love.

A Fulfilling Life Is Not Necessarily a Perfect One

None of us has a perfect life. None of us. And the temptation to judge your insides by other people's outsides can be overwhelming. The fact is, outside appearances can be deceiving. Many of us already know this firsthand. So be careful not to fall into the fallacy that everyone out there has more money, a more fulfilling job, a better relationship, or children who are better behaved. When it comes down to it, none of us knows the complete story of others' lives. So what sense does it make to draw unnecessary comparisons? They only make you feel bad and can delude you into thinking that you're coming up short when, in fact, you may have more good things going right than you realize. For all you know, if you probed more deeply, you'd discover scenarios that you'd just as soon leave on their doorstep . . . and *your* situation may start to look really good despite the negatives!

In the end, comparisons are fruitless. They're just another way to focus on the external, or at least the appearance of the external, when in truth creating a fulfilling life is an inside job. That doesn't mean you don't work to bring it into form . . . of course you do! But it begins inside by answering these questions: *What do I want? What makes me feel genuine joy? What fills me up on all levels?* Build a life that is centered on Self.

> **Build a life that is centered on Self.**

Decide, for yourself, what elements are fulfilling to you. Painting portraits on weekends? Outings with your kids? The fact that your parents live nearby and you get to see them often? Maybe you enjoy your career; the city or town in which you live; frequent visits to the ballet—or the rodeo? It doesn't matter what it is, just that it's fulfilling to *you*.

Thomas Moore, in his book *The Re-Enchantment of Everyday Life*, talks about satiating the soul:

> The soul needs to be fattened, not explained, and certain things are nutritious, while others are without taste or benefit. Good food for the soul includes especially anything that promotes intimacy: a hike in nature, a late-night conversation with a friend, a family dinner, a job that satisfies deeply, a visit to a cemetery. Beauty, solitude, and deep pleasure also keep the soul well fed.

Even mindless television, beauty magazines, and roughhousing with your dog, in the right dose, can be part and parcel of a plan to keep you fulfilled. It need not be elaborate; it just needs to fit for you. Be alive, imagine, execute, deliver, and love. Be free. Be awake.

"There was a time," writes French novelist Monique Wittig, "when you were not a slave. Remember that. You walked alone, full of laughter, you bathed bare-bellied . . . You say there are no words to describe this time, you say it doesn't exist. But remember. Make an effort to remember. Or, failing that, invent."

Resources

Here are some useful resources for additional assistance and information. In fact, I used many of these titles in researching this book; you'll find many of them also listed in the Bibliography.

Introduction
The Verbally Abusive Relationship: How to Recognize It and Respond to It by Patricia Evans, Bob Adams, Inc., 1992.

Chapter One
Social Intelligence: The New Science of Human Relationships by Daniel Goleman, Bantam Books, 2006.

Chapter Two

Books
The Batterer: A Psychological Profile by Donald G. Dutton, Ph.D., with Susan K. Golant, Basic Books, 1995.

Why Does He Do That? Inside the Minds of Angry and Controlling Men by Lundy Bancroft, Berkeley Books, 2002.

How to Recognize Emotional Unavailability and Make Healthier Relationship Choices by Bryn Collins, M.A., L.P., MJF Books, 1997.

The Verbally Abusive Relationship: How to Recognize It and How to Respond by Patricia Evans, Bob Adams, Inc., 1992.

Men Who Hate Women & The Women Who Love Them by Susan Forward, Ph.D., Bantam Books, 1986.

Living with the Passive-Aggressive Man by Scott Wetzler, Ph.D., Fireside/Simon & Schuster, 1992.

The Sociopath Next Door by Martha Stout, Ph.D., Broadway Books, 2005.

Snakes in Suits: When Sociopaths Go to Work by Paul Babiak, Ph.D., and Robert D. Hare, HarperCollins, 2006.

When Men Batter Women: New Insights into Ending Abusive Relationships by Neil Jacobson, Ph.D., and John Gottman, Ph.D., Simon & Schuster, 2007.

But He Never Hit Me: The Devastating Cost of Non-Physical Abuse to Girls and Women by Jill Murray, Ph.D., iUniverse, 2007.

Is It Love or Is It Addiction? by Brenda Schaeffer, Hazelden, 1997.

Love, Infidelity, and Sexual Addiction by Christine Adams, iUniverse, 1992.

Trapped in the Mirror: Adult Children of Narcissists and Their Struggle for Self by Elan Golomb, Ph.D., William Morrow, 1992.

"Not to People Like Us": Hidden Abuse in Upscale Marriages by Dr. Susan Weitzman, Basic Books, 2000.

If You Loved Me, You'd Stop!: What You Need to Know When Your Loved One Drinks Too Much by Lisa Frederiksen, KLJ Pub, 2009.

Web Sites
www.lovefraud.com.
www.al-anon.alateen.org: Al-Anon Family Group Headquarters.

Chapter Three
"Not to People Like Us": Hidden Abuse in Upscale Marriages by Dr. Susan Weitzman, Basic Books, 2000. Dr. Weitzman offers a helpful section on expectations and narcissistic rage.

Do I Have to Give Up Me to Be Loved By You? by Jordan Paul and Margaret Paul, Hazelden, 2002. You shouldn't have to give yourself up for anyone. This book helps you sort through the dilemmas we face in terms of bending to the expectations of others, overidentifying with others, and losing ourselves in others' expectations.

Reviving Ophelia: Saving the Selves of Adolescent Girls by Mary Pipher, Ph.D., Ballantine Books, 1994. Dr. Pipher discusses the distress caused by giving up our own identities to meet the expectations of others.

The Tending Instinct by Shelley E. Taylor, Henry Holt & Co., 2003. UCLA researcher Shelley Taylor asserts that women's ways of dealing with stress are more tend-and-befriend than fight-or-flight. However, if we're not careful, we can take care of others to our detriment.

Chapter Four

Books

The Price of Motherhood: Why the Most Important Job in the World Is Still the Least Valued by Ann Crittenden, Metropolitan Books, 2001.

The Tending Instinct by Shelley E. Taylor, Henry Holt & Co., 2003.

Women's Ways of Knowing: The Development of Self, Voice and Mind by Mary Field Belenky, Blythe McVicker Clinchy, Nancy Rule Goldberger, and Jill Mattuck Tarule, Basic Books, 1986. A brilliant study of women's developing identity and personal power.

The Second Shift by Arlie Hochschild with Anne Machung, Avon Books, 1990.

The Way We Really Are: Coming to Terms with America's Changing Families by Stephanie Coontz, Basic Books, 1997.

Kidding Ourselves: Breadwinning, Babies, and Bargaining Power by Rhona Mahony, Basic Books, 1995.

Coming Home: The Return to True Self by Martia Nelson, New World Library, 1993.

The Secret Life of Bees by Sue Monk Kidd, Penguin Putnam, 2002. A great novel that embodies women's inner journey and celebration of the sacred feminine.

Women's Reality: An Emerging Female System in a White Male Society by Anne Wilson Schaef, HarperCollins, 1992. Schaef validates what many women feel but are afraid to say.

The Power of Now: A Guide to Spiritual Enlightenment by Eckhart Tolle, New World Library, 1999.

To Be a Woman: The Birth of the Conscious Feminine, edited by Connie Zweig, Jeremy P. Tarcher, 1990.

Women Who Run with the Wolves: Myths and Stories of the Wild Woman Archetype by Clarissa Pinkola Estes, Ballantine Books, 1992.

The Way of Woman: Awakening the Perennial Feminine by Helen M. Luke, Doubleday, 1995.

Articles
The Framingham, Massachusetts, study on self-silencing and its relationship to women's health was reported in the July 2007 issue of *Psychosomatic Medicine*. Dr. Dana Crowley Jack's research was detailed in *The New York Times*, October 2, 2007.

Web Site
www.bethwilsonlifecoach.com: Visit my site to listen to my number one Internet radio show, *Quantum Leaps*, for lively discussions on the value of women's currency, the importance of women gathering, and much, much more! In particular, check out "Beyond Finances: The Value of Women's Currency," and "Where There's Women, There's Gathering."

Chapter Five

Books
Controlling People: How to Recognize, Understand and Deal with People Who Try to Control You by Patricia Evans, Adams Media, 2002.

Emotional Intelligence: Why It Can Matter More Than IQ by Daniel Goleman, Bantam Books, 1995.

Courage to Change, Al-Anon Family Headquarters.

Codependent No More: How to Stop Controlling Others and Start Caring for Yourself by Melody Beattie, Hazelden, 1992.

Energy and Personal Power by Shirley Gehrke Luthman, Mehetabel & Co., 1982.

Women and Self-Esteem: Understanding and Improving the Way We Think and Feel About Ourselves by Linda Tschirhart Sanford and Mary Ellen Donovan, Doubleday, 1995.

Facing Love Addiction: Giving Yourself the Power to Change the Way You Love by Pia Mellody, Andrea Wells Miller, and J. Keith Miller, HarperCollins, 1992.

Is It Love or Is It Addiction? by Brenda Schaeffer, Hazelden, 1997.

Web Sites

al-anon.alateen.org: Al-Anon 12-Step Program.

www.bethwilsonlifecoach.com: Go to my Web site to listen to my number one Internet radio show, *Quantum Leaps*, especially the episodes "He's Just No Good for You," "The Power of Being Seen and Heard," "The Zen and Art of Intimate Relationships" "2008 I Can Hardly Wait!" "Listening with Heart 360," and "Marriage: A History."

Chapter Six

Books

Women Who Run with the Wolves by Clarissa Pinkola Estes, Ph.D., Ballantine Books. 1992. Dr. Estes has a superb section about innocence and naïveté in terms of women's empowerment and susceptibility to destructive individuals.

But He Never Hit Me: The Devastating Cost of Non-Physical Abuse to Girls and Women by Jill Murray, Ph.D., iUniverse. 2007.

The Sociopath Next Door by Martha Stout, Ph.D., Broadway Books, 2005.

Just Like a Woman: How Gender Science Is Redefining What Makes Us Female by Dianne Hales, Bantam Books, 1999.

Snakes in Suits: When Sociopaths Go to Work by Paul Babiak, Ph.D., and Robert D. Hare, HarperCollins, 2006.

SuperWoman: Simple Steps to Find the Real You and Become a SuperME, SuperPARTNER, SuperMOM...SuperWOMAN! by Kelly Wade-Arnel, just love publishing, 2006.

Without Conscience: The Disturbing World of Psychopaths Among Us by Robert D. Hare, The Guilford Press, 1999.

"Not to People Like Us": Hidden Abuse in Upscale Marriages by Dr. Susan Weitzman, Basic Books, 2000.

The Bonds of Love: Psychoanalysis, Femininsm, and the Problem of Domination by Jessica Benjamin, Pantheon Books, 1988.

The Battered Woman by Lenore E. Walker, HarperCollins,1979. According to the author, "The learned helplessness theory has three basic components: information about what will happen; thinking or cognitive representations about what will happen (learning, expectations, belief, perception); and behavior toward what does happen."

The Gift of Fear: Survival Signals That Protect Us from Violence by Gavin de Becker, Little Brown, 1997.

Creating Balance in Your Child's Life by Beth Wilson Saavedra, Contemporary Books, 1999.

The Domestic Assault of Women: Psychological and Criminal Justice Perspectives by D. G. Dutton, University of British Columbia Press, 1995.

Power vs. Force: The Hidden Determinants of Human Behavior by Michael R. Hawkins, M.D., Ph.D., Hay House, 2002.

Article
"Frustration and Learned Helplessness," by Martin Seligman, *Journal of Experimental Psychology and Animal Behavior Processes*, 104, no. 2 (April 1975).

Videos
Sleeping with the Enemy
Alice Doesn't Live Here Anymore
28 Days
Pleasantville
Practical Magic

Chapter Seven

Separation Violence
Separation violence is very real, so if you are concerned for your safety or your children's safety, please call the Domestic Violence Hotline: (800) 799-7233. It is staffed twenty-four hours a day by trained counselors who can provide crisis assistance and information about shelters, legal advocacy, health care centers, and counseling.
www.feminist.org/911/crisis.html: Visit this site to find domestic violence assistance within your home state.

Financial and Divorce Strategy Assistance
www.bloomonline.com: Barb Scala, J.D., C.L.C. Barb can assist you with divorce coaching to decide if you want to leave or stay, how to take more control over your life, and how to strategize in terms of a divorce. She also has access to a variety of resources.

www.discoverthedspot.com: Laura Campbell has compiled a clear-inghouse of divorce information that is available through her site. She is a skilled divorce coach.

www.momference.com: A wealth of information for every stage of divorce and separation including parenting advice, divorce strategies, financial assistance, and networks of support. They also offer monthly virtual conferences via the computer on a variety of topics with skilled professionals for an engaging event.

I also recommend Suze Orman's books: *Women and Money: Owning the Power to Create Your Destiny* and *The Nine Steps to Financial Freedom: Practical and Spiritual Steps So You Can Stop Worrying*.

Books

When Men Batter Women: New Insights into Ending Abusive Relationships by Neil Jacobson and John Gottman, Simon & Schuster, 1998.

The Gift of Fear: Survival Signals That Protect Us from Violence by Gavin de Becker, Little Brown, 1997.

The Price of Motherhood: Why the Most Important Job in the World Is Still the Least Valued by Ann Crittenden, Metropolitan Books, 2001.

The Everything Divorce Book: Know Your Rights, Understand the Law, and Regain Control of Your Life by Mary L. Davidson, Adams Media, 2003.

Divorce and Money: Everything You Need to Know by Gayle Rosenwald Smith, Perigee Trade, 2004.

Two Homes by Claire Masurel and Kady Macdonald Denton, Candlewick Press, 2003.

Making Divorce Easier on Your Child: 50 Effective Ways to Help Children Adjust by Nicholas Long and Rex L. Forehand, Contemporary Books, 2002.

Coercive Control: How Men Entrap Women in Personal Life by Evan

Stark, Oxford University Press, 2007.

Divorced from Justice: The Abuse of Women and Children by Divorce Lawyers and Judges by Karen Winner, HarperCollins, 1996.

When the Bough Breaks: The Cost of Neglecting Our Children by Sylvia Ann Hewlett, Perennial, 1992.

The Transcendent Child: Tales of Triumph over the Past by Lillian B. Rubin, Harper Paperbacks, 1997.

The Batterer as Parent: Addressing the Impact of Domestic Violence on Family Dynamics by Lundy Bancroft and Jay G. Silverman, Sage Publications, Inc., 2002.

Creating Balance in Your Child's Life by Beth Wilson Saavedra, Contemporary Books, 1999.

Article

"Why They Stay: A Saga of Spouse Abuse" by H. E. Marano, *Psychology Today*, 29, no. 3.

Web Site

www.bethwilsonlifecoach.com: The *Quantum Leaps* Internet radio show offers two shows on divorce: "Make Transition Matter" and "Don't Do It Alone!"

Chapter Eight

Books

The Domestic Assault of Women: Psychological and Criminal Justice Perspectives by D. G. Dutton, University of British Columbia Press, 1995.

The Woman's Comfort Book: A Self-Nurturing Guide for Restoring Balance in Your Life by Jennifer Louden, HarperCollins, 1992, 2004.

Change Your Brain, Change Your Life by Dr. Daniel Amen, Three Rivers

Press, 1998. Dr. Amen offers progressive and effective strategies for coping with and improving depression.

Anatomy of the Spirit: The Seven Stages of Power and Healing by Carolyn Myss, Three Rivers Press, 1996.

Women's Bodies, Women's Wisdom by Dr. Christiane Northrup Bantam Books, 2006.

Emotional Sobriety: From Relationship Trauma to Resilience and Balance by Tian Dayton, Ph.D., Health Communications, 2007.

A Woman's Worth by Marianne Williamson, Ballantine Books, 1994.

Kitchen Table Wisdom: Stories That Heal by Rachel Naomi Remen, M.D., Riverhead Books, 1996.

Videos
Shirley Valentine
My Brilliant Career
What the Bleep Do We Know?
The Devil Wears Prada

Chapter Nine

Shaping of the Feminine Identity
Reviving Ophelia by Mary Pipher, Ph.D., Ballantine Books, 1994.

The Way We Never Were by Stephanie Coontz, Harper Collins, 1992.

The Way We Really Are by Stephanie Coontz, Basic Books, 1997.

Marriage, A History by Stephanie Coontz, Penguin Books, 2005.

Listening with Heart 360: The New Paradigm for Women by Elizabeth Diane and Andrew Marshall, Robert D. Reed, 2008.

The Feminine Mystique by Betty Friedan, W. W. Norton & Co, 1963.

The Second Stage by Betty Friedan, Summit Books, 1981.

The Erotic Silence of the American Wife by Dalma Heyn, Random House, 1992.

The Second Shift by Arlie Hochschild with Anne Machung, Avon Books, 1990.

"Holistic Politics: Difference Is Our Strength" by Audre Lorde, *Ms. Magazine*, 1996.

Gift from the Sea by Anne Morrow Lindbergh, Vintage Books, 1978 (originally written in 1955).

Boundaries

Are You the One For Me?: Knowing Who's Right & Avoiding Who's Wrong by Barbara DeAngelis, MJF Books, 1992.

The Gift of Fear: Survival Signs That Protect Us from Violence by Gavin de Becker, Little Brown, 1997.

Controlling People: How to Recognize, Understand and Deal with People Who Try to Control You by Patricia Evans, Adams Media, 2002.

Boundaries: Where I End and You Begin by Anne Katherine, Fireside/Parkside Publishing, 1991.

Motherhood

The Erotic Silence of the American Wife by Dalma Heyn, Random House, 1992.

Restoring Balance to a Mother's Busy Life by Beth Wilson Saavedra, Contemporary Books, 1996, offers images of motherhood that are geared toward creative self-definition rather than external standards that may or may not fit for a woman and her family.

Momfulness: Mothering with Mindfulness, Compassion, and Grace by Denise Roy, M.A., John Wiley & Sons, 2007.

The Mother Dance by Harriet Lerner, HarperCollins, 1998.

Ourselves as Mothers: The Universal Experience of Motherhood by Sheila Kitzinger, Addison-Wesley Publishing, 1995.

Reinventing Ourselves After Motherhood by Susan Lewis, Contemporary Books, 1999.

Redefining Ourselves

If Women Ruled the World, edited by Sheila Ellison, Inner Ocean Publishing, 2004.

The Chalice and the Blade by Riane Eisler, Ph.D., HarperCollins, 1987.

Reinventing Womanhood by Carolyn G. Heilbrun, W.W. Norton & Co., 1993.

Videos

Dr. Quinn, Medicine Woman
Steel Magnolias
Becoming Jane

Chapter Ten

Books

Dangerous Relationships: How to Identify and Respond to the Seven Warning Signs of a Troubled Relationship by Noelle Nelson, Ph.D., Perseus Publishing, 1997.

Transitions: Making Sense of Life's Changes by William Bridges, Da Capo Press, 2004.

Joint Custody with a Jerk: Raising a Child with an Uncooperative Ex by Julie A. Ross and Judy Corcoran, St. Martin's Press, 1996.

Custody Chaos, Personal Peace: Sharing Custody with an Ex Who Is Driving You Crazy by Jeffrey P. Wittman, The Berkeley Publishing Group, 2001.

Divorce Poison: Protecting the Parent-Child Bond from a Vindictive Ex by Richard A. Warshak, HarperCollins, 2001.

When Things Fall Apart: Heart Advice for Difficult Times by Pema Chodron, Shambala Publications, 1997.

Web Site

www.bloomonline.com: Barb Scala, transformation and divorce coach.

www.discoverthedspot.com: divorce coach Laura Campbell's clearinghouse of divorce information.

Chapter Eleven

Books

The Body Has a Mind of Its Own: How Body Maps in Your Brain Help You Do (Almost) Everything Better by Sandra and Matthew Blakeslee, Random House, 2007. Science writers Sandra and Matthew Blakeslee examine the findings in neuroscience that confirm the fact that harsh and cruel words, rejection, and invalidating behaviors not only hurt our feelings but can also inflict psychic damage by disrupting the equilibrium of "body maps" in the brain. *Quantum Leaps*, Episode 15, February 21, 2008.

Snakes in Suits: When Sociopaths Go to Work by Paul Babiak, Ph.D., and Robert D. Hare, HarperCollins Publishers, 2006.

When Men Batter Women: New Insights into Ending Abusive Relationships by Neil Jacobson, Ph.D., and John Gottman, Ph.D., Simon & Schuster, 2007.

If the Buddha Dated: A Handbook for Finding Love on a Spiritual Path by Charlotte Kasl, Ph.D., Penguin Putnam, 1999.

Power vs. Force: The Hidden Determinants of Human Behavior by David R. Hawkins, MD, Ph.D., Hay House, 2002.

Skills Training Manual for Treating Borderline Personality Disorder by Marsha M. Linehan, Guilford Press, 1993, includes a discussion of the brain function of sociopaths based on the research of Niels Birbaumer and Ranganatha Sitaram at the University of Tubingen in Germany.

Women's Reality: An Emerging Female System in a White Male Society by Anne Wilson Schaef, HarperCollins, 1992.

Real Moments by Barbara DeAngelis, Ph.D., Dell Publishing, 1994.

We Have to Talk: Healing Dialogues Between Men and Women by Samuel Shem, M.D., and Janet Surrey, Ph.D., Basic Books, 1998.

16 Steps to Self-Empowerment by Charlotte Kasl, Ph.D., www.charlottekasl.com. Dr. Kasl offers support groups in North America based on her empowerment model.

Article
"The Thing Called Love" by Lauren Slater, *National Geographic*, February 2006,

Web Site
www.bethwilsonlifecoach.com: Check out the episode of my *Quantum Leaps* Internet radio show called "The Body Has a Mind of Its Own" with guests Sandra and Matthew Blakeslee.

Chapter Twelve

Books
Restoring Balance to a Mother's Busy Life by Beth Wilson Saavedra, Contemporary Books, 1996.

Care of the Soul by Thomas Moore, HarperCollins, 1992

The Re-Enchantment of Everyday Life by Thomas Moore, HarperCollins, 1996.

The Woman's Comfort Book: A Self-Nurturing Guide for Restoring Balance in Your Life, by Jennifer Louden, HarperCollins Publishers, 1992, 2004.

The Woman's Retreat Book and *Comfort Queens* by Jennifer Louden

Emotional Sobriety: From Relationship Trauma to Resilience and Balance by Tian Dayton, Ph.D., Health Communications, 2007.

Girlfriends Are the Best Friends of All: A Tribute to Laughter, Secrets, Girl Talk, Chocolate, Shopping . . . and Everything Else Women Share by Suzanne Moore, Blue Mountain Arts, 2004.

A Woman's Book of Life: The Biology, Psychology, and Spirituality of the Feminine Life Cycle by Joan Borysenko, Ph.D., Riverhead Books, 1996.

Web Sites

www.bethwilsonlifecoach.com: Check out the episode of my *Quantum Leaps* Internet radio show called "Why Women Gather."

www.gathercentral.com: Workshops and unique gathering groups for women.

Chapter Thirteen

Books

The Seven Principles for Making Marriage Work by John Gottman, Ph.D., and Nan Silver, Orion Publishing Group, 2000.

Are You the One For Me?: Knowing Who's Right & Avoiding Who's Wrong by Barbara DeAngelis, Ph.D., MJF Books, 1992.

The Dance of Intimacy: A Woman's Guide to Courageous Acts of Change in Key Relationships by Harriet Goldhor Lerner, Ph.D., HarperCollins, 1986.

The Dance of Anger: A Woman's Guide to Changing the Patterns of

Intimate Relationships by Harriet Goldhor Lerner, Ph.D., HarperCollins, 1985.

Emotional Intelligence: Why It Can Matter More Than IQ by Daniel Goleman, Bantam Books, 1995.

Social Intelligence: The New Science of Human Relationships by Daniel Goleman, Bantam Books, 2006.

The Resilient Self: How Survivors of Troubled Families Rise Above Diversity by Steven J. Wolin, M.D., and Sybil Wolin, Ph.D., Villard Books, 1993.

The Pleasers: Women Who Can't Say No and the Men Who Control Them by Dr. Kevin Leman, Dell Publishing, 1995.

What Smart Women Know by Steven Carter, M. Evans & Co., 1996.

Web Sites
www.thinkyourselfthin.com: Debbie Johnson calls her weight loss program for improving self-image and self-love "Think Yourself Loved." Very relaxing and affirming.

www.bethwilsonlifecoach.com: Go to my Web site to learn more about the Quantum Leaps Aficionados Pod, and to find out about a group in your area or how you can start one.

Chapter Fourteen
Coming Home: The Return to True Self by Martia Nelson, New World Library, 1993.

The Re-Enchantment of Everyday Life by Thomas Moore, HarperCollins, 1996.

The Creation of Feminist Consciousness: From the Middle Ages to Eighteen-seventy by Gerda Lerner, Oxford University Press, 1993.

Norma Jean the Termite Queen by Sheila Ballantyne, Ballantine Books, 1985. A humorous and clever tale of motherhood and holding onto one's identity despite the daily demands and challenges.

Composing a Life: Life as a Work in Progress by Mary Catherine Bateson, Grove/Atlantic, Inc., 1989.

Divine Daughters: Liberating the Power and Passion of Women's Voices by Rachel Bagby, HarperSanFrancisco, 1999.

■ ■ ■ ■ ■

Don't forget to play the theme song from *Chariots of Fire* or *Rocky*, or "I Will Survive"—whatever reminds you that you have done more than survive . . . you've thrived! Congratulations on your hard-won wisdom and incredible experience.

Bibliography

Adams, Christine. *Love, Infidelity, and Sexual Addiction*. Lincoln, Neb.: iUniverse, 1992.

Amen, Daniel G., M.D. *Change Your Brain, Change Your Life*. New York: Three Rivers Press, 1998.

American Psychiatric Association. *Diagnostic and Statistical Manual of Mental Disorders DSM-IV-TR*. Arlington, Va.: American Psychiatric Publishing, Inc., 2000.

Babiak, Paul, Ph.D., and Robert D. Hare, Ph.D.. *Snakes in Suits: When Psychopaths Go to Work*. New York: Regan Books, 2006.

Bagby, Rachel. *Divine Daughters: Liberating the Power and Passion of Women's Voices*. San Francisco: HarperSanFrancisco, 1999.

Ballantyne, Sheila. *Norma Jean the Termite Queen*. New York: Ballantine Books, 1985.

Bancroft, Lundy. *Why Does He Do That?: Inside the Minds of Angry and Controlling Men*. New York: Berkeley Books, 2002.

———— and Jay G. Silverman. *The Batterer as Parent: Addressing the Impact of Domestic Violence on Family Dynamics*. Thousand Oaks, Calif.: Sage Publications, Inc., 2002.

Bateson, Mary Catherine. *Composing a Life: Life as a Work in Progress*. New York: Grove/Atlantic, Inc., 1989.

Beattie, Melody. *Codependent No More: How to Stop Controlling Others and Start Caring for Yourself*. Center City, Minn.: Hazelden, 1992.

Belenky, Mary Field, Blythe McVicker Clinchy, Nancy Rule Goldberger, and Jill Mattuck Tarule. *Women's Ways of Knowing: The Development of Self, Voice and Mind*. New York: Basic Books, 1986.

Benjamin, Jessica. *The Bonds of Love: Psychoanalysis, Feminism, and the Problem of Domination.* New York: Pantheon Books, 1988.

Bernstein, Albert J., Ph.D.. *Emotional Vampires: Dealing with People Who Drain You Dry.* New York: McGraw Hill, 2001.

Blakeslee, Sandra, and Matthew Blakeslee. *The Body Has a Mind of Its Own: How Body Maps in Your Brain Help You Do (Almost) Everything Better.* New York: Random House, 2007.

Borysenko, Joan, Ph.D. *A Woman's Book of Life: The Biology, Psychology, and Spirituality of the Feminine Life Cycle.* New York: Riverhead Books, 1996.

Bridges, William. *Transitions: Making Sense of Life's Changes.* New York: Da Capo Press, 2004.

Brizendine, Louann, M.D. *The Female Brain.* New York: Broadway Books, 2006.

Brooks, Gary R., Ph.D. *The Centerfold Syndrome: How Men Can Overcome Objectification and Achieve Intimacy with Women.* San Francisco: Jossey-Bass Publishers, 1995.

Carns, Patrick, Ph.D. *Don't Call It Love: Recovery from Sexual Addiction.* New York: Bantam Books, 1992.

Carter, Steven. *What Smart Women Know.* New York: M. Evans & Co., 1996.

Chodron, Pema. *When Things Fall Apart: Heart Advice for Difficult Times.* Boulder, CO: Shambala Publications, 1997.

Collins, Bryn, M.A., L.P. *How to Recognize Emotional Unavailability and Make Healthier Relationship Choices.* New York: MJF Books, 1997.

Coontz, Stephanie. *Marriage: A History.* New York: Penguin Books, 2006.

———. *The Way We Never Were: American Families and the Nostalgia Trap.* New York: HarperCollins, 1992.

———. *The Way We Really Are: Coming to Terms with America's Changing Families.* New York: Basic Books, 1997.

Courage to Change. Virginia Beach, Va.: Al-Anon Family Headquarters.

Crittenden, Ann. *The Price of Motherhood: Why the Most Important Job in the World Is Still the Least Valued*. New York: Metropolitan Books, 2001.

Davidson, Mary L. *The Everything Divorce Book: Know Your Rights, Understand the Law, and Regain Control of Your Life*. Avon, Mass.: Adams Media, 2003.

Dayton, Tian, Ph.D. *Emotional Sobriety: From Relationship Trauma to Resilience and Balance*. Deerfield Beach, Fla.: Health Communications, 2007.

DeAngelis, Barbara, Ph.D. *Are You the One For Me?: Knowing Who's Right & Avoiding Who's Wrong*. New York: MJF Books, 1992.

———. *Real Moments*. New York: Dell Publishing Group, 1994.

de Becker, Gavin. *The Gift of Fear: Survival Signals That Protect Us from Violence*. Boston: Little Brown, 1997.

Diane, Elizabeth, and Andrew Marshall. *Listening with Heart: The New Paradigm for Women*. Bandon, Oreg: Robert D. Reed Publishers, 2008.

Dutton, Donald G., Ph.D., with Susan K. Golant. *The Batterer: A Psychological Profile*. New York: Basic Books, 1995.

Dyer, Wayne W., Ph.D. *The Power of Intention: Learning to Co-Create Your World Your Way*. Carlsbad, Calif.: Hay House, 2004.

Eaker, Elaine D., ScD, Lisa M. Sullivan, Ph.D., et al. "Marital Status, Marital Strain, and Risk of Coronary Heart Disease or Total Mortality: The Framingham Offspring Study" *Psychosomatic Medicine*, July 18, 2007.

Eisler, Riane, Ph.D. *The Chalice and the Blade*. New York: HarperCollins, 1987.

———. *The Real Wealth of Nations*. San Francisco: Berrett-Koehler Publishers, 2007.

————. *Sacred Pleasure: Sex, Myth and the Politics of the Body.* San Francisco: HarperSanFrancisco, 1995.

Ellison, Sheila. *If Women Ruled the World: How to Create the World We Want to Live In.* Maui, Hawaii: Inner Ocean Publishing, 2004.

Estes, Clarissa Pinkola, Ph.D. *Women Who Run with the Wolves: Myths and Stories of the Wild Woman Archetype.* New York: Ballantine Books, 1992.

Evans, Patricia. *The Verbally Abusive Relationships: How to Recognize It and Respond to It.* Holbrook, Mass.: Bob Adams, Inc., 1992.

————. *Controlling People: How to Recognize, Understand, and Deal with People Who Try to Control You.* Avon, Mass.: Adams Media Corporation, 2002.

Fisher, Helen, Ph.D. *Anatomy of Love.* New York: Ballantine Books, 1992.

Flinders, Carol Lee. *At the Root of This Longing: Reconciling a Spiritual Hunger and a Feminist Thirst.* San Francisco: HarperSanFrancisco, 1998.

————. *Enduring Grace: Living Portraits of Seven Women Mystics.* San Francisco: HarperSanFrancisco, 1993.

————. *Rebalancing the World: Why Women Belong and Men Compete and How to Restore the Ancient Equilibrium.* San Francisco; HarperSanFrancisco, 2003.

Forward, Susan, Ph.D. *Men Who Hate & The Women Who Love Them.* New York: Bantam Books, 1986.

Frederiksen, Lisa. *If You Loved Me, You'd Stop! What You Need to Know When Your Loved One Drinks (or Uses) Too Much.* KLJ Pub, 2009.

Friedan, Betty. *The Feminine Mystique.* New York: W. W. Norton & Co., 1963.

————. *The Second Stage.* New York: Summit Books, 1981.

Goldberger, Nancy, Jill Tarule, Blythe Clinchy, and Mary Belenky, editors. *Knowledge, Difference, and Power: Essays Inspired by Women's Ways of Knowing.* New York: Basic Books, 1996.

Goleman, Daniel. *Social Intelligence: The New Science of Human Relationships.* New York: Bantam Books, 2006.

————. *Emotional Intelligence: Why It Can Matter More Than IQ.* New York: Bantam Books, 1995.

Golomb, Elan, Ph.D. *Trapped in the Mirror: Adult Children of Narcissists and Their Struggle for Self.* New York: William Morrow & Co., 1992.

Gottman, John, Ph.D. *Why Marriages Succeed or Fail . . . and How You Can Make Yours Last.* New York: Simon & Schuster Paperbacks, 1994.

Gottman, John, and Nan Silver. *The Seven Principles for Making Marriage Work.* Great Britain: Orion Publishing Group, 2000.

Hales, Dianne. *Just Like a Woman: How Gender Science Is Redefining What Makes Us Female.* New York: Bantam Books, 1999.

Hare, Robert D. *Without Conscience: The Disturbing World of Psychopaths Among Us.* New York: The Guilford Press, 1999.

Hawkins, David R., M.D, Ph.D. *Power vs. Force: The Hidden Determinants of Human Behavior.* Carlsbad, Calif.: Hay House, 2002.

Heilbrun, Carolyn G. *Reinventing Motherhood.* New York: W.W. Norton & Co., 1993.

Hendricks, Gay, Ph.D., and Kathlyn Hendricks, Ph.D. *Conscious Loving: The Journey to Co-Commitment.* New York: Bantam Books, 1990.

Herman, Judith, M.D. *Trauma and Recovery: The Aftermath of Violence—from Domestic Abuse to Political Terror.* New York: Basic Books, 1997.

Hewlett, Sylvia Ann. *When the Bough Breaks: The Cost of Neglecting Our Children.* New York: Perennial, 1992.

Heyn, Dalma. *The Erotic Silence of the American Wife.* New York: Random House, 1992.

Hochschild, Arlie, with Anne Machung. *The Second Shift.* New York: Avon Books, 1990.

Jacobson, Neil, Ph.D., and John Gottman, Ph.D. *When Men Batter Women: New Insights into Ending Abusive Relationships.* New York: Simon & Schuster, 2007.

Kasl, Charlotte, Ph.D. *If the Buddha Dated: A Handbook for Finding Love on a Spiritual Path.* New York: Penguin Putnam, 1999.

———. *If the Buddha Married: Creating Enduring Relationships on a Spiritual Path.* New York: Penguin Putnam, 2001.

Katherine, Anne. *Boundaries: Where You End and I Begin.* New York: Fireside/Parkside Publishing, 1991.

Kidd, Sue Monk. *The Secret Life of Bees.* New York: Penguin Putnam, 2002.

———. *The Dance of the Dissident Daughter: A Woman's Journey from Christian Tradition to the Sacred Feminine.* NewYork: HarperCollins, 1996.

Kim, Elizabeth. *Ten Thousand Sorrows: The Extraordinary Journey of a Korean War Orphan.* New York: Doubleday/Random House, 2000.

Kitzinger, Sheila. *Ourselves as Mothers: The Universal Experience of Motherhood.* New York: Addison-Wesley, 1995.

Kurtz, Ernest, and Katherine Ketcham. *The Spirituality of Imperfection: Storytelling and the Search for Meaning.* New York: Bantam Books, 2002.

Leman, Kevin. *The Pleasers: Women Who Can't Say No—and the Men Who Control Them.* New York: Dell Publishing, 1995.

Lerner, Gerda. *The Creation of Feminist Consciousness: From the Middle Ages to Eighteen-seventy.* New York: Oxford University Press, 1993.

Lerner, Harriet, Ph.D. *The Dance of Anger: A Woman's Guide to Changing the Patterns of Intimate Relationships*. New York: HarperCollins, 1985.

———. *The Dance of Intimacy: A Woman's Guide to Courageous Acts of Change in Key Relationships*. New York: HarperCollins, 1986.

_____. *The Mother Dance*. New York: HarperCollins, 1998.

Lewis, Susan. *Reinventing Ourselves After Motherhood*. Chicago: Contemporary Books, 1999.

Levy, Ariel. *Female Chauvinist Pigs: Women and the Rise of Raunch Culture*. New York: Free Press/Simon & Schuster, 2005.

Lindbergh, Anne Morrow. *Gift from the Sea*. New York: Vintage Books, 1978.

Linehan, Marsha M. *Skills Training Manual for Treating Borderline Personality Disorder*. New York: Guilford Press, 1993.

Lissette, Andrea, M.A., CDVC, and Richard Krauss, Ph.D. *Free Yourself from an Abusive Relationship: 7 Steps to Taking Back Your Life*. Berkeley, Calif.: Hunter House Publishers, 2000.

Lombard, Jay, Ph.D., and Christian Renna, Ph.D., with Armin A. Brott. *Balance Your Brain, Balance Your Life*. Hoboken, N.J.: John Wiley & Sons, 2004.

Long, Nicholas, and Rex L. Forehand. *Making Divorce Easier on Your Child: 50 Effective Ways to Help Children Adjust*. Chicago: Contemporary Books, 2002.

Lorde, Audre. "Holistic Politics: Difference Is Our Strength." *Ms. Magazine*, 1996.

Louden, Jennifer. *The Woman's Comfort Book: A Self-Nurturing Guide for Restoring Balance in Your Life*. New York: HarperCollins, 1992, 2004.

———. *The Woman's Retreat Book*. San Francisco: HarperSanFrancisco, 1997.

Luke, Helen M. *The Way of Woman: Awakening the Perennial Feminine.* New York: Doubleday, 1995.

Luthman, Shirley Gehrke. *Energy and Personal Power.* San Rafael, Calif.: Mehetabel & Co., 1982.

Mahoney, Rhona. *Kidding Ourselves: Breadwinning, Babies, and Bargaining Power.* New York: Basic Books, 1995.

Marano, H.E. "Why They Stay: A Saga of Spouse Abuse," *Psychology Today,* 29, no. 3.

Mason, Paul T., M.S., and Randi Kreger. *Stop Walking on Eggshells: Taking Your Life Back When Someone You Care About Has Borderline Personality Disorder.* Oakland, Calif.: New Harbinger Publications, 1998.

Masurel, Claire and Kady Macdonald Denton. *Two Homes.* Cambridge, Mass.: Candlewick Press, 2003.

Mellody, Pia, Andrea Wells Miller, and J. Keith Miller. *Facing Love Addiction: Giving Yourself the Power to Change the Way You Love.* New York: HarperCollins, 1992.

Miller, Mary Susan, Ph.D. *No Visible Wounds: Identifying Nonphysical Abuse of Women by Their Men.* New York: Fawcett Columbine, 1995.

Mitchell, Edgar, Ph.D. *The Way of the Explorer: An Apollo Astronaut's Journey Through the Material and Mystical Worlds.* Franklin Lakes, N.J.: New Page Books, 2008.

Moore, Suzanne. *Girlfriends Are the Best Friends of All: A Tribute to Laughter, Secrets, Girl Talk, Chocolate, Shopping . . . and Everything Else Women Share.* Boulder, CO: Blue Mountain Arts, 2004.

Moore, Thomas. *Care of the Soul.* New York: HarperCollins, 1992.

_____. *The Re-Enchantment of Everyday Life.* New York: HarperCollins, 1996.

Moss, Richard, M.D. *The Black Butterfly: An Invitation to Radical Aliveness.* Berkeley, Calif.: Celestial Arts, 1986.

Murray, Jill, Ph.D. *But I Love Him: Protecting Your Teen Daughter from Controlling, Abusive Dating Relationships.* New York: Regan Books, 2000.

———. *Destructive Relationships: A Guide to Changing the Unhealthy Relationships in Your Life.* San Diego: Jodere Group, 2002.

———. *But He Never Hit Me: The Devastating Cost of Non-Physical Abuse to Girls and Women.* Lincoln, Neb.: iUniverse, 2007.

Myss, Caroline, Ph.D. *Anatomy of the Spirit: The Seven Stages of Power and Healing.* New York: Three Rivers Press, 1996.

Nelson, Martia. *Coming Home: The Return to True Self.* Novato, Calif.: New World Library, 1993.

Nelson, Noelle, Ph.D. *Dangerous Relationships: How to Identify and Respond to the Seven Warning Signs of a Troubled Relationship.* Cambridge, Mass.: Perseus Publishing, 1997.

Northrup, Christiane, M.D. *Women's Bodies, Women's Wisdom.* New York: Bantam Books, 2006.

Parker-Pope, Tara. "Marital Spats, Taken to Heart," *New York Times,* October 2, 2007.

Paul, Jordan and Margaret Paul. *Do I Have to Give Up Me to Be Loved By You?* Center City, Minn: Hazelden, 2002.

Paul, Pamela. *Pornified: How Pornography Is Transforming Our Lives, Our Relationships, and Our Families.* New York: Henry Holt, 2005.

Pipher, Mary, Ph.D. *Reviving Ophelia: Saving the Selves of Adolescent Girls.* New York: Ballantine Books, 1994.

Remen, Rachel Naomi, M.D. *Kitchen Table Wisdom: Stories That Heal.* New York: Riverhead Books, 1996.

Ross, Julie A. and Judy Corcoran. *Joint Custody with a Jerk: Raising a Child with an Uncooperative Ex.* New York: St. Martin's Press, 1996.

Roy, Denise, M.A. *Momfulness: Mothering with Mindfulness, Compassion, and Grace.* New York: John Wiley & Sons, 2007.

Rubin, Lillian B. *The Transcendent Child: Tales of Triumph over the Past.* New York: Harper Paperbacks, 1997.

Saavedra, Beth Wilson. *Restoring Balance to a Mother's Busy Life.* Chicago: Contemporary Books, 1996.

———. *Meditations for New Mothers.* New York: Workman Publishing, 1992.

———. *Creating Balance in Your Child's Life.* Chicago: Contemporary Books, 1999.

Samenow, Stanton E., Ph.D. *Inside the Criminal Mind.* New York: Crown Publishers, 2004.

Sanford, Linda Tschirhart and Mary Ellen Donovan. *Women and Self-Esteem: Understanding and Improving the Way We Think and Feel About Ourselves.* New York: Doubleday, 1995.

Schaef, Anne Wilson. *Women's Reality: An Emerging Female System in a White Male Society.* New York: HarperCollins, 1992.

Schaeffer, Brenda. *Is It Love or Is It Addiction?* Center City, Minn.: Hazelden, 1997.

Seligman, Martin. "Frustration and Learned Helplessness," *Journal of Experimental Psychology and Animal Behavior Processes,* 104, no. 2 (April 1975).

Shem, Samuel, M.D, and Janet Surrey, Ph.D. *We Have to Talk: Healing Dialogues Between Men and Women.* New York: Basic Books, 1998.

Shlain, Leonard. *The Alphabet Versus the Goddess: The Conflict Between Word and Image.* New York: Penguin Putnam, 1998.

Siegel, Daniel J. *The Developing Mind: How Relationships and the Brain Interact to Shape Who We Are.* New York: Guilford Press, 1999.

Slater, Lauren. "The Thing Called Love," *National Geographic,* February 2006.

Smith, Gayle Rosenwald. *Divorce and Money: Everything You Need to Know*. New York: Perigee Trade, 2003.

Stark, Evan. *Coercive Control: How Men Entrap Women in Personal Life*. New York: Oxford University Press, USA, 2007.

Stout, Martha, Ph.D. *The Sociopath Next Door*. New York: Broadway Books, 2005.

Tannen, Deborah. *The Argument Culture: Moving from Debate to Dialogue*. New York: Random House, 1998.

Taylor, Shelley. *The Tending Instinct*. New York: Henry Holt & Co., 2002.

Thoele, Sue Patton. *Heart Centered Marriage: Fulfilling Our Natural Desire for Sacred Partnership*. Berkeley, Calif.: Conari Press, 1996.

Tolle, Eckhart. *The Power of Now: A Guide to Spiritual Enlightenment*. Novato, Calif.: New World Library, 1999.

Wade-Arnel, Kelly. *SuperWoman: Simple Steps to Find the Real You and Become a SuperME, SuperPARTNER, SuperMOM...SuperWOMAN!* Lighthouse Point, Fla.: just love publishing, 2006.

Warshak, Richard A. *Divorce Poison: Protecting the Parent-Child Bond from a Vindictive Ex*. New York: HarperCollins, 2001.

Weitzman, Susan, Ph.D. *"Not to People Like Us": Hidden Abuse in Upscale Marriages*. New York: Basic Books, 2000.

Wetzler, Scott, Ph.D. *Living with the Passive Aggressive Man*. New York: Fireside/Simon & Schuster, 1992.

Wilbur, Ken, editor. *The Holographic Paradigm and Other Paradoxes: Exploring the Leading Edge of Science*. Boulder, Colo.: Shambala Publications, 1982.

Williamson, Marianne. *A Woman's Worth*. New York: Ballantine Books, 1994.

Winner, Karen. *Divorced from Justice: The Abuse of Women and Children by Divorce Lawyers and Judges*. New York: HarperCollins, 1996.

Wittman, Jeffrey P. *Custody Chaos, Personal Peace: Sharing Custody with an Ex Who Is Driving You Crazy.* New York: Berkeley Publishing Group, 2001.

Wolf, Naomi. *The Beauty Myth: How Images of Beauty Are Used Against Women.* New York: Doubleday, 1991.

Wolin, Steven J., M.D., and Sybil Wolin, Ph.D. *The Resilient Self: How Survivors of Troubled Families Rise Above Diversity.* New York: Villard Books, 1993.

Zweig, Connie, editor. *To Be a Woman: The Birth of the Conscious Feminine.* Los Angeles: Jeremy P. Tarcher, 1990.

Acknowledgments

I would like to acknowledge the support and enduring humor of my family, not only in terms of my success and times of great happiness, but also during the turbulent years when destructive individuals taught me many a hard lesson.

A special "I cannot tell you how blessed I am to be your mother" to my children, Alexander, Sara, and Matthew. You are such amazing people. I love you with all my heart.

To the dispersed and always present members of my extended family, thank you. I could never have done it without you. Each and every one of you is an extraordinary individual in your own right . . . so glad I get to share the adventure with you!

A heartfelt thank-you to my lively agent, Penny Nelson, whose genuine enthusiasm for *He's Just No Good for You* helped to move it out into the world. Both Penny and my "Publishing Goddess" and editor, Mary Norris, immediately saw the value of this book. Their vision, good-natured ways, and professional expertise have been invaluable.

I'd also like to extend special wishes to Sherryl Lin Haldy, the beyond-capable and energetic executive producer for my Internet radio show, *Quantum Leaps*. Our work together has been a joy!

Thank you to the brilliant Beth Sullivan, the delightful Brendan Kelly, the wonderful Sue Wilson, and jubilant Deborah Genovesi for their encouragement and continued support in the world of media.

My dear "sisters in crime" have contributed their love, time, energy, and many talents to help me with my work and also to come more fully into being. Deepest thanks to Deirdre Mueller, Audrey White, Shelley Singer, Lisa Molinelli, Jan Taylor, Sandrine Stievenard, Helena Messenger, Maris Allen, Teresa Bentley, Petra Bittag, Karen Gray, Morgan Green, and Lucienne Rasetti.

Thank you to the many men and women who have graced my life on the path and readily opened themselves to remarkable personal growth: Allison Teisch, Scott Cantor, Jennifer Clifford, Melania Levitsky, Cara Stone and Rob Garrity, Katherine Robertson, Mary Beasley, Nancy Morris, Sue Bammer, Patricia Weeks, Aimee Stanich, Stacy Mahlstedt, Trisha Keith, Barb Herz, Alma Goldchain, Amy Lebovitz, Judy London, Shelley Gordon, Joan Anway, Kari Henley, Kate Hoppe, Anita Stansbury, Elizabeth Diane, Merrily Shade Brown, and many of the members of the LIP Network.

To the extraordinary men in my life whose presence has touched me in too many ways to mention: Walter "Buddy" Wilson, Paul Wilson, Brian Wilson, Michael Wilson, Eric Lieberman, Fernand Rasetti, Todd Nelson, Ned Green, Brad Pearsall, Dave Ciliberto, Louis D'Agrosa, Andrew Taylor, Johnnie LeBord, and Rene Parsell. Thanks for being real men with hearts of gold!

To Karen Winner: Your personal and professional commitment to women is exemplary.

My sincere thank-you to Dr. "Mo" Hannah for many enlightened conversations as well as a meaningful collaboration.

—Beth Wilson

To the many beautiful minds and hearts who have surrounded me throughout my life and taught me the true meaning of love:

My three living children, Will, Alexis, and Jesse, and my beloved angel child, Monique Therese Hannah;

My life partner, Joe Lombardo, who epitomizes love in action;

My many sources of theoretical inspiration, especially Harville Hendrix, Ph.D., Helen Hunt, Ph.D., and Lundy Bancroft;

The many courageous colleagues who have worked with me to make the Battered Mothers Custody Conference possible: attorneys Barry Goldstein, Joan Zorza, Richard Ducote, Robin Yeamans, Wendy Murphy, and Karen Winner; authors Angela Shelton and Amy Neustein, Ph.D.; producer Garland Waller; my dear fellow activists Marcia Pappas, Liliane Miller, Paige Hodson, and Renee Beeker; my

longtime friend and colleague, Dr. Joe Marrone; my "real" sisters, Marian and Marita, and my "true" brother, Bob, and the hundreds of Siena College students I've taught over the years and who, collectively, have taught me more than I have taught them. Finally, I thank the countless clients and couples I have counseled who have allowed me to share and benefit from their struggles to love and be loved.
—Mo Therese Hannah, Ph.D.

Index

potential and, 75
The Predator, 36–39
predators, 178–83
public *vs.* private behavior,
15
recognizing, 21–22
red flags and benefit of the
doubt, 87–88
The Respondaholic woman
and, 72–73
The Self-Righteous Pro-
gressive, 31–33
The Sex Addict, 41–43
tools of, 8–9
willfulness and, 186
willingness and, 185–86
mind games, 12
minimizing, 14
mistakes, 218–19
Moore, Thomas, 230
motherhood
as defined by external
sources, 162–63
devising your own version
of, 164–66
divorce and, 163–64
judgments about character
and, 163–64
pressure to conform, 163
sex and, 163, 164
Superwoman and, 163
value of, 115–16
Murray, Jill, 83–84, 95
Myss, Caroline, 161
myths, 88–89

N

narcissism, 34–35
narcissistic rage, 53–54
Nelson, Martia, 226

Nelson, Noelle, 172
New Age Man, The, 33–34,
187–88
Nice Guy, The, 35–36
*"Not to People Like Us":
Hidden Abuse in
Upscale Marriages*, 30

O

opposites, 76–77
Optimist, The, 75
Orman, Suze, 57

P

parents, 50–53
passive-agressive behavior,
27–29
Perfect Wife, The, 49–50
perfectionism, 210
personal growth
fulfillment *vs.* perfection,
229–30
new relationships, 227–28
success and, 224–25
ups and downs, 225–26
Peter, Lawrence J., 8
physical abuse, 9–11
Pillar of the Community, The,
29–31
Pipher, Mary, 66–67, 68–69,
146, 148
politics, 31–33
possessiveness, 15–16
*Power vs. Force: The Hidden
Determinants of Human Behavior*, 186
predators
being nice and, 97–98
criticism for falling for,
89–90

About the Authors

Best-selling author, speaker and life coach, **Beth Wilson** has built a reputation on sound advice. Her innovative style has won her international acclaim. She understands the importance of relationships in women's lives—and the ways in which these vital bonds can make them susceptible to bad news individuals.

As author of the bestselling book, *Meditations for New Mothers*, Beth extended a lifeline to mothers around the globe. She followed it with *Meditations for Mothers of Toddlers* and *Restoring Balance to a Mother's Busy Life*, which introduced mothers to the idea that they could "sacrifice for their children without sacrificing themselves." Not surprisingly, balance is the topic Beth is asked to speak about the most—whether on television and radio appearances or to live audiences. Her fourth book, *Creating Balance in Your Child's Life* continues to be popular with the media as well as parents concerned about stress and its affect on their children. She is also author of *Meditations During Pregnancy*.